A SENSE OF JUSTICE

Legal Knowledge and Lived Experience in Latin America

EDITED BY SANDRA BRUNNEGGER AND
KAREN ANN FAULK

D0166919

STANFORD UNIVERSITY PRESS
Stanford, California

Stanford University Press
Stanford, California

Printed in the United States of America on acid-free, archival-quality paper

Library of Congress Cataloging-in-Publication Data

A sense of justice: legal knowledge and lived experience in Latin America / edited by Sandra Brunnegger and Karen Ann Faulk.
     pages cm
  Includes bibliographical references and index.
  ISBN 978-0-8047-9796-2 (cloth : alk. paper) — ISBN 978-0-8047-9907-2 (pbk : alk. paper)
  1. Law—Social aspects—South America. 2. Justice—Social aspects—South America. I. Brunnegger, Sandra, editor. II. Faulk, Karen Ann, editor.
  KH99.S46 2016
  340'.115098—dc23

                                                                    2015034973

ISBN 978-0-8047-9911-9 (electronic)

Typeset by Newgen in 10/13.5 Minion

Cover photo: From commemoration of the AMIA Jewish Community Center bombing in Buenos Aires. Gustavo Castaing

CONTENTS

Acknowledgments   vii

Contributors   ix

Introduction: Making Sense of Justice   1
          Karen Ann Faulk and Sandra Brunnegger

PART ONE   MEMORY AND JUSTICE UNDER CONSTRUCTION

Chapter 1   Transitional Justice, Memory, and the Emergence
            of Legal Subjectivities in Colombia   25
            Juan Pablo Vera Lugo

Chapter 2   Pursuing Justice in Jewish Buenos Aires   50
            Karen Ann Faulk

PART TWO   THE SPACES OF LEGALITY

Chapter 3   Justice, Rights, and Discretionary Space in Brazilian
            Policing   79
            Graham Denyer Willis

Chapter 4   Imaginaries of Judicial Practice among Legal Experts
            in Argentina   99
            Leticia Barrera

PART THREE   DIFFERING SCALES
OF JUSTICE

Chapter 5   The Craft of Justice-Making through the Permanent
Peoples' Tribunal in Colombia   123
Sandra Brunnegger

Chapter 6   On Justice, Insecurity, and the Right to the City in
Brazil's Oldest Metropolis   147
Marta Magalhães Wallace

Chapter 7   Water Justice, Mining, and the Fetish Form of Law
in the Atacama Desert   170
Alonso Barros

Conclusion: Justice at the Limits of Law   203
Mark Goodale

Index   221

ACKNOWLEDGMENTS

The edited book project grew out of a conference organized at the Centre for Research in the Arts, Social Sciences and Humanities (CRASSH) at the University of Cambridge, which was further supported by *Social & Legal Studies*, St. Edmund's College, and the Society for Latin American Studies. The project also received support from the Fortes Fund (Division of Social Anthropology, University of Cambridge) and the People Programme (Marie Curie Actions) of the European Union's Seventh Framework Programme FP7/2007–2013. It benefitted from a Carson fellowship from the Rachel Carson Center for Environment and Society at the Ludwig Maximilian University and an APART fellowship from the Austrian Academy of Sciences. This generous support is gratefully acknowledged by the editors.

We would also like to thank the many people who have provided support, intellectual and otherwise. Of course, this book wouldn't be what it is without the thoughtful contributions of each of the chapter authors who provided their written contributions and productive insights over the course of the project's development. We are grateful to Michelle Lipinski at Stanford University Press for her careful readings of the manuscript and faith in the project. Special thanks are due to Mark Goodale for his careful and generous guidance and intellectual inspiration. Finally, we would like to thank all those who accompanied us along the way, both personally and professionally, without whom this project would not have been possible.

CONTRIBUTORS

Leticia Barrera is a researcher from CONICET (Argentina's National Research Council) at Instituto Superior de Estudios Sociales. Her scholarly work focuses on the production and circulation of knowledge among legal experts. Her works include the book *La Corte Suprema en escena: Una etnografía del mundo judicial* (Buenos Aires, Siglo XXI Editores, 2012); "Relocalizing the Judicial Space: Place, Access and Mobilization in Post-Crisis Argentina" (*Law, Culture and the Humanities*, 2012); and "Performing the Court: The Politics of Judicial Transparency in Argentina" (*PoLAR: The Political and Legal Anthropology Review*, 2013).

Alonso Barros is a lawyer (PUCCh) with a doctoral degree from the University of Cambridge and 20 years of native title research and advocacy among the Mesoamerican and Andean peoples. He currently serves as Senior Research Associate at the Fundación Desierto de Atacama (Chile), a nonprofit organization for cultural and environmental protection.

Sandra Brunnegger, a social anthropologist, is a Fellow and Lecturer at St. Edmund's College, Cambridge. She is currently a Fung Global Fellow at Princeton University. She writes on human and indigenous rights, indigenous legal systems, transitional justice, environmental concerns, and social movements.

Karen Ann Faulk is an anthropologist and research professor with the Centro de Estudios Sociológicos at the Colegio de México. In addition to several articles and book chapters, she is the author of the book *In the Wake of Neoliberalism: Citizenship and Human Rights in Argentina* (Stanford University Press, 2013), an ethnography of postneoliberal justice in Argentina.

Mark Goodale is Professor of Cultural and Social Anthropology at the University of Lausanne and Series Editor of Stanford Studies in Human Rights. He is the author or editor of 12 books, including *Anthropology and Law: A Critical Introduction* (NYU Press, 2017).

Marta Magalhaes Wallace is a research associate in social anthropology and a teaching associate in Latin American Studies at the University of Cambridge. She has done work on processes of urban transformation, heritage-making, citizenship, and violence in Brazil. She is currently working on a new project about crisis, austerity, and mental health in contemporary Europe.

Juan Pablo Vera Lugo is currently a PhD candidate at Rutgers University and an assistant professor in social anthropology at the Pontificia Universidad Javeriana in Colombia.

Graham Denyer Willis is a University Lecturer in Development and Latin American Studies and a Fellow of Queens' College, University of Cambridge. His book *The Killing Consensus: Police, Organized Crime and the Regulation of Life and Death in Urban Brazil* was published by the University of California Press in 2015.

FIGURE 0.1   Areas of detail. Map created using stepmap.com. Printed with permission.

INTRODUCTION

Making Sense of Justice

Karen Ann Faulk and Sandra Brunnegger

TOWARD AN ANTHROPOLOGY OF JUSTICE

Latin America is as culturally diverse as it is geographically vast. Yet, the nations of Latin America share important historical and institutional characteristics. Perhaps most significantly, countries across the region continue to grapple with the legacies of colonialism—from the classical era of Iberian colonialization to the neocolonial domination enacted through economic penetration in the early twentieth century. At the approach of the twenty-first century, Latin Americans found themselves constrained by the demands of international lending agencies and awash in the flood of cultural and material products made ever more readily available by multinationals striving to captivate and capitalize on the "emerging markets" opened by neoliberal reform. The continent has also had to contend with the legacies of state violence and dictatorial regimes that sought to strip society of its vibrant forms of popular organizations, preemptively crushing opposition and laying the foundation for the economic restructuring that was to come.

These shared processes of emergence paved the way for a diversity of forms of resistance. In the Chilean Atacama Desert, residents have undertaken a prolonged struggle for their right to groundwater. Family members of bombing victims in Buenos Aires brought a case against the state of Argentina before an international human rights body and are still working through a slow process of attempted resolution. In Colombia, some victims of political violence are turning increasingly to the courts for resolution in the wake of devastating personal tragedy, while others reject the state's ability to fairly adjudicate their grievances and construct instead a nonstate tribunal to consider the damages they have suffered to both persons and property. In all of these cases, the protagonists are seeking one thing: justice. But what exactly does "justice" mean for those involved in each of these examples? If achieved, what would justice look like? Invocations of 'justice' are generative not only of a sense of a defined goal or a means of resolution, but they also often raise essential questions of what justice can or should look like. How can "justice" be determined or evaluated? How is it best achieved? What norms or procedures can or must govern its enactment? Who has the authority to decide what "justice" is?

This book answers these questions through grounded ethnographic explorations of a range of cases in contemporary Latin America. The particular experiences of each nation and population in Latin America form a backdrop to the complex ways in which (in)justice is lived and imagined today. "Justice" serves as the ultimate goal and fundamental rationale for a wide variety of actions and causes. Non-governmental organizations, organizations from across the political spectrum, and public protests may all appeal to ideas of "justice"—environmental, social, racial, global, economic, and so on—and only in some cases are legal channels (i.e., the criminal or civil "justice" systems) seen as the first, most appropriate, or only avenue for enacting change.

The chapters in this book examine the negotiations and social interactions involved in the "production of justice" by which we refer to the multiple processes whereby socially contentious issues may be settled. The implementation of justice and the search for it are inextricable from—and sometimes a matter of—social and economic inequality, human rights abuses, organized or casual crime, violence, corruption, patronage, or other forms of structural exclusion. Asymmetries in different groups' experiences with justice engender practical and theoretical disagreements over acceptable forms of resolution. Indeed, those seeking justice are constrained by available channels and the underlying assumptions that bolster and define institutionalized forms of redress. As a whole, this book explores what "justice" means to different groups and individuals and the wide variety of methods they use in their struggle to achieve it. The authors find that definitions of "justice" often emerge from the interplay between holistic visions of rightful redress and the practical limitations of available channels for implementing resolutions.

The question of what justice is and the nature of its essential character have lain at the core of political philosophy for millennia (Gaus 2004: 253). In his book *A Theory of Justice*, John Rawls refers to "the sense of justice" as a moral capacity for good. In particular he sees that "[a] capacity for a sense of justice . . . would appear to be a condition of human sociability" (2003: 433). As such, debates over the nature of justice often take place in the abstract. Philosophers from Plato to Rawls have treated justice as, in Justyna Miklaszewska's words, "a theoretical concept [and one] that needs to be implemented in the real world" (2011: 119). In recent years, Amartya Sen has proposed a deviation from the prevailing domain of abstract or utopian justice theories, as for him, "[j]ustice is ultimately connected with the way people's lives go, and not merely with the nature of the institutions surrounding them" (2010: x). Sen's relational vision of justice offers a more grounded or practical approach through his interest in choice, human agency, and diversity. His concept of agency has, however, been criticized as thin and too abstract (e.g., Gasper 2002: 20) and lacking in "anthropological richness" (Giovanola 2005: 262). Studying justice ethnographically, as this book does, allows us to move away from abstract concepts and to access close-textured descriptions of the meanings of justice and their impact in social life (Clarke 2009; Comaroff and Roberts 1981; Geertz 1983; Hirsch 2006; Rosen 1989).

Philosophical treatments of the ancient and multivalent concept of justice have often reduced it to its manifestation in formal and codified legal systems (aka justice systems). This notion is inherently tied to a modern, liberal idea of the state based on the rule of law and a particular kind of state-subject relationship. In its early days, legal anthropologists and the anthropology of law were key in stepping in to highlight the historically and culturally derived assumptions embedded in this concept of justice, broadening the scope to include non-Western forms of assuring and restoring social harmony. Indeed, the field of anthropology has a long history of analyzing mechanisms of dispute management and their relationship to broader cultural systems (see Malinowski 1926; Nader 1997; Starr and Collier 1989). More recently, a number of important studies have examined justice as a political concept (Mamdani 2001; Wilson 2001), a field of contention (Borneman 1997; Niezen 2010; Payne 2008), and a space for social innovation (Richland 2008) and resistance (Besky 2014; Godoy 2006). Anthropology has also drawn attention to the intersections between custom-based forms of law and the formal legal orders of nation-states or international bodies (Merry 1997; Moore 1978; Nader 1990) and alternative forms of justice that emerge in the absence of effective judicial practice (Godoy 2006; Goldstein 2003, 2004). For example, in his book *Outlawed: Between Security and Rights in a Bolivian City*, Daniel Goldstein explores the complexities of the now state-sanctioned "community justice" in Cochabamba, Bolivia. Importantly, he shows how the marginal neighborhoods in his study are largely excluded from official forms of protection like effective policing and legal recourse as victims of crime, even as they remain subject to legal regulations governing their actions and options (Goldstein 2012). The ethnography of law has also been fundamental in exploring the functioning of law within society and the construction of legal truths through documentation and in the production of technocratic knowledge (Maurer 2005; Riles 2004, 2006).

Likewise, the anthropology of human rights has importantly drawn attention to the cultural and sociohistorical assumptions embedded in the concept of human rights. Mark Goodale has traced anthropology's long history of hesitation with the celebratory narrative of progress and universal good that accompanied the modern manifestation of human rights, as formalized in the wake of World War II (Goodale 2006, 2009; see also Messer 1993). While international institutions and funding agencies still tend to espouse a notion of human rights as a universal constant—indeed, that human rights be applicable equally in all times and places is a fundamental element of their contemporary form—anthropologists and other scholars have raised important questions about the historical particularity and neocolonialist potential of a singular, universal notion of rights (Baxi 2006; Clarke 2009). Rather than abandoning the notion of human rights, ethnographic studies of the practice of human rights[1] and the way human rights look and are implemented on the ground reveal the multiplicity of ways that people understand, mobilize, resist, adapt, and transform the discourse of human rights in defining and contesting the status quo (see Englund 2006; Faulk 2013; Goodale and Merry 2007; Merry 1997; Tate 2007; Wilson 1997).

Building off the anthropologies of law and human rights, what is at stake in an anthropology of justice is a deeper recognition of the multiple ways in which "justice" is understood. It can perhaps go without saying that the idea of justice is not a singular, universal idea but a complex, locally variable, and ever-changing concept. In their book *Mirrors of Justice*, Clarke and Goodale argue that there has been an "empirical pluralizing of justice" in the post–Cold War era (2010: 2). This is partly the result of the dissection of the concept of justice into codified variations that are then often treated separately by non-governmental organizations (NGOs) or international regulatory, legal, or governing agencies. Through this division of justice into disparate categories—local, popular, transitional, economic, and so on—we both gain an implicit recognition of the multiplicity of its meaning and lose sight of how this partitioning occludes its own arbitrariness and the very different ways that people interpret it (Clarke and Goodale 2010: 2). For example, transitional justice may be as much about economic inequality as it is about politics, so why could they be separated? Clarke and Goodale focus on the "multiple languages of justice" by considering the complex and interlocking relationship between local meanings of justice and international or normative visions of law, justice, and human rights (2010: 2).

This book expands on this focus with ethnographic attention to the variability in the meanings of justice, or what we might call "justice pluralism," which we use to refer to the coexistence of a plurality of meanings, ideas, and experiences attached to justice within spatial settings, scales, and layers. These meanings are frequently contested, so differences over the practical course of the law will play themselves out, in part, through attempts to specify justice's conceptual entailments and demands. As such, "justice pluralism" is broader than the related but more narrow concept of legal pluralism, which focuses specifically on legal systems, including the coexistence of different forms of law within a social field and the pluralistic qualities within systems and institutions of law (Merry 1988). Even taking a broad view of "legal system" to include "nonlegal forms of normative ordering" (Merry 1988: 870), justice pluralism differs from legal pluralism by focusing not on systems of social regulation but rather on the notions and ideas of proper action to redress a perceived wrong. Yet, the concept of legal pluralism per se has been criticized for begging the question of how to define "law." In Merry's words, "Where do we stop speaking of law and find ourselves simply describing social life?" (1988: 878). With calls to do away with the concept of legal pluralism due to these definitional problems, Tamanaha suggests we should "accept as 'legal' whatever . . . [is] identified as legal by the social actors" (2008: 396). Thus, "legal pluralism exists whenever social actors identify more than one source of 'law' within a social arena" (2008: 396). This book's approach is similar to Tamanaha's in that "justice pluralism" refers to what individual actors or movements invoke or characterize as justice.

This book joins a body of scholarship focused on the multiple and dialogic construction of legal cultures across Latin America. *Cultures of Legality: Judicialization and Political Activism in Latin America*, by Javier Couso, Alexandra Huneeus, and Rachel Sieder, and *The Judicialization of Politics in Latin America*, by Rachel Sieder, Alan Angell, and Line Schjolden both ask relevant questions about the changing face of politics and justice and explore the multiple ways in which the legal system is used, understood, and invoked in the actions of social movements across the region. In particular, *Cultures of Legality* exposes the disjunctions between the demands for justice and "legal cultures." This book's contribution is in its focuses on the meaning(s) of justice and their origins, whether or not they include judicialization.

This book also offers grounded, ethnographic explorations of the concepts of justice in practice and how these concepts may (or may not) rely on the justice that the law can provide *but are neither limited to nor fully encompassed by it*. To the extent that concepts of justice do rely on or appeal to systems of law, this books aims to destabilize representations that construct a dichotomy between formal and informal legal systems. The chapters demonstrate ethnographically the multiple ways in which different systems interact, and the boundaries between them become blurred and often unsettled. Likewise, Goodale and Merry (2007) have drawn attention to the interplay between local understandings of justice and the assumptions inherent within the national and international systems of law or mediation with which they are engaged. However, they also reject a reified division between the "global" (or dominant culture) and the "local" understandings and point out the theoretically productive space between and among global and local normativities (2007). At the heart of these normativities lie the participants

who interpret their actions and the events that animate them through certain un
derstandings of justice, understandings that are constructed within the space of
the interplay among different systems.

Latin America provides fertile terrain for the exploration of the meanings of
justice and a new theorization of justice as an analytic category. This is not to say
that Latin America is unique or homogeneous. Indeed, as Walter Mignolo pointed
out, the very category of "Latin America" is more a historically constructed conceptual unit than a geographic reality. An archaeology of the concept of justice as it
has been understood, undermined, imposed, implemented, and resisted throughout the region further exposes what Mignolo has signaled as the inextricable
coupling of modernity/coloniality (Mignolo 2005: 11), especially as it pertains to
morality and law. In other words, using "justice" as a theoretical lens reveals how
the colonizing process of imposing similar moral and legal precepts was shared
across the region, even as it draws attention to the differences produced from their
implementation in diverse social topographies.

Likewise, while Latin American nations share many features with other postcolonial countries, certain elements of a common history unite the widely varied
localities of the region and allow for a productive exploration of the divergences
that arise out of these commonalities. Here we mention specifically three of these
elements and how they have served as focal points in recent struggles for justice,
although others could no doubt be added.[2] The first is the upsurge in indigenous
movements and demands for recognition and respect of indigenous peoples,
lands, and culture (Postero 2007; Sullivan and Brunnegger 2011; Warren 1998;
Yashar 2005). As Chapters 5 and 7 demonstrate, the interplay between indigenous
and hegemonic forms of law and their constructive expression in visions of justice is complex and dynamic. Another feature that has been a prominent subject of justice activism is the region's enduring legacy and continued reliance on
extractivist economics. As New Left governments have come into power in the
twenty-first century, challenges to the privatization of state-run industries to (often foreign) private corporations have intensified, and efforts to increase national
industry and value-added processing have been given new life (for an overview,
see Burbach, Fox, and Fuentes 2013). Taking the idea of justice as a lens illuminates how the long history and lingering legacy of extractivism condition contemporary tensions (see Chapter 7) and inform New Left governments' attempts
to rectify historical injustices and forge a new, inclusive social foundation (see the
Conclusion). Finally, the broad reach and impressive diversity of accountability
movements across the region following (or, in some cases, during ongoing) political violence can be productively explored through the central demand of "justice"
that the movements so clearly articulate. As many of the chapters in this book

document, the call for justice made by these movements is omnipresent but not univocal. Exploring what activists and institutions consider to be "justice" offers a powerful lens for understanding what is at stake and what is in store for present-day Latin America.

Taking an analytical view of the diversity of justice in contemporary Latin America, two major themes emerge that underlie and structure how justice is perceived, received, and achieved. The first concerns legal subjectivity, or the effects of legal discourses and practices on the construction of self-identity or the administrative categorizing of others. Actors' settings are integral to the concepts of justice they promote, demonstrating how these concepts lie at the heart of individuals' and collective bodies' subjectivities and experiences. As Chapters 1, 5, and 7 explain, this process can be particularly contentious in situations with a plurality of state and nonstate legal systems, or competing legal logics. The second theme that a look at contemporary Latin America highlights is the role of the production, circulation, and legitimizing force of authoritative legal knowledge. The variety of understandings necessitates that the study of justice must also include attention to the kinds of legal knowledge accepted as valid, especially in cases where multiple knowledges coexist. Chapters 2, 3, 4, and 6 examine how actors become entangled in predetermined webs of authoritative knowledge and legal practices, even as they provide critical reflections on the process. In addition to these two themes, the chapters demonstrate a shared concern for the spatialization of justice. The ethnography that forms the heart of each chapter reveals the importance that space plays in the formation and actualization of ideas of justice. As a whole, this book argues that the production of legal subjectivities and authoritative knowledges are intertwined and that their instantiation in spaces, both concrete and conceptual, is fundamental to understanding the complex ways in which justice is defined and practiced in Latin America today. In the following sections we explore each of these themes in turn.

Legal Subjectivities

Aihwa Ong argues that an anthropology of the present "should analyze people's everyday actions as a form of cultural politics embedded in specific power contexts." Understandings of justice are part of the "reciprocal construction" of "cultural institutions, projects, regimes, and markets that shape people's motivations, desires, perceptions, and struggles *and make them particular kinds of subjects*" (1999: 5–6, emphasis added). This book takes up this way of conceptualizing politics as the claim- and constituency-making character of habitual action, in exploring the "reciprocal construction" of cultural institutions, projects, and regimes with those forces behind the actions—the motivations, desires, and perceptions   of the subjects that engage with them. Specifically, it adopts the concept of legal subjectivity to refer to the understanding of the self as a legal subject.[3] This includes self-perception as an active legal subject, in having the ability to utilize systems of law to achieve redress for perceived wrongs against the self, and passively, in seeing the self as subject to the restrictions and norms that systems of law impose. People's engagements with codified channels for achieving justice shape their subjectivity. In a related way, the sense of what is fair, or what is owed, feeds into the construction of formal systems, even as involvement in legal claims-making alters, informs, or reinforces the legal subjectivity of those engaged with the system.

In Latin America, hegemonic or state-controlled legal systems have foregrounded individual rights since the early postindependence era. While colonial and transitional postcolonial jurisprudence often focused more on substantive justice concerned primarily with restoring social cohesion and stability (Adelman 1999), the irruption of liberalist political and legal philosophy onto the American continent soon pushed the idea of preestablished, formalized, rational jurisprudence to center stage. Combined with the increasing incorporation of the individual as the ideal and only legitimate rights-bearing subject, legal jurisprudence became hegemonic as the primary legitimate system of justice ("La Justicia"/ "A Justiça"). More recently, the place of the individual in making claims to legal rights has been forcefully reasserted in the international sphere, as activists from across Latin America have utilized international organizations and transnational support networks in asserting rights being denied to them or violated by the nation-state. However, the dominance of French or Anglo ideas of jurisprudence, so formative to national legal systems across Latin America and to the emerging sphere of international law, have always existed alongside of and in tension with other, alternative systems. Often these have been in the form of ethnic community-based systems; in other cases, lack of access to effective and timely forms of legal justice has engendered the emergence or revival of alternative, non-state-based forms of seeking justice (see Chapter 5).

Legal subjectivity is influenced by the selective use, definition, and interpretation of law by actors in accordance with their perceptions of justice, and these understandings are often brought about by enacting or embodying alternative imaginings of justice and authority. Legal subjectivity, in such contexts, is particularly open to variation, and it is this variation that produces a dialectic tension with formalized, state-centered systems of law. One visible effect of these tensions can be seen in the wave of new constitutions across Latin American countries over the past two decades, which increasingly include subjects and provisions not traditional to Western law (see the Conclusion). The inclusion of some forms of collective rights has been particularly revealing, underscoring and recognizing that multiple understandings of rights coexist in Latin American societies. However, predictably, even new formalizations like the 2008 Ecuadorian Constitution, which, in response to push-back from alternative visions of justice, radically departs from Western law's homocentrism by affording equal rights to Nature, still fail to encompass the range of legal subjectivities and understandings of rights that are produced in the interstice between formal systems of law and lived experiences with justice.

An anthropology of justice needs to pay close attention to the lived experience of justice and its role in the production of legal subjectivities. While recognizing that the production of selves as legal subjects is in part determined by the structure of the law itself, the chapters in this book focus on the lived experience of justice and how perceptions of justice and forms of legal subjectivity influence interactions with the law. We need to ask: What does justice mean for the actors? What form of justice might satisfy those with an unsatisfied grievance? Do the methods used to achieve justice affect the value of the outcome to those seeking it? Finding contextually specific answers to these questions expands our understanding of what a legal subject is and of how different engagements with justice affect subjects' self-conception. In other words, the refraction of subjectivity through specific empirical or ethnographic cases sheds light on the role of justice in shaping subjectivity. This book maps the limits of legal subjectivities. Magalhães Wallace (Chapter 6), for instance, reflects on "subjectivity and citizenship," framing the question "What makes a citizen?" in the context of people's attempts to secure justice and greater "security" for themselves in Salvador, Brazil. In Chapter 7, Barros discusses the Atacameños of the Chilean desert and traces the relationship between "resistance and subjectivity" as people claim their rights in litigation. Chapter 1, by Vera Lugo, connects subjectivity to memory and shows subjects representing themselves through a narration of their experience, in the process constructing themselves as the victims of political violence and as legal subjects. The settings in which justice is delivered, which are often in Latin America enacted within local communities or otherwise outside of centralized legal systems, affect participants' sense of right and their self-understanding. The diversity of people's concepts of and experiences with justice demands attention to what this idea means in particular cases and forces a recognition of the plurality of forms of legal subjectivity. The chapters united here explore how a focus on lived experiences with justice provides a means for accessing the transformative potential of the space between the justice available through state-centered legal systems and the needs and understandings of those who seek it.

Authoritative Legal Knowledge

In many cases, the sense of justice as held by those who seek it can be only partly fulfilled through formal systems of law. The multiple and layered components of justice and the interplay between them are often lost when we consider justice only through established, state-directed forms of law and punishment. Yet, while multiple senses of what justice entails often exist within a community, rarely are those seeking justice able to access or achieve recognition for all aspects equally. Certain forms of resolution often gain precedence over others, leading to unequal or incomplete resolution for those affected. We can better make sense of these multiple senses of justice through an attention to the way legal knowledges are produced and legitimated.[4] As Brigette Jordan observed, "For any particular domain several knowledge systems exist, some of which, by consensus, come to carry more weight than others, either because they explain the state of the world better for the purposes at hand ('efficacy') or because they are associated with a stronger power base ('structural superiority'), and usually both" (1993: 152). In using the idea of authoritative legal knowledge, we refer to the production and legitimization of certain forms of legal meaning and procedures over others. "Authoritative" here denotes the legal meanings that have been endowed with the power of legitimacy and the formalization of procedures by which such meanings may emerge. Authoritative legal knowledge, then, is that knowledge considered most legitimate, significant, approved, or valued by social actors. Much like the "legal instrumentalism" that Annelise Riles (2006) has shown pervades even critical engagement with international human rights regimes, the dominance of authoritative legal knowledge infuses and permeates the idea of justice in many cases. We see authoritative legal knowledge as dependent on, or subject to, legal practices and to discourses of its authority (its relation to authorization) in order to maintain itself. In the case of authoritative legal knowledges, Jordan's "efficacy" corresponds to how certain structures and mechanisms of achieving justice can become hegemonic by being the only ones made available for individuals and communities (local, national, and international). In other cases, these structures derive structural superiority by being associated with a stronger power base, yet access to this form of justice is nonetheless limited, or the systems designed to enact it are weak, inefficient, or ineffective. However, as this book demonstrates, in both cases, authoritative legal knowledge structures *but does not encompass* all aspects of the concept of justice as defined and sought by those who seek it.

In using the concept of authoritative legal knowledges, we ask: How do legal knowledge(s) come to be authoritatively established? What kind(s) of legal knowledge are accepted as valid, reproduced, negotiated, and circulated? How are "legal cultures" formed, validated, and maintained? What particular kinds of knowledge are produced by legal proceedings? Specifically, what is rejected, altered, or manipulated by those seeking to use legal systems to address grievances? Further, how does the production and diffusion of legal knowledge—that is, the use of such knowledge—serve to "produce" justice? In this process, as the chapters demonstrate, knowledge will never be of any one type, but rather different authoritative knowledges will interact. Chapter 3, for instance, examines the practical interactions of the police and nonstate armed groups, describing a "trans-legal space" out of which working forms of the law, of justice, of the acceptable, and of the corrupt emerge through constant friction. Alonso Barros's work (Chapter 7) on communities in Chile's Atacama Desert examines ideas of knowledge as bestowed by "traditional" ownership of water sources. In considering experts in the juridical field in Argentina, Leticia Barrera opens the question of authoritative legal knowledge as such in Chapter 4.

Several of the authors in this book also address questions relating to the underlying processes by which "authoritativeness" of persons and procedures arises and of the relationship between authority-production and subjective experience with practices of law. It is in this interstice between legal subjectivity and authoritative legal knowledges that an anthropology of justice has the most to offer. Subjectivity and knowledge cannot be separated; all knowledge is inescapably experiential and intersubjective as actors produce and process knowledge through their lived experiences and contextualized social interactions (Benjamin 1989). The interpolation of individuals/communities as legal subjects by authoritative legal forms is, as a result, both creative of certain subjectivities and productive of the spaces that lead to resistance. It is creative of subjectivities in that authoritative knowledge can become "incorporated into people's experiences of themselves and their worlds, shaping desires, decisions, and actions" (Gammeltoft 2014: 166). On the other hand, challenges to the authority of legal knowledge can emerge from the breach between the justice that legal authority can provide and the needs and understandings of what justice is to those who seek it.

In outlining an anthropology of justice, the essential recognition is that notions of justice can be layered and varied even within the same community, and authoritative forms of knowledge, through the institutionalized privileging of particular aspects, can suppress more complete or inclusive forms of resolution. However, this should not obscure the ways in which authoritative knowledges are constructed through "an ongoing social process that both builds and reflects power relationships within a community of practice" (Jordan 1993: 152). When law is authoritative, ideas of justice influence the way in which formal systems of law are used or experienced by participants. Certainly authoritative legal knowledges

carry an obfuscating weight. Pierre Bourdieu called the process by which the au
thority of a knowledge system and the power relationships supporting it come
to be accepted as natural, inevitable, or singular "misrecognition" (1984; Jordan
1993: 153). Without denying the power of misrecognition, we focus more on the
disconnect between authoritative legal knowledges and those who question, resist,
or reinterpret the practices they engender by asserting ideas of justice that are not
adequately encompassed within the authoritative framework. Anthropologists/
ethnographers are well equipped to direct the focus toward what participants
understand as just and how practices of law can be used to enact local, alternate, or
uncodified understandings of justice. Attention to how people conceive of, define,
and search for justice shows how these ideas influence the way participants use,
value, or experience formal systems of law. Rather than forming separate domains,
authoritative legal knowledge is often contested precisely through the selective use
of formal legal structures. Laws and legal structures can themselves be used to produce expanded notions of justice that go beyond or may even be at odds with their
framing or intention (see Chapter 5). Ethnographic attention to these expanded
notions of justice and the nonexclusivity of law in concept and in practice can
serve to highlight how "justice" transcends a formal/informal dichotomy.

Spatializing Justice

Another theme that runs throughout the book is how issues of space—
theoretical, methodological, and physical—are central to the ways in which justice
is conceived, articulated, and practiced. Edward Soja argued for the need to over-
come what he calls an "ontological distortion" in social theory and knowledge production over the past hundred years.[5] This distortion, he says, has focused attention
"primarily on the social and temporal or historical aspects of being and much less
on life's fundamental spatiality" (2010: 70). He draws on Foucault in noting:

> The tendency to see time as dynamic and developmental, and space as relatively
> fixed and dead background arose in Western thought in the last half of the
> nineteenth century and continued, almost entirely unrecognized, to shape our
> thinking up to the present. . . . There is no good reason to presuppose that our
> existence as social and historical beings is axiomatically more important, more
> basic, than our existence as spatial beings, yet nearly all streams of philosophical
> thought, from the social sciences to Marx's scientific socialism, privilege the social
> and historical nature of reality over its fundamental spatiality. (70)

Soja utilizes the insights of Henri Lefebvre and David Harvey in attempting
to restructure the ontology of Western knowledge, giving equal attention to the

up-to-now relatively neglected third point in the "triple dialectic" of knowledge, consisting of the social/societal, the temporal/historical, and the spatial/geographical. In applying this perspective to justice, which he takes as a broad category that includes the general principles of fairness and democracy (74), he argues that the modern Western concept of "justice," with its roots in the seventh century BCE Athenian polis, was first and foremost the right to participate in the social life—politics, economics, religion, and culture—of a *city*, and thus inseparable from a sense of spatiality. While this constitutes only one (albeit a widely influential) version of justice, the broader point—that the meaning and experience of "justice," however conceived, take place in and through physical and conceptual spaces—has important theoretical and practical implications.

The chapters in this book consider how subjects view and experience justice, or the lack thereof, within and through spatial imaginaries and embodied practices of being-in-space. That these conceptual and physical spaces are socially constructed and produced at least in part in dialogue with ideas of (in)justice perhaps goes without saying—and is precisely the point. A far cry from Rawls's ahistorical and aspatial idea of justice, this book explores how "justice" emerges from the spaces of lived experience. Each chapter shows how the physical spaces inhabited and traversed by the subjects involved—from courtrooms to prisons to plazas to dry river beds—influence (and are often influenced by) the kind of justice that is sought. Many of the chapters also focus on the conceptual spaces of justice, or how justice is mapped by those who seek it. Additionally, the ethnography that informs each chapter forms a methodological space that engages the researcher in the concrete and imagined pathways that "justice" follows.

ORGANIZATION OF THE BOOK

Although the themes of legal subjectivity, authoritative legal knowledge, and space are shared across the chapters, this book is divided into three parts that each represent particular conceptual points of engagement. Chapters 1 and 2 highlight how ideas and practices of memory and justice come together in the on-the-ground construction of particular legal subjectivities. Chapter 1 focuses on Colombia—specifically on how legal narratives are selectively appropriated in debates over the rights of victims of conflict-related violence. In this case, as in many others, defining victims' rights has been a process fraught with tension and manipulated for political ends. Vera Lugo focuses on how state agencies and grassroots movements draw on codified narratives of transitional justice—what it is, who it is for, and how it is meant to operate—in defining and legitimizing their goals. The chapter also pays careful attention to the role of memory in localizing notions of justice.

For the Uribe administration, demobilizing the internationally condemned para-military forces became a political necessity to maintain credibility. The structure put into place to achieve this focused on reparation and reconciliation. Vera Lugo explores how memory, the performance of memory, and legal frameworks are utilized by grassroots movements and by the state in articulating localized claims as to what constitutes the limit and scope of legitimate rights.

Chapter 2 also highlights the intricate relationship between memory and justice. In 1994, a bomb attack blew apart the Argentine Jewish Mutual Aid Association building in Buenos Aires. Family members of those killed spent the next two decades struggling to achieve one thing: justice. But as Faulk describes in Chapter 2, for those most deeply affected by the bombing, what constitutes "justice" and how best to achieve it remain a complex issue. The chapter traces the actions of four different organizations formed in the wake of the attack and proposes that each is guided by their adherence to a multilayered vision of what constitutes justice. Divisions among the goals and actions of these different groups can be explained through attention to the validity that each places on certain forms of knowledge creation, showing the intricate link between authoritative knowledge and a sense of justice.

The chapters in Part 2 deal directly with how legality and legal knowledges are defined in spatialized terms. These spaces of legality are themselves productive, defining and delimiting the limits of the legal and interpolating the subjects who act within them. In Chapter 3, Graham Denyer Willis examines the ways in which types of authoritative knowledge are questioned, reinterpreted, and resisted. Using examples from the day-to-day functioning of Brazilian police operations, Willis explores the translegal space of discretionary police activity and social relations that can span the state, politics, and criminal actors. By exploring these translegal spaces, Willis shows why a discourse of human and citizens' rights fails to resonate with Brazilian police workers, for whom ideas of "justice" are deeply impacted by the challenges of inadequate pay and lack of protection from the violence they are meant to control.

In Chapter 4, Leticia Barrera explores the sites within which legal forms of knowledge are themselves constituted and transmitted to new practitioners. By focusing on the formation and opinions of legal experts from within (judicial agents) and without (legal scholars) the field of judicial practice, Barrera traces the literal and symbolic divide over how "justice" and the workings of the Argentine Supreme Court are perceived by those working within and for the court and those outside of it. However, her ethnography also suggests that the spaces where these knowledges of the Court are produced rely on intersubjective encounters that continuously redefine the position of the Court within a rapidly shifting social and political field.

Part 3 contains three chapters that illuminate the complex interplay between state-controlled systems of law and local interpretations and activism. As Sally Engle Merry notes, "Law empowers powerful groups to construct normative orders that enhance their control over resources and people, but also provides to less privileged people avenues for protest and resistance" (2006: 109). Chapters 5 and 7 take a critical look at the dominant legal structures governing the status and use rights of indigenous territories and, especially, the role of transnational organizations in the definition and enforcement of these rules.

Chapter 5 focuses on two Permanent Peoples' Tribunal (PPT) prehearings and the PPT process in Colombia. Brunnegger shows how these hearings, designed to poll popular opinion on the actions of transnational corporations on legally recognized indigenous land, can also be read as generative sites of knowledge practices of storytelling and testimony, and she focuses on the legitimacy-creating dynamics at play in the hearing's legally framed pursuit of justice. By serving as spaces for expressing and mobilizing the pain and outrage that corporate incursions into their land have provoked, these hearings allowed participants to assert alternative forms of knowledge and to establish networks in which these knowledges and senses of belonging are negotiated, legitimized, and reinforced. By reading these hearings as sites of knowledge production, Brunnegger reconceptualizes the dynamics of the interrelated practices that comprise knowledge-making in these justice-seeking processes, emphasizing how "knowledge turns into a fictitious commodity . . . capable of creating and reproducing a network of social relations around the (legal and moral) acknowledgment of wrongdoing."

Chapter 6 also considers the interplay between state-level legal structures and local interpretations and activism. Marta Magalhães Wallace explores the way in which ideas about insecurity have come to modulate public discourse on justice and citizenship in Salvador, Brazil, inflecting the experience of life in the city and the values that underpin the resident's image of a good citizen and the meanings they give to ideas of justice. Considering the city in terms of a dystopian landscape, Magalhães Wallace illuminates how feelings of insecurity permeate residents' perceptions of their city and create a citizen-subjectivity based on notions of the human person (*pessoa humana*). In this light, she shows how legal formalizations designed to enact laws such as the constitutionally guaranteed "right to the city" must contend with local realities that are not always amenable to the principles it sets out to foster.

Chapter 7 follows the Atacameños of the Chilean desert as they assert their rights to their land and, crucially, the scarce water that manages to reach it. Alonso Barros explores the social life of water and the types of authoritative knowledge constructed around and about its proper and legitimate uses. The debates, we are shown, tap into and flow out of indigenous cosmologies, neoliberal ideologies, and corporate fetishization of commodities and of its own self-interests. Fundamentally, Barros explains how laws governing water usage deepen racialized conflicts by fetishizing nature/culture binaries in the form of law.

In the Conclusion, Mark Goodale offers a critical reflection on the changing nature of law and justice in Movimiento al Socialismo (MAS)-era Bolivia. Crucially, and with implications that reach well beyond that country's borders, he shows how the senses of justice embedded in projects of alternative modernization are a response to the *lack* of justice in the lived experiences of the subject-citizens of the "neoliberal world order." "Justice," then, becomes a "paradoxically opaque moral, cultural, and legal category [and] a way to create space within which at least the possibility of [some social good] can be envisioned." As the Bolivian case demonstrates, however, the revolutionary potential that lurks within the space between the idea and lived reality of justice is not easily transformed into effective, more "just" forms of postrevolution governance. The very nature of the transition from imagined potential into practical action brings change into the ideas as well as the institutions. Goodale's reflections on Bolivia and beyond highlight how the anthropology of justice has an inherently dual formation. Fundamentally, it seeks to describe and understand justice ethnographically as a social, cultural, and political category. In doing so, however, the anthropology of justice can also remove the false promise of the veil from the iconic blind figure of Western justice's eyes, uncovering the entrenched structural inequalities that condition the possibilities and limits of lived experiences with "justice" in the contemporary world.

PLURALIZING JUSTICE

The chapters in this book speak to broader questions about the limits of state power, human rights, and international law. The interplay of justice, law, and rights in Western thought is evidenced in the semiotic—all three concepts overlapping in the Latin *jus*, meaning both "right" and "law," with the latter two still inseparable in both Spanish (*derecho*) and Portuguese (*direito*).[6] The book explores the links between and the limits on how these concepts manifest in lived experience and aims to promote a dialogue on the range of definitions of "justice." At the same time, the book reassesses the nature of the nation-state as it is sidelined (or sometimes devolves its authority) to other formal or nonformal justice systems. The chapters contained herein propose a new agenda for discussions of the diversity of forms of justice possible in contemporary Latin America.

An examination of contemporary Latin America reveals the plurality of meanings of "justice" and suggests a theoretical approach to studying these meanings in contexts across the globe. Paying attention to the on-the-ground construction of legal subjectivities and authoritative legal knowledge opens the way to a deeper analysis of what justice means in particular cases and for those who would seek it. A sense of justice is constructed through the embodied expression of memory, mapped out spatially, and continuously negotiated in dialogic practice. An anthropology of justice has the potential to shed light on how these aspects coexist in producing and transforming what justice can and must entail for those who seek it, providing both a reconceptualization of what justice delivers and the many forms it can take. Understanding the dynamic processes of construction of what justice entails and the concept's power to generate alternative futures is essential to achieving meaningful resolution to social conflict and to constructing cooperative rather than oppressive forms of law.

NOTES

1. Goodale usefully defines the practice of human rights as "all of the many ways in which social actors across the range talk about, advocate for, criticize, study, legally enact, vernacularize, and so on, the idea of human rights in its various forms" (2007: 24).

2. Our thanks to an anonymous reviewer for this suggestion.

3. This book analytically differentiates legal subjectivity from legal consciousness. Legal consciousness has been defined in many ways in sociolegal studies. It has been understood as people's attitude toward the law, often in the context of resistance and the study of power relations (e.g., Coutin, Mallin, and Merry 2014; Ewick and Silbey 1998). Merry argues that "legal consciousness describes the way an individual conceives of his/her relationship to the law and how that shapes who he/she is" (Coutin, Mallin, and Merry 2014: 4) and that legal subjectivity is a "dimension of legal consciousness" (ibid.). This book builds on this approach to legal subjectivity but relates it specifically to people's understandings of their relationship to various systems of redress and their strivings toward justice (whether "justice" relies on these systems or not). In this specific sense, then, "subjectivity" is rather "the basis of agency" (Ortner 2006) and legal subjectivity as the degree to which the subject's engagement with legal structures encompasses (or fails to encompass) their sense of achieved justice.

4. Goldman used his ethnographic research with the World Bank to explore how "authoritative green knowledge" was created and how it operated as the dominant or authoritative knowledge, structuring funding decisions and programs in Laos. He uses the concept of authoritative green knowledge to refer both to a "certain understanding of environmentalism (e.g., environmentally sustainable development), and to the particular set of facts that are produced to differentiate, classify, and categorize populations and their natural environments" (2001: 194). Likewise, this book maintains that authoritative legal knowledge encompasses both a certain understanding of the legal system and the production and dissemination of legal instruments and their role in legitimizing particular visions of justice.

5. The so-called spatial turn, or the appreciation of the spatial dimensions of social life, has been widely discussed in the social sciences and humanities. Since Giddens first stated in 1979 that "most forms of social theory have failed to take seriously enough not only the

temporality of social conduct but also its spatial attributes" (202), substantial attention has been paid to analyzing space as an analytical concept (see von Benda-Beckmann, von Benda-Beckmann, and Griffiths 2009: 1). This also includes legal anthropology because space is inscribed into law as "legal practice serves to produce space, yet, in turn, is shaped by a sociospatial context" (Blomley 1994: 51).

6. The moral correctness of "rights," whatever their culturally and historically specific content may be, is further expressed in the linkage in English of "right" and "just"; a just action is also a right (i.e., correct) one. The linkage of "exact/perfect in form" with "fair," such as the Spanish *justo*, also lends linguistic credence to an innate perfection of law.

WORKS CITED

Adelman, Jeremy. 1999. *Republic of Capital: Buenos Aires and the Legal Transformation of the Atlantic World*. Stanford, CA: Stanford University Press.

Baxi, Upendra. 2006. *The Future of Human Rights*. 2nd ed. Oxford: Oxford University Press.

Benjamin, Walter. 1989. "On the Program of the Coming Philosophy." In *Philosophy, Aesthetics, History*, edited by Gary Smith, 1–12. Chicago: University of Chicago Press.

Besky, Sarah. 2014. *The Darjeeling Distinction: Labor and Justice on Fair-Trade Tea Plantations in India*. Berkeley: University of California Press.

Blomley, Nicholas K. 1994. *Law, Space and the Geographies of Power*. New York: Guilford.

Borneman, John. 1997. *Settling Accounts: Violence, Justice and Accountability in Postsocialist Europe*. Princeton, NJ: Princeton University Press.

Bourdieu, Pierre. 1984. *Distinction: A Social Critique of the Judgment of Taste*. Translated by Richard Nice. Cambridge, MA: Harvard University Press.

Burbach, Roger, Michael Fox, and Federico Fuentes. 2013. *Latin America's Turbulent Transitions: The Future of Twenty-First Century Socialism*. London: Zed.

Clarke, Kamari Maxine. 2009. *Fictions of Justice: The International Criminal Court and the Challenge of Legal Pluralism in Sub-Saharan Africa*. Cambridge: Cambridge University Press.

Clarke, Kamari Maxine, and Mark Goodale, eds. 2010. *Mirrors of Justice: Law and Power in the Post–Cold War Era*. Cambridge: Cambridge University Press.

Comaroff, John, and Simon Roberts. 1986. *Rules and Processes: The Cultural Logic of Dispute in an African Context*. Chicago: University of Chicago Press.

Couso, Javier, Alexandra Huneeus, and Rachel Sieder, eds. 2010. *Cultures of Legality: Judicialization and Political Activism in Latin America*. Cambridge: Cambridge University Press.

Coutin, Susan Bibler, Sean Mallin, and Sally Engle Merry. 2014. "Technologies of Truth, Law, and Inequalities." Interview. *PoLAR: Political and Legal Anthropology Review Online*, June 12. http://www.polaronline.org/virtual-issues/law-and-inequalities/interview-coutin-merry/.

Englund, Harri. 2006. *Prisoners of Freedom: Human Rights and the African Poor*. Berkeley: University of California Press.

Ewick, Patricia, and Susan Silbey. 1998. *The Common Place of Law: Stories from Everyday Life*. Chicago: University of Chicago Press.

Faulk, Karen Ann. 2013. *In the Wake of Neoliberalism: Citizenship and Human Rights in Argentina*. Stanford, CA: Stanford University Press.

Gammeltoft, Tine. 2014. *Haunting Images: A Cultural Account of Selective Reproduction in Vietnam*. Berkeley: University of California Press.

Gasper, Des. 2002. "Is Sen's Capability Approach an Adequate Basis for Considering Human Development?" Working Paper Series 360, Institute of Social Studies, The Hague.

Gaus, Gerald F. 2004. "The Diversity of Comprehensive Liberalisms." In *The Handbook of Political Theory*, edited by Gerald F. Gaus and Chandran Kukathas, 110–114. London: Sage.

Geertz, Clifford. 1983. "Local Knowledge: Fact and Law in Comparative Perspective." In *Local Knowledge: Further Essays in Interpretive Anthropology*, edited by Clifford Geertz, 167–234. New York: Basic Books.

Giovanola, Benedetta. 2005. "Personhood and Human Richness: Good and Well-Being in the Capability Approach and Beyond." *Review of Social Economy* 63 (2): 249–267.

Godoy, Angelina Snodgrass. 2006. *Popular Injustice: Violence, Community, and Law in Latin America*. Stanford, CA: Stanford University Press.

Goldman, Michael. 2001. "The Birth of a Discipline: Producing Authoritative Green Knowledge, World Bank-Style." *Ethnography* 2 (2): 191–217.

Goldstein, Daniel M. 2003. "'In Our Own Hands': Lynching, Justice, and the Law in Bolivia." *American Ethnologist* 30 (1): 22–43.

———. 2004. *The Spectacular City: Violence and Performance in Urban Bolivia*. Durham, NC: Duke University Press.

———. 2012. *Outlawed: Between Security and Rights in a Bolivian City*. Durham, NC: Duke University Press.

Goodale, Mark. 2006. "Toward a Critical Anthropology of Human Rights." *Current Anthropology* 47 (3): 485–511.

———. 2007. "Locating Rights, Envisioning Law between the Global and the Local." In *The Practice of Human Rights: Tracking Law between the Global and the Local*, edited by Mark Goodale and Sally Engle Merry, 1–38. Cambridge: Cambridge University Press.

———. 2009. *Surrendering to Utopia*. Stanford, CA: Stanford University Press.

Goodale, Mark, and Sally Engle Merry, eds. 2007. *The Practice of Human Rights: Tracking Law between the Global and the Local*. Cambridge: Cambridge University Press.

Hirsch, Susan F. 2006. *In the Moment of Greatest Calamity: Terrorism, Grief, and a Victim's Quest for Justice*. Princeton, NJ: Princeton University Press.

Jordan, Brigette. 1993. *Birth in Four Cultures*. 4th ed. Prospect Heights, IL: Waveland.

Malinowski, Bronislaw. 1926. *Crime and Custom in Savage Society*. London: Rowman and Littlefield.

Mamdani, Mahmood. 2001. *When Victims Become Killers: Colonialism, Nativism, and the Genocide in Rwanda*. Princeton, NJ: Princeton University Press.

Maurer, Bill. 2005. *Mutual Life, Limited: Islamic Banking, Alternative Currencies, Lateral Reason*. Princeton, NJ: Princeton University Press.

Merry, Sally Engle. 1988. "Legal Pluralism." *Law and Society Review* 22 (5): 869–896.

———. 1997. "Legal Pluralism and Transnational Culture: The Ka Ho'okolokolonui Kanaka Maoli Tribunal, Hawai'i, 1993." In *Human Rights, Culture and Context: Anthropological Perspectives*, edited by Richard A. Wilson, 28–48. London: Pluto.

———. 2006. "Anthropology and International Law." *Annual Review of Anthropology* 36: 99–116.

Messer, Ellen. 1993. "Anthropology and Human Rights." *Annual Review of Anthropology* 22: 221–249.

Mignolo, Walter. 2005. *The Idea of Latin America: Blackwell Manifestos*. Malden, MA: Blackwell.

Miklaszewska, Justyna. 2011. "Contemporary Theories of Justice: Between Utopia and Political Practice." *Polish Journal of Philosophy* 5 (2): 119–122.

Moore, Sally Falk. 2000. *Law as Process: An Anthropological Approach*. Berlin: LIT Verlag.

Nader, Laura. 1990. *Harmony Ideology—Injustice and Control in a Zapotec Mountain Village*. Stanford, CA: Stanford University Press.

———, ed. 1997. *Law in Culture and Society*. Berkeley: University of California Press.

Niezen, Ronald. 2010. *Public Justice and the Anthropology of Law*. Cambridge: Cambridge University Press.

———. 2011. "The Social Study of Human Rights—A Review Essay." *Comparative Studies in Society and History* 53 (3): 682–691.

Ong, Aihwa. 1999. *Flexible Citizenship: The Cultural Logics of Transnationality*. Durham, NC: Duke University Press.

Ortner, Sherry. 2006. *Anthropology and Social Theory: Culture, Power, and the Acting Subject*. Durham, NC: Duke University Press.

Payne, Leigh A. 2008. *Unsettling Accounts: Neither Truth nor Reconciliation in Confessions of State Violence*. Durham, NC: Duke University Press.

Postero, Nancy. 2007. *Now We Are Citizens*. Stanford, CA: Stanford University Press.

Rawls, John. 2003. *A Theory of Justice*. Cambridge, MA: Harvard University Press.

Richland, Justin. 2008. *Arguing with Tradition: The Language of Law in Hopi Tribal Court*. Chicago: University of Chicago Press.

Riles, Annelise. 2004. "Real Time: Unwinding Technocractic and Anthropological Knowledge." *American Ethnologist* 31 (3): 392–405.

———. 2006. "Anthropology, Human Rights, and Legal Knowledge: Culture in the Iron Cage." *American Anthropologist* 108 (1): 52–65.

Rosen, Lawrence. 1989. *The Anthropology of Justice: Law as Culture in Islamic Society*. Cambridge: Cambridge University Press.

Sen, Amartya. 1999. "Global Justice: Beyond International Equity." In *Global Public Goods: International Cooperation in the 21st Century*, edited by Inge Kaul, Isabelle Grunberg, and Marc Stern, 116–125. Oxford: Oxford University Press.

———. 2011. *The Idea of Justice*. Cambridge, MA: Harvard University Press.

Sieder, Rachel, Alan Angell, and Line Schjolden. 2005. *The Judicialization of Politics in Latin America*. New York: Palgrave Macmillan.

Soja, Edward W. 2010. *Seeking Spatial Justice*. Minneapolis: University of Minnesota Press.

Starr, June, and Jane Fishburne Collier. 1989. *History and Power in the Study of Law: New Directions in Legal Anthropology*. Ithaca, NY: Cornell University Press.

Sullivan, Kathleen M., and Sandra Brunnegger. 2011. "Introduction (Symposium: Negotiating Rights between Peoples and States in Latin America)." *Studies in Law, Politics, and Society* 55 (1): 3–17.

Tamanaha, Brian Z. 2008. "Understanding Legal Pluralism: Past to Present, Local to Global." *Sydney Law Review 30 (3): 375–411.*

Tate, Winifred. 2007. *Counting the Dead: The Culture and Politics of Human Rights Activism in Colombia*. Berkeley: University of California Press.

Von Benda-Beckmann, Franz, Keebet von Benda-Beckmann, and Anne Griffiths. 2009. "Space and Legal Pluralism: An Introduction." In *Spatializing Law: An Anthropological Geography of Law in Society*, edited by Franz von Benda-Beckmann, Keebet von Benda-Beckmann, and Anne Griffiths, 1–29. Burlington, UK: Ashgate.

Warren, Kay. 1998. *Indigenous Movements and Their Critics: Pan-Maya Activism in Guatemala*. Princeton, NJ: Princeton University Press.

Wilson, Richard, ed. 1997. *Human Rights, Culture and Context: Anthropological Perspectives*. Chicago: Pluto.

———. 2001. *The Politics of Truth and Reconciliation in South Africa: Legitimizing the Post-Apartheid State*. Cambridge: Cambridge University Press.

Yashar, Deborah J. 2005. *Contesting Citizenship in Latin America: The Rise of Indigenous Movements and the Postliberal Challenge*. Cambridge: Cambridge University Press.

PART ONE   MEMORY AND JUSTICE
UNDER CONSTRUCTION

1 TRANSITIONAL JUSTICE, MEMORY, AND THE EMERGENCE OF LEGAL SUBJECTIVITIES IN COLOMBIA

Juan Pablo Vera Lugo

Modern and contemporary Colombian history has been shaped by internal conflict. The country has experienced different cycles of violence since the late 1940s: bipartisan violence during the 1950s, the rise of guerrillas in 1964 in the context of the Cold War, and the emergence of drug trafficking and paramilitary groups from the early 1980s until the present. Over the past three decades, paramilitaries, guerrillas, and the state security forces have been behind the disappearance of 27,000 civilians[1] and have forcibly displaced more than 4.7 million Colombian peasants, members of the indigenous groups, and Afro-Colombian communities,[2] who have lost approximately 16 million acres of land.[3] In Colombia, most victims and targets of violence belong to the poorest strata, which comprise 49 percent of Colombia's population of 45 million; the various armies are made up of this large pool of individuals.

Many attempts have been made to achieve peace through amnesties and pardons with different armed groups that have rebelled against the state. However, a dramatic turn in this history took place between 2003 and 2005. Álvaro Uribe was the first Colombian president to initiate a peace process with paramilitary groups—an army born in the heart of the drug trafficking in the mid-1980s for the protection of illegal businesses and later used by landlords and regional political elites as private armies for their protection against guerrilla groups (Romero 2003; Ronderos 2014). Negotiations started in July 2003 and ended with the partial demobilization of the paramilitary forces in 2005. During the same year, Law 975, or the so-called Justice and Peace Law, was enacted, incorporating transitional justice mechanisms and emphasizing the disarmament, demobilization, and reintegration (DDR) of combatants.[4] At the same time, and continuing from 2005 to 2010, the Colombian government neglected to address the rights of the victims and decidedly stigmatized social movements and organizations. Although this changed in 2011 with the enactment of the Victims Law and Land Restitution Act, this chapter focuses on the unexpected consequences of the Justice and

Peace Law from 2005 to 2010. Interestingly, during this time a number of social agents, organizations, and institutions appropriated and mobilized a narrative of transitional justice and interpretations of its meaning, thereby challenging the normative purpose of the law and making Colombian victims visible before the international community and to the broader community of victims themselves. Surprisingly, this visibility remains limited within Colombian society as a whole because the majority of the nation's population remain indifferent to the lives and fates of their fellow citizens and refuse to investigate these disappearances.

A key dimension of transitional justice is encouraging perpetrators to confess to crimes and human rights violations in exchange for light sentences, with the goal of achieving truth and reparation for victims of violence. Transitional justice attempts to establish or reestablish first-generation human rights—and sometimes, as has been debated in Colombia, second-generation human rights—emphasizing retributive rather than restorative justice (Uprimny et al. 2006). However, transitional justice goes beyond this legal frame and is linked to a set of practices related to truth commissions, institutional reforms, reparation programs, human rights archives, memorialization, public policy, museums, amnesties, pardons, and criminal prosecutions (Hinton 2010; Payne 2008; Wilson 2001).[5] Colombia's case is somewhat different, given that the transitional justice approach has been implemented during the ongoing internal conflict as a means to achieve peace. Even given the plethora of studies about Colombian violence, state violence has received scant scholarly attention (Corradi, Fagen, and Garretón Merino 1992; Taussig 1992).[6] No attempts have been made to understand the mechanisms through which the Colombian state has reactualized and masked itself in order to preserve its legitimacy and perpetuity (Corrigan and Sayer 1985; Taussig 1992). In describing Colombian contemporary violence, Victoria Sanford (2004) has argued that in the context of paramilitary violence in the late 1980s and the 1990s, what initially appears to be simply a privatization of state violence is revealed in practice as state violence by proxy (Sanford 2004)—that is, state forces' support for and involvement with the creation and actions of the paramilitary groups.

And yet, Colombian institutions have remained legitimate for the majority of Colombian society despite the state's use of force against the civilian population. Accordingly, rather than considering Colombia as a failed state,[7] this chapter argues that the Colombian state has been fairly successful in imposing its power and legitimacy. How did this happen? The answer is that transitional justice has worked as a renewed legal ideology for the state and has granted the state legitimacy as it implemented paramilitary demobilization using the framework of transitional justice. This idea calls attention to a cyclical and dynamic conception of legitimacy-making, where both state and nonstate actors appropriate and invest legal capital in asserting their own particular causes.

Traditionally, lawyers, policy makers, and social science scholars have been interested in exploring the application of international standards and the efficacy of transitional justice rulings. However, from an ethnographic point of view, this chapter highlights how both expert and nonexpert groups appropriate this particular juridical language (Merry 2006)[8] and explores how it is socially transformed and contested. By exploring the work of one governmental institution and one non-governmental organization, we will see how discourses about the rights of the victims of political violence work as a site of appropriation of legal narratives to mediate specific social and political struggles. From 2008 to 2010, the members of the Grupo de Memoria Histórica (Historical Memory Center, or GMH) and the Movimiento Nacional de Víctimas de Crímenes de Estado (National Movement of State Crime Victims, or MOVICE) had a strong influence on the adoption and circulation of transitional justice meanings and practices. Victims of state violence became victim-activists in the process of articulating their victimhood. The rights to justice and memory can become powerful instruments of state victims' struggles for legitimacy, while remaining particular objects of aspiration and performance for the state itself. The victims of state actors discussed in this chapter represent the most extreme and paradoxical form of victimization because often they are unable to mobilize their claims within traditional institutional mechanisms.

BECOMING A VICTIM OF COLOMBIAN POLITICAL VIOLENCE

Although humanitarian programs that provided assistance to internally displaced people in Colombia existed before 2005, these programs were not part of a consistent and structured public policy.[9] On the contrary, to be recognized as a *victim* was to put oneself in a marginal social position—one in which legal and citizenship guarantees are lacking. Victimhood in Colombia, then, has been the object of different forms of stigmatization because it entails what Kristeva (1982) and Panourgiá (2009) refer to as "abject subjectivities," a troubling anomaly to the sovereign order.

However, since the implementation of the law in 2005, the concept of being a *victim* has gained a different social significance, legitimacy, and meaning. Before that year, the main humanitarian concern of local institutions and international agencies was the forced internal displacement of the population (IDP). This shift is discernible through the news and broadcast media about Colombia's ongoing humanitarian crisis since 2005.[10] The emergence of the concept of being a victim reframed within the transitional justice paradigm subsumed the internal displace-ment phenomena and other complex and varied forms of victimization.

In this new context, the concept of being a victim has become a realm of con-testation. For some—mostly left wing—organizations, the concept of being a vic-tim fails to acknowledge the heroic role of social groups and countless unknown people in the struggle for the democratization of Colombian society. For others, broadly defined as the right-wing rural elite and urban upper and middle classes, the concept of being a victim recasts the rights of people who have been de-prived of them by subversive groups such as Fuerzas Armadas Revolucionarias de Colombia (Revolutionary Armed Forces of Colombia, or FARC). Some grassroots organizations and non-governmental organizations (NGOs) demand recognition of specific forms of victimization, such as in the case of ASFAMIPAZ (Asociación Colombiana de Familiares de Miembros de la Fuerza Pública Retenidos y Libera-dos por Grupos Guerrilleros), which is composed of the families of kidnapped police officers, or groups such as MOVICE and its claims against state violence. These groups mobilize their own victimization in demanding justice and the right to know what has happened to their loved ones.

Many social organizations exist today that demand justice, truth, and redress for victims of state crimes and paramilitary groups. From 2008 to 2010, the num-ber of social, academic, and political organizations formed around the concept of transitional justice increased dramatically. Practices based on memories—in personal archives, local museums, and public acts—and reports by people who consider themselves victims also increased. This new class of victims demanded basic citizenship rights—the rights to life and education—as well as the rights to know the truth and to justice and redress.

Victims' mobilization of their experiences and the intersection between this and the role the state forces play in their victimization produce a conjuncture that includes both the right not to be harmed and the rights derived from any harm they have incurred. This is very evident and further complicated in Colombia, where many victims and victims' relatives have endured recurring experiences of state actors' violence. From the victims' perspective, the image of the state is a contradictory one: the state possesses the power to take away everything, but, paradoxically for victims, the state is the only entity that can, and should, enact its restitution. The testimonials of survivors who have been victims of state actors or state actors by proxy provide a rich source of state representations as corrupt and against society, but they also preserve the idea that the state must do justice and recognize its weaknesses. Yet, it is the law that, as discursive formation and state language, also empowers the survivors of political violence when it comes to claiming their rights through transitional justice, human rights, or constitutional rights discourse.[11]

In this context, state victims and victim-activists have to struggle not only against the constant threat to their lives but, fundamentally, against stigmatization, which produces both political marginalization and social ostracism. One of the most frequent claims of victims of state agents is what they call *la lucha por la dignidad* (struggle for their dignity). Dignity, which embodies the very sense of restituted self for victims, is a central aspect of the agentive mobilization of survivors and their relatives and advocates in Colombia, and it plays a central role in the emotional mobilization of victimhood. Incorporating dignity into the frame of rights discourses is calling for the rehumanization of the victims of state violence and also for a particular sense of justice. For victims and survivors, dignity requires that the state acknowledge their suffering and the harm it has done to them. Dignity is also related to truth and the restitution of their *buen nombre* (good name). This means the historical recognition of state crimes and the active and successful application of an acceptable form of justice.

The articulation and understanding of victims' and survivors' histories and organizations is complicated because they occur within the struggle for historical representation between survivors and perpetrators (Tate 2007).[12] One of the main factors related to the how victims are rendered invisible culturally and socially has been the systematic process of naming, whereby the state relegates these particular social actors to the boundaries of political illegitimacy through a discourse of criminalization or illegality (Panourgiá 2009; Scott 1998). The struggle over the representation of victims and survivors has been shaped by the state criminalization of political opposition and illegal groups supposedly acting beyond state reach. In this sense, the governmental interpretation of violence has become the representational space where meanings are contested but also a specific place of state making (Desmond and Goldstein 2010).

The collapse of peace talks between the administration of Andrés Pastrana (1998–2002) and the FARC guerrillas in the late 1990s led to the loss of social and political credibility of the guerrillas' will to peace among the Colombian population and general public opinion. Eventually, the failure of the peace talks led to the moral and political justification of state persecution of the country's grassroots and social organizations. The public discourse also changed after September 11, 2001, to reflect the war on terror. Since then, Colombian counterinsurgency efforts and state violence increased a concentration on Colombian social, economic, and security policies as the main pillars of Colombian development with the implementation of "Plan Colombia," a Colombian and U.S. military and diplomatic

US$7.5 billion ('Transnational Institute 2001) initiative aimed at combating Co
lombian drug cartels and guerrilla groups (Ramírez 2011). The polarization of
Colombian society during this period sought also to increase the dissemination of
international and humanitarian discourses, intensifying the social representations
of "victims" associated with Colombian conflict and rooted in a historical struggle
over the meaning and the legitimacy of their political recognition.[13]

At this time, many targets of violence were affiliated with grassroots organizations, opposition groups, local leaders, and unions, as well as local businesspeople,
politicians, and peasants suspected of collaborating with subversive groups, paramilitary groups, or state armed forces. In the public discourse, state agents usually justify violence against guerrilla groups and those designated as terrorists and
amigos del terrorismo (friends of terrorism). In the case of victims of state actors,
some survivors, victims' relatives, and civic organizations challenge this representation by presenting themselves as *victims of state crimes*. Confronted with the
situation of being associated with left-wing groups that are allegedly allied with
guerrillas, these individuals and groups insisted that the state must recognize their
suffering. But how are these new transnational legal narratives transforming and
distinguishing the victim as deserving of legitimacy and political justification?
How are these postconflict legal discourses transforming the social and political
spaces in which victims and survivors have traditionally been positioned by the
state and represented by society, while the conflict endures?[14]

TRANSITIONAL JUSTICE APPROPRIATIONS

When individuals try to identify themselves as victim-activists in the context of
transitional justice in Colombia, discursive mobilization challenges their position
in the social milieu. Transitional justice and human rights can be understood as
resources or forms of social capital where appropriation is mediated through the
work of human rights activists and governmental and non-governmental institutions.[15] This mediation is produced through different means that usually end
when the harm inflicted upon survivors and victims' relatives is *recognized* as
something beyond a criminal act. Survivors become "victims" not just through
their engagement with the realm of law but also through the actual resignification
enacted by the use of transitional justice discourse.

Using a discourse of transitional justice started to frame the way in which some
victim-activists thought about their experiences. This process is not the same for
everyone, and it takes place in different contexts and organizations. We will focus
on GMH and MOVICE to demonstrate how this resignification is made possible
through two different practices and ends.

MOVICE is a good example of transforming the transitional justice legal paradigm into an instrument for human rights struggles. One MOVICE member said
the following:[16]

> I think there is a transformation in the victim. Here, there is a reality. The
> majority of the victims share a common characteristic: they are poor people or
> people with limited resources. What we are trying to do here is to help the victim
> make the transition from being a victim to becoming a political actor. And this
> transition consists in going beyond obtaining economic redress and becoming a
> person who is able to demand rights. We find victims that are aware of this, but
> there are others that have to understand that their dignity is dependent upon the
> acknowledgement that they have other rights. When they understand that, they
> fight for their dignity and that of their loved ones.

In 2005, MOVICE began to organize different associations of victims of state
crimes into one national movement. This organization was formed in reaction to
the Justice and Peace Law. According to its most visible representatives, MOVICE
emerged in response to the "absence of legal instruments for the recognition and
reparation of victims."[17] Today, MOVICE's goal is the legitimation and historical
visibility of "state crime victims."[18]

Although state agent victims' organizations are not new in Colombia,
MOVICE brought together victims and organizations associated with state crimes
that existed throughout the country, and in doing so facilitated the incorporation of debates about transitional justice. Between 2006 and 2008, the movement
gathered rural and urban groups and consolidated a central organization with five
"chapters" across Colombia's regions. MOVICE's members' main role since then
has been to raise awareness among survivors and victims' relatives about their
rights, to show them the legal means of making their claims, and, most of all,
to allow survivors to recognize themselves as victims.[19] This has been the most
challenging work for MOVICE, given that prosecution of state agents and paramilitary members is done without political and security guaranties. Particularly
in rural areas, where victims are more isolated from institutional influence and
protection, the work of an organization that protects and encourages victims to
denounce crimes is constantly threatened.

On the other hand, the Grupo de Memoria Historica (Historic Memory Group,
or GMH) was created as part of the Comisión Nacional de Reparación y Reconciliación (Reparation and Reconciliation National Commission, or CNRR) with
the mandate to produce reports on Colombia's internal conflict.[20] GMH's goal was
to explore the violence that occurred Colombia since 1965 by studying emblematic cases of crimes committed by each of the different armed actors, including the

state. From 2008 to 2011, GMH produced 11 reports that attempted to account for the complexity of political violence and other documents related to land tenancy and distribution, production of *casos emblematicos* (emblematic cases), and different methodologies in order to work with victims and survivors. The work of this institution was quite different from MOVICE. GMH does not try to get legal truth but what they call the "historical reconstruction from the point of view of the victims."[21] Even so, the Attorney's Office and other legal institutions today are using the reports produced by GMH in order to support cases against paramilitary and state forces. In these cases, although it was not their original function, historical reconstructions have been used to accomplish legal truths. The following statement by a GMH research assistant is revealing:

> It is very difficult to build memory when you are part of the state. While it is difficult to gain legitimacy, especially within the universe of victims' organizations, what I believe is that the work of memory from state institutions has broader impacts than those efforts from the NGOs. Especially in terms of diffusion I think the state reaches sectors that traditionally do not get information like this—for example, the reports we are producing. However, the Group is not responsible for the truth or legal truth, because the truth is very difficult to investigate in the midst of the conflict. Instead, we try to work in cases that have already been investigated, although this is never the case because, in the end, everything remains to be said. So, our actual interest is memory, but that does not mean that in the process we do not find truths. Still, our role is to help reconstruct the historical memory. We try to make this clear everywhere. Also, we try to distinguish historical truth from judicial truth. However, what is happening is that many of the reports we are doing are taken as judicial truth or are attached to court records. We just want to contribute a bit to the historical clarification.

It is in the process of making these reports that survivors of political violence and other crimes use their testimonies, through different techniques and methodologies implemented by the GMH, to reconstruct and reconfigure the memories of lived events. Survivors appropriate and internalize different legal discourses associated with transitional justice and human rights narratives in the process of the production of these reports, especially in legitimizing a place for the production of memory, which has been traditionally neglected. These documents have been the main sources of influence in the production of forms of self-representation—currently a rich site of social and political transformation. Although some reports have been contested, they have become important tools for rendering victims visible.

The articulation of these processes is made possible through the prior existence of various networks, victims' associations, and different social actors that have been involved in the regulation and implementation of these juridical discourses. On the one hand, activists and social leaders such as those in MOVICE work with survivors in order to collect historical and personal experiences that can be recorded for archival or legal purposes. On the other hand, some researchers and research assistants, such as those in GMH, mediate between public institutions and social organizations in order to link them to larger processes of juridical and historical reconstruction. One GMH researcher explains:

> The difference between the GMH and MOVICE is clear. The first is purely political. . . . For MOVICE, the work of the GMH, being connected to the CNRR, like it or not, is linked to what they call a process of legitimation of paramilitarism and to a logic of implementation of impunity in the country. For "historical memory" (GMH), its work is to begin to open doors and dialogues between civil society and state. The (GMH) academic perspective allowed the Group to be an interlocutor, political mediators symbolically, but it does not give the GMH political legitimacy, given the readings that MOVICE members would make.

Another difference between these organizations is in what they consider to be the purpose of memory production, particularly the use of such production. While the GMH works to recover the memory of victims regardless of the perpetrators of the violence, MOVICE privileges victims of state agents, given the prerogative the state has over directing its actions and the state's assertions that these actions fall within the bounds of its monopolistic hold over the legitimate use of force. Members of the GMH argue that any report represents fragmented pieces of Colombian violence and that its purpose is to publicize the multiplicity and complex sources of violence in Colombia. MOVICE, by contrast, sees the process of memorialization as a way to support legal claims against the state in national and international scenarios.

The two organizations also had dramatically different ideas of what constituted "justice." While the executive director of the CNRR,[22] the institution encompassing the GMH, claimed publicly that victims of violence seek reconciliation and want to forgive the aggressors, the victims of state violence brought together in MOVICE instead seek to reinstate the truth and demand legal justice and social repudiation of the state crimes in order for justice to be done. Paradoxically, it is for this reason that victims are often considered to be problematic and undesirable. Even members of the CNRR claimed that victims of state agents were taking advantage of their own victimization. Nonetheless, in spite of these differences and each in its own way, victim-activists have come together to mobilize legal and political claims, elaborate methods and techniques of memory compilation and assembly, develop workshops of psychosocial attention, and engage in debates about memory and legal battles against state impunity and social neglect.

TRANSITIONAL SUBJECTIVITIES, VICTIM-ACTIVISTS LEGAL TALK, AND STATE REPRESENTATIONS

Between 2008 and 2010, a widespread dissemination of transitional justice language occurred through academic seminars, forums and public debates, and governmental and non-governmental memory initiatives conducted by communities and social organizations. The numerous seminars about memory, books and reports released about Colombian and international experiences, and political mobilization and public performances demonstrate how important these two years were in increasing the visibility of the victims and international awareness of the Colombian situation. During this time, the author met several members of the victims' organizations, public servants, experts, scholars, human rights activists, and social researchers involved in the intense debates about the production of memory and the application of the Justice and Peace Law. Among the practices and uses of memory within MOVICE and GMH, particularly those related to reports, performances, and public happenings, what was most striking was the particular, and at that time new, appropriation of the transitional justice discourse related to victims' rights.

One MOVICE representative explained how she addressed the different audiences to whom she presented MOVICE's truth and justice initiatives:

> Let's say there are two definitions when we talk about a victim: one is used when one is referring to a natural disaster and there has been physical and psychological harm. And, let's say, when it comes to political violence, the victim is the subject itself. For us, the concept of victim is related to the law. This means that the victim is also the subject of rights and therefore of political action. . . . Victims' rights to truth, justice, and integral reparation bring with them a reconfiguration of the meaning and a creation of the concept of victim. . . . We believe that when one has been a victim, . . . one has the possibility of fixing the historical terms of what has happened.

By characterizing the realm of victimhood as within the sphere of the law, this person is able to elicit a particular way of presenting the subject as someone with rights. Also, the relationship among subject, law, and politics becomes evident in the mobilization of law as part of a specific political strategy, one that includes its particular connection to the past. This narrative of victimhood was expressed systematically in human rights workshops, seminars, and street manifestations. In this sense, the speaker's words were articulated within public scenarios whose context shaped the very nature of the individual's speech. Legal language was also embedded in an ideological realm where the law enables the victim-activist to imagine that a different social horizon (worldview) is possible—a future where justice can be achieved. But here, something else is also evident: legal language allows the speaker to mobilize emotion, power, and new social meanings.

In such a situation, law indexes the narrative and allows acknowledgment of the fact that the victim's reality has been disrupted because the legal discourse affirms that a different social horizon is possible. In this particular context of victims' organizations, the audience defines the appropriation and performance of legal language in the hands of victims and their relatives. Usually, these narratives are addressed to other victims, government and human rights representatives, students, and social researchers. Clearly, it is not a universal move, but it takes place in the world of humanitarian relations where some victims/survivors are in constant contact with governmental and non-governmental institutions and experts and have familiarity with NGOs and institutional bureaucracy.

Human rights activists and victim-activists have been exposed to the meanings of transitional justice through state agencies, NGOs, workshops, and the everyday circulation of these meanings, which have thereby defined new forms of legal subjectivity, or their ways of framing their political expectations and conceiving of themselves as victims and bearers of rights. As Kulick and Schieffelin (2004) point out, "By analyzing ways in which praxis come to be acquired, and performativity actually operates in situated interactions, language socialization can document not only how and when they are acquired, but also how and when they are acquired differently from what was intended, or not acquired at all" (353; see also Payne 2008). Here, legal language appears, for both victim-activists and human rights activists, as a key tool in the mobilization of power and new social meanings. Because law is not just constitutions, bills, statutes, and sentences but also consists of a socially constructed reality, it is important to consider law as operating through its social and linguistic circulation and its permanent enacting and mobilization by social actors. In this sense, transitional justice can be seen as a powerful legal language that circulates throughout society and is capable of framing ideas and actions. Likewise, transitional justice is part of the social production of meaning. These ideas are particularly relevant to this analysis as a basis for exploring the agentive potential and the social and cultural values that are at stake when victims and activists demand a particular set of rights and profound political transformations.

Transitional justice also allows for the mobilization of emotions. Testimony as a therapeutic performance empowers the victim when it is produced in public.[23] It can allow the victims to confront their experiences, and it enables them to invoke the state, seen here as a contradictory entity but one that has taken something away from the victim. The state as agent (Abrams 1988; Taussig 1987) appears in the horizon of legal language. This fictional reality of the state is socially powerful and is identifiable not only in those discourses and practices that produce the state form as a concrete entity but also in actual social and subjective life (Aretxaga 2003: 402). In this sense, Aretxaga argues, "If the state appears and acts as having a life of its own, then we are in the presence of a fetish and must ask for the powerful ways in which the fetish works" (Aretxaga 2003: 401). In the Colombian case, paramilitary crimes or state agent crimes exacerbate the fetish of the state given the difficulty (and near impossibility) of pointing at concrete perpetrators apart from the state itself. As one MOVICE human rights victim-activist affirmed:

> We all are sons and daughters of the state, aren't we? We believe that we are the sons and daughters, all of us Colombians, of the state. In particular terms, we believe the state is like our father. He is the guarantor of all our rights. That he has to ensure that I will be okay. That protects me so. We say that the state can be seen also from the point of a responsible paternity, in terms of the guarantees of the rights of Colombians. When we speak of the crimes of the state, we say that the father has acted directly against Colombians. And that can be said to have been the way the state has been built in Colombia.

Here also, the representation of the state as a father extends the sociopolitical realm of victimhood to a wide scope of patriarchy as a social system (Jimeno 2007). The state's legitimacy is at stake because the father is the one who makes the rules and is also the first one to overlook them (Gutierrez and Stoller 2001; Jimeno 2007). When survivors' and victims' relatives are victims of the state, it represents a more radical experience in which the sense of (in)justice is relentless given the exacerbation of the state arbitrarily—as the recognition of the perpetrators is both diffuse and extremely concrete at the same time. However, justice, truth, and redress become a process through which victims enter the arena of state language in order to question the state lost authority ruling.[24] And yet, victims' appropriation and reinterpretation of the meaning of transitional justice is also a place where the state is formed.

In Colombia, the articulation of the Peace and Justice Law ironically contributes to the legibility and emergence of narratives about transitional justice and victimhood among traditionally excluded social actors (Linke 2006: 211) who become aware of their own visibility as subjects of rights and citizenship. This process of reinscription, within the state's symbolic order, not only transforms the political landscape but also the sense of self of the victims of political violence. Ortner describes the cultural and social formations that shape, organize, and provoke specific modes of affect, thought, perception, fear, desire, and so on as a process of subjectivation (Ortner 2006: 31). Survivors, in calling themselves "victims," attribute meaning to their identities, which brings with it the beginning of a path toward *reconocimiento* (acknowledgment): an aspirational aim that becomes a personal goal and struggle.

Here, then, the concept of transitional subjectivities expresses the process through which legal language and legal practices enact particular ways of thinking, agency, and emotion framed in the mobilization of juridical discourse and its symbolic power (Aretxaga 2003). As stated above, law belongs to an ideological realm where specific subjects and ideas are embedded. In the same way, human rights and transitional justice discourses operate through configurations of particular kinds of subjects and objects of intervention, but they also impact victims' narratives by the interpellation of their collective history and personal experiences. As a human rights activist recalls:

> There are victims that help other victims understand that there are relationships, that what happened to them is part of a regular action. When there is an acknowledgment that their rights where infringed, in that moment they become political actors. Still, the most difficult problem for victims' organizations is the victims' acknowledgment of their victimization. This is a major challenge because there are victims who believe that what was inflicted on them was an isolated event. For example, in September they killed someone, in February they killed other, but sometimes people don't recognize a coherent reason or cause behind the crimes. I believe that people from the Oriente Antioqueño didn't know—as they do today—that what happened to them a few years ago was the same thing that happened to young people in Soacha last year. But with the work of NGOs and victims' organizations people acknowledge today the quotidian nature of these crimes.

In this interpretation, the process of becoming a victim as a political actor does not start when the act of violence is perpetrated but when there is an acknowledgment of its political nature. This social process of becoming has also been shaped by the latent forces historically oppressed by Colombian state power and from the material condition of the social conflict. However, legal language plays a central role in the victim's mobilization, and the roles of both governmental and non-governmental institutions are central in the political and legal process of becoming—from a subject of violence to a victim-activist against political violence. But how do these personal experiences and political articulations intersect in the realm of state power and legitimacy? How is it that the very sensorial experience is placed in the realm of the body politic? How do notions of justice come into being for victims and victim-activists? In the next section, I explore the process of becoming a victim-activist in the context of ongoing political violence through the appropriation of a discourse of transnational justice, and particularly through the role of truth and memory as counterhegemonic tools.

LAW AND MEMORY: A SENSE OF JUSTICE
AND THE REORDERING OF THE POLITICAL

The appropriation of legal language also holds agentive and creative potential. As Mertz (1994) argues, "Legal language affords a key site for advancing the social-linguistic project of unpacking the social creative character of language use and structure" (441). In the framework of victims' legal claims, the mobilization of the right to truth implies the recognition by the state of the events and crimes, as well as the rights of victims to produce their own memory—as counterintuitive as it might seem that such an important cultural process has to be legitimized by political rights frameworks. In this context, the intertextual practices transform the very normative aspiration of Law 975 (Vera 2015). The recognition of the value of their experiences as something that can and should be told enables the reinterpretation of the victims' experiences. The active role that some of the participants play in this endeavor transforms victims into activists within their own community and organizations.

The concept of memory as a counterpoint of the right to truth enacts the most powerful tool against silence or official interpretation of events. It can be argued that the right to truth as a hegemonic and dominant feature of Western law becomes a cultural articulation of the past and of memory.[25] Within this framework, it can also be said that survivors and their relatives become *subjects in transition* (Theidon 2007)—from a surviving subject with anonymous and untold experiences to a recognized subject as a victim of political violence. But this ongoing process of formation can also be grasped in the work of memory and the adjustment of survivors to the political demands of their visibility (Payne 2008).

Before such an appropriation takes place, however, mediation between the organizations and the survivors and their relatives is necessary. In this sense, testimonies play an important role in the construction of archives and databases, both for MOVICE and for the historical purposes of the GMH. In the latter case, for example, the survivors who have been chosen to develop the reports in processes of historical reconstruction articulate different narratives and academic paradigms through workshops and interviews. For instance, GMH has produced its own repertory of tools and methodologies in order to rebuild historic memory.[26] In a different way, MOVICE approaches the victims using what they call "psychosocial attention." In this way, the victims use pictures or objects that are meaningful to them in order to remember in public settings their relatives and family members. Through this exercise, a file is produced aimed at constructing a collectively held human rights violation archive. The outcome of this institutional work is portrayed in terms of rights language. The production of memory as a right becomes particularly important in the process of self-representation in particular public settings. Subjects become aware of their own rights, and it is acknowledged that their rights have been denied or violated. The use of juridical language operates by moving from a narrated testimony to a juridical claim.[27] Here, the words of one MOVICE human rights victim-activist are poignant:

> The memory we are trying to build comes from the very victims . . . from the stories and narrations about what they experience in everyday life and in their territories. We want to show that there is responsibility and a regular way of action, which were manifested as crimes against humanity. We want to show that this was an institutional policy. . . . We only have memory. . . . In our juridical strategy, stories are the only things we have. . . . It is what the victims have said.

Personal memory and rights' discourses emerge as an uncanny combination. Memory appears as a category somehow charged with legitimacy. Memory as a right and the right to memory constitute the ambiguous form of articulation of the past, the present, and the law, and this becomes the work of transitional justice in Colombian context. The law allows transforming memory into another kind of depositary. On the one hand, it is within this realm of mobilization of the past in the present that the (subaltern and marginal) victim is embodied as a political subject. Through declarations and testimonies, their story not only acquires a historical value but also a juridical one. Therein lies the power of testimonies that both GMH and MOVICE recognize. On the other hand, there is the creation of consciousness about the right to remember. When the victim speaks and retells his or her story, the testimony indexes the language of rights. Consequently, the tension between law and memory becomes the site of an ideological battle for the monopoly of the interpretation of the past through juridical categories. The mobilization of victims' speech becomes their own discourse in this process. The past is shaped in terms of specifically dispersed testimonies and mobilized for social legitimation. Political and social mobilization of their claims becomes a practice that enables them to produce new meanings within the framework of transitional justice and human rights discourses.

As a result, the right to memory becomes a way of making sense of the historical reconstruction of the past, not as something marginal but as a central element in the recovery of a history that has been stigmatized. *El derecho a la memoria* (right to memory), as articulated by victims, is what gives remembrance legitimacy and power. The right to memory becomes a site of struggle. For survivors, impunity and the void in the law become an empty historical space. Nevertheless, history finds its way in both the absence and the presence of the law because the law oppresses the victims but also allows them to speak and be recognized as legitimate *personas* through their sense of justice. In the case of victims' exposure to state agent violence, justice does not only suggest *verdad histórica* (historical truth) but also *verdad juridica* (judicial truth, according to victims). Here, the sense of justice is represented in the institutional scenario; they want perpetrators to be brought before a judge in order to be prosecuted. But at the foreground persist the ideas and representations of state corruption and illegitimacy state rulings; the active process of producing historical truth, while very rich in its own particular signification, becomes enmeshed with those of the state and legal meanings.

This constant ambiguity is constitutive of the relationship between law and memory, because the testimonies, and sometimes the rulings and sentences in favor of the victims, question a silenced history and, at the same time, the state legitimacy. However, a new juridical rationality seems to emerge, which is then rearticulated to produce all kinds of surprising effects, including making history and transforming the past into a place of confrontation. In the words of one of the victims' MOVICE representatives:

> There is hope in justice, although in Colombia the judicial process is slow and corrupt. . . . We believe that without justice, memory will not be consolidated. . . . That's the reason why we do not renounce the right to know the truth.

Without justice, memory cannot be unfolded. This idea also makes visible the gap between the totalizing view of the governmentalized gaze of the state and what Linke (2006) defines as the formative power of sensual experience, which acknowledges the order of significance of a reflexive, meaning-making subjectivity: "This approach forces us to reconsider any assumption we may hold about the presumed unity of national states: for subjects can successfully resist or evade the homogenizing tendencies of the modern state apparatus" (216). However, this occurs not in the sense of the expectation of the acquisition of rights but as in the case of the MOVICE—through the formative personal and subjective scope where people become aware of some particular rights. The language of rights attains a new meaning and use for the victims.

Rights discourses can be used not only to make claims but also to empower the victims as they talk through the "language of power." A great part of the constitution of legal discourse serves the purpose of making a traumatic and frightening experience more articulated. In the case of the perpetrators of passionate crimes, Miriam Jimeno (2004) has shown that legal language allows for the rationalization and provision of meaning to life experiences. Victim-activists, on the other hand, make reference to their experience and to the different narratives within which these are embedded.

Memory and legal narratives are produced by means of different strategies. It is in the interest of different institutions (such as MOVICE, GMH, ICTJ) to seek out different experiences of victimization. Survivors of different armed actors participate in workshops (in which they share their experiences in different ways, according to the aim that the collection of testimonies may have) and in regional or local meetings, to narrate, write, or otherwise (re)collect their experiences. Throughout these processes, survivors are also invited to academic conferences and seminars, social encounters, and acts of remembrance and rallies that make them visible in the public sphere or, in the case of MOVICE, to public events to denounce the crimes.[28]

All of these settings constitute new spaces where survivors appeal to the law and its institutions, but they are also the places where the state reactualizes itself, this time, under transitional justice mechanisms, meanings, and practices. These settings also constitute a site where discourse (as law) is filled with different forms of emotion and acquires its power and brings about the possibility of justice. The articulation of rights' discourses with lived experience furnishes survivors with a form of acknowledging their victimization. This kind of speech becomes authorized and legitimized by its insertion in the dominant legal discourse. Bourdieu (2009) describes this process in a wider scale—heterodoxy vis-à-vis doxa—as "the capacity of the heretical speech to objectify unformulated experiences, to make them public—a step on the road to officialization and legitimation—and, when the occasion arises, to manifest and reinforce their concordance" (171). In Colombian context, the appropriation and rearticulation of memory through transitional justice talk have placed the victims on the road to recognition of their more basic civil and political rights.

Many of these juridical narratives are produced around testimonies and memory, both in its therapeutic and political aspects. Yet, there is something distinctive going on with memory in contemporary Colombia in the sense that memory is embedded in the languages of transitional justice and human rights. This recognition of victims, which does not take place suddenly, requires social work and a process of configuration by those who are objected. This process involves the most complex relationship between the state agents' ideological representations of the conflict and the traditionally excluded and marginalized subjects that, in such tension, become active political actors.

CONCLUSION: LAW, LANGUAGE, AND STATE LEGITIMACY

This chapter analyzed two major aspects of the process of the appropriation of legal language, particularly those related to the framework of transitional justice, by victims of state violence and emergent human rights activists. One of these concerns how legal language appears as a bearer of social meaning—a particularly special one and powerful. As Elizabeth Mertz (1994) argues:

> In legal language can be found a crucial "crossroad" where social power and language interact. Law is, in effect, the locus of a powerful act of linguistic appropriation where the translation of everyday categories into legal language produces powerful changes. Through legal language, the state imposes its interpretation and appropriation (of physical and symbolic power), and social actors' struggle to shift existing power relations. (441)

In the Colombian transitional justice discourse, appropriations have produced powerful changes in the way people address and interpret the conflict and the contemporary social context.

The other aspect developed is the process of signifying social reality through legal language, which does not depend solely on the production of law. The law has to be actively used by people in order to produce specific legal discourses and practices. In this process of articulation, there is a complex relationship between hegemony and human action. As such, from an ethnographic standpoint, law cannot be conceived as a top-down oppressive machine. Instead, it should be understood as produced within processes of appropriation, interpretation, and even fleeting empowerment. As Gal (1989) explains, in referring to subaltern language, "Because linguistic practices provide access to material resources, they become resources in their own right. In studies of local-level politics, ethnographers have long noted the importance of oratory and verbal skill in the acquisition of power" (353). In this sense, the performativity of law plays a crucial part in shaping the practices and beliefs of victims and human rights activists.

In depicting how nonexpert groups appropriate a singular legal language, we saw how, in the Colombian case, the appropriation, articulation, and reinterpretation of the transitional justice discourses and practices by historically vulnerable populations challenge the normative production of the Justice and Peace Law. The exposure to and relationship with GMH and MOVICE became the main source of articulating legal meaning for these traditionally marginalized actors. In the process of assuming the cost of making their situation explicit by presenting themselves as victims of state agents, some survivors and civic organizations decided to transit from a marginal position to a context of political struggle. The configuration of new forms of self-representation as victims necessarily involved the emergence of a legal and political consciousness in the context of stigmatized political and social stereotypes. The increasing circulation of discourses about the rights of victims in different social spheres, then, has had unintended effects with regards to the normative purposes of the law, because it has placed a very powerful language in the hands of traditionally excluded social actors.

Clearly, this chapter does not do justice to the victims' struggles; neither does it exhaust the forms of Colombians' struggle for justice and reparation. I have attempted to present the relationship between legal meanings and their reception in particular social contexts, contexts that are articulated through experiences of suffering and resistance. We saw the hegemonic character of some legal discourses, such as those of human rights and transitional justice, with regards to the experience of people in a context of violence and exclusion. Legal contexts and discourses are crucial sites for the construction of hegemony because they provide the resources and spaces to establish, give legitimacy to, and authorize the legal meaning of things, subjects, and actions. This scheme perhaps refutes the idea that legal discourses can be key in carrying out counterhegemonic political struggles, because to what extent can we affirm that the law has the potential to transform itself? And to what extent is the mobilization of the law against itself a reproduction of hegemony?

In reference to the victims of state actors, we can see the emergence of a powerful relationship among law, activism, and recognition. The manner in which victim-activists mobilize rights discourses happens through a process of acknowledgment and then a mobilization of that acknowledgment. The effects of this acknowledgment and its mobilization are key to this milieu. Even if legal discourses have allowed victims and social activists to give a name to the unnamable, to rationalize and externalize their experiences, and if survivors are now able to mobilize their rights, they do so in the face of an institution that overlooks its own law. The articulation of this rationale confronts forces that are outside and through the law in its most complex expression: violence.

These juridical discourses, embedded in the ideological production of regimes of truth, in this case human rights and transitional justice, only show their full potential when agents and subaltern groups adopt them. The process of being recognized as subjects of the law has become the only site of struggle and resistance against the different armed actors and political violence. Paradoxically, the importation of mechanisms of transitional justice has become, like multicultural-ism in 1991 with the enactment of the last Colombian Constitution, a dispositive through which Colombian state legitimacy recreates itself.[29]

The case of victims of political violence in Colombia reflects the relationship between hegemony and contestation. Hegemony comes with its own constitutive contestation (Williams 1977). As always, social reality is more complex than the dispositive produced to contain it. When it comes to the processes by which the paramilitary groups were demobilized, the consequences in Colombia have been more social and political than juridical. Even if the actual application of Justice and Peace Law has brought former combatants into society, without truth, justice, or redress, survivors and victims' organizations of many kinds have learned to use a special juridical language. This language, which is mobilized by numerous social actors, has come to articulate a diverse social movement that has gained consciousness of its rights and that has, thereby, allowed the hope of attaining their rights and new forms of citizenship.

In this sense, when talking of emancipation and its relationship to hegemony, subverting meaning, reconfiguring it, and making the law and its formal contents a semantic battlefield by means of disseminating a multiplicity of discourses, as Deleuze (2005) suggests, is to create a most combative version of emancipation. "Meaning," says Deleuze, "is never a beginning or an origin, but a product, that does not need to be discovered or restored but produced with a new machinery" (16). Much of the Colombian reconciliation process could be nurtured in this granted right to remember that has begun to challenge the dominant representa-tion of the Colombian conflict.

NOTES

1. According to UN statistics, Colombia is among the countries with the highest number of people who have disappeared in the world. UN High Commissioner for Human Rights in Colombia, "Legal Tools for the Protection and Defense of the Rights of the Victims of Enforced Disappearances to Truth at National and International Levels," May 23, 2011.
2. As of May 2011, the Government of Colombia had registered more than 3.7 million IDPs in the country. NGOs such as the Consultancy for Human Rights and Displacement (CODHES) estimate that the actual number of people displaced by internal armed conflict since the mid-1980s is more than 5 million.
3. Human Rights Watch, June 10, 2011, http://www.hrw.org/news/2011/06/10/colombia -victims-law-historic-opportunity.
4. The Colombian Constitutional Court (S-370/2006) introduced the scope of truth, justice, and redress into Law 975, framing this statute in a transitional justice approach.
5. Transitional Justice emerged from World War II postwar experiences and was trans-planted into new legal forms in postconflict contexts such as Rwanda, Guatemala, or South Africa. The dissemination of transitional justice mechanisms has gone hand in hand with

the proliferation of political conflicts around the world after the end of the Cold War. The postconflict era in Latin American has especially enriched its applicability and application. The period after the Argentinean and Chilean dictatorships and the Peruvian and Guatemalan conflicts in particular brought together new discussions and appropriation of TJ practices and narratives with different outcomes.

6. The use of state violence has been located in the period called *La Violencia* from 1948 to 1958. Yet, there is no consensus about the chronology of La Violencia. Anthropologists and historians in the late 1970s attributed the origin of political violence to the *bananeras* massacre in 1928 (Arocha 1979; Sánchez and Meertens 2001), which was perpetrated by the army in defending the interests of the United Fruit Company, later immortalized by Gabriel García Márquez in *One Hundred Years of Solitude*. Analyses like those of Corradi, Fagen, and Garretón Merino are unable to encompass contexts such as Colombia, where dictatorship was not necessary in order to impose fear. However, Michael Taussig (1992, 2006) is able to describe such dimensions as part of a permanent state of emergency in Colombian society.

7. I agree with Greg Beckett (2010) when he affirms that the discursive formation of "state failure" paradigm is in itself a mode of power (50).

8. In fact, this process of empowerment through the law by marginalized groups is not unique to Colombia. In the early 1990s, multiculturalist discourse was a fashionable example of this appropriation of multicultural and social rights.

9. In the case of the demobilization process triggered by the Peace and Justice Law, the perpetrators, not the victims, were the centers of the policy. During the period from 2002 to 2008, and even before, there was no integral policy for victims of political conflict. All this changed with the ratification of the Victims Law and Land Restitution Act of 2011 by President Juan Manuel Santos (2010–2014). This policy might be changing the place of victims in the Colombian violence narrative. It is also worth noting that MOVICE did not support the law because the new law "did not represent the real claims of the victims."

10. From 2008 to 2010, I collected and analyzed media documentation, congressional database debates, laws and statues produced from 2005 to 2010. I want to thank especially Ingrid Díaz, Daniela Botero, Natalia Ladino, Catalina Garcia, and Catalina Martinez for their collaboration in collecting this material. Also I thank Javeriana University for funding the project "Políticas y tecnologías de la memoria: Lecturas oficiales y no oficiales de la memoria en medio del conflicto colombiano" from 2008 to 2010. The discussion in this chapter was made possible by its generous support.

11. Law as discourse entails a field of subjects and objects with its own rules and norms (Foucault 2002), while law as language implies the articulation and practice of legal meanings, concepts, statements, and emotions.

12. The social representation of victims and perpetrators also constitutes a battlefield of significations because the ongoing cycle of victim-perpetrator-victim makes it difficult to define the line between them.

13. This struggle over meaning also occurs in a context where forced disappearance and crime are justified by certain state and social conventions. Colombian analyst Francisco Gutierrez (2002) has pointed out how people's articulation of victimization is related to the idea of "who knows what he might have been involved in" (57). Here, social indifference toward victims follows from such neutralizing rationale.

14. Other groups—for instance, the movement Hijas e Hijos por la Memoria y Contra la Impunidad (Sons and Daughters for Memory and against Impunity)—have chosen not to

mobilize the concept of victim or any other idea of victimhood, at least discursively, but instead call attention for the transformation of Colombian political culture.

15. By asking the question "How do transnational human rights ideas become part of local social movements and local legal consciousness?," Sally Merry (2006) points out, "Intermediaries who translate global ideas into local situations and retranslate local ideas into global frameworks play a critical role in this process [of appropriation and transplantation]. They foster the gradual emergence of a local rights consciousness among grassroots people and greater awareness of national and local issues among global activists. These actors include political elites, human right lawyers, feminist activists and movement leaders, social workers and academics" (265).

16. All interviews were conducted in confidentiality and the names of interviewees withheld by mutual agreement.

17. http://www.movimientodevictimas.org/index.php.

18. Through the enactment of the Justice and Peace Law, the Colombian government tried to separate itself, at least symbolically, from its responsibility in recent Colombian conflicts. However, the result of the implementation of the law was ironic in that it has actually revealed the links among paramilitary groups, traditional political parties, businesspeople, and the armed forces.

19. http://www.movimientodevictimas.org/index.php.

20. http://www.memoriahistorica-cnrr.org.co/s-home/.

21. http://www.memoriahistorica-cnrr.org.co/s-home/.

22. Eduardo Pizarro was CNRR executive director from 2006 to 2010.

23. When discussing the relationship between law and memory, I argue that the law plays a role in the rearticulations of victims' traumatic experiences. As Ochs and Capps (2001) point out, "The fundamentalistic tendency lends consistency to otherwise fragmented experience and allows us to assess what is happening in an expedient manner. Adherence to a dominant narrative is also a community-building in that it presumes that each member ascribes a common history. Reliance solely on a dominant narrative, however, may lead to oversimplification, stasis, and irreconcilable discrepancies between the story one has inculcated and one's encounters in the world. . . . Psychological disorders such as posttraumatic stress, depression, and anxiety involve silencing would-be narratives that deviate from the dominant story by which one lives" (32).

24. Here, Butler's notion of interpellation is useful in order to grasp the *formative* aspect of the mediation between legal discourses and subjects: "As a form of power, subjection is paradoxical. To be dominated by a power external to oneself is a familiar and agonizing form power takes. To find, however, that what 'one' is, one's very formation as a subject, is in some sense dependent upon that very power as what presses on the subject from the outside, as what subordinates, sets underneath, and relegates to a lower order. This is surely a fair description. But, if following Foucault, we understand power as *forming* the subject as well as providing the very condition of its existence and the trajectory of its desire, the power is not simply what we oppose but also, in a strong sense, what we depend on for our existence and what we harbor and preserve in the beings that we are" (Butler 1997: 1–2).

25. While the right to truth is derived from due process and legal guarantees, the right to memory is a concept developed in the context of national jurisdictions and the human rights framework. As Ignacio Briceño argues, "Memory as a right is recognized by the domestic legal systems, but never created, since the fundamental rights emanate from qualities inherent of man that all states should recognize, promote, and secure with clear

obligations. Therefore, the right to memory is a truly radical new regulatory paradigm, a new civil, social, and cultural right embedded and integrated in the set of fundamental rights, although not expressly insured in the constitutional texts. However, it is not necessary that a right be expressly set in the formal or conventional international law to be social, human, or fundamental. Rights can be derived from values, principles, and historical reasons that feed the positive constitutional and international law. One of the qualities of the right to memory is that it allows the transformation of the subjects of memory into active agents that change and strength their involvement with the concept of citizen, reconceptualizing the subject historically excluded by making him or her a valid subject of cultural identity construction" (2011: 4). The mobilization of the right to truth in Colombia has been appropriated interchangeably with the right to memory, producing new debates on the right of victims to produce their own narratives and about the *deber de memoria del estado* (state duty of memory) (Antequera 2011). Catalina Martinez (2012) also states that "the duty of memory and the right to memory are concepts that are still under discussion. Both rely on the 'right to truth' that human right stipulated in local laws and transitional processes, which individually or collectively, can be accepted or rejected" (33).

26. The tool box is called "Recordar y Narrar el Conflicto: Herramientas para Reconstruir la Memoria Histórica." Grupo de Memora Histórica—CNRR, Bogota 2009.

27. This narrative differs from those of other victims among peasants and indigenous communities in rural areas when in juridical settings such as the *incidentes de reparación* (reparation incidents) where victims are asked to speak about the way their life was before the tragic experience. However, in such public forums, the control of speech did not allow extensive forms of reminiscence (Paula Rodriguez, former GMH research assistant, in a personal interview).

28. There is another major actor in the spread and articulation of networks and meaning of transitional justice: the International Center for Transitional Justice, or ICTJ. The active role of this organization has been key in the production and dissemination of the ideology of transitional justice. It has produced several reports and books where the research was done in conjunction with the victims' memories.

29. In July 2013, President Juan Manuel Santos acknowledged for the first time the human rights violations committed by state agents before the Colombian Constitutional Court after the release of the GMH general report *Basta ya: Colombia memorias de violencia, memoria y dignidad* the day before.

WORKS CITED

Abrams, Philip. 1988. "Notes about the Difficulty of Studying the State." *Journal of Historical Sociology* 1 (1): 58–89.

Antequera, José. 2011. *La memoria histórica como relato emblemático*. Bogotá: Agencia Catalana de Cooperación.

Aretxaga, Begoña. 2003. "Maddening States." *Annual Review of Anthropology* 32: 393–410.

Arocha, Jaime. 1979. *La violencia en el Quindío*. Bogotá: Tercer Mundo.

Beckett, Greg. 2010. "Phantom Power: Notes on Provisionality in Haiti." In *Anthropology and Global Counterinsurgency*, edited by John D. Kelly, 39–51. Chicago: University of Chicago Press.

Bourdieu, Pierre. 1998. "Rethinking the State: Genesis and Structure of the Bureaucratic Field." In *Practical Reason: On the Theory of Action*. Stanford, CA: Stanford University Press.

————. 2009. *Outline of a Theory of Practice.* Cambridge: Cambridge University Press.

Briceño, Ignacio. 2011. "El derecho a la memoria histórica como nueva categoría de derecho social fundamental implícito." *Periódico Biblioteca del Congreso Nacional de Chile,* September 13, 2011.

Butler, Judith. 1997. *Theories in Subjection: The Physic Life of Power.* Stanford, CA: Stanford University Press.

Corradi, Juan E., Patricia Weiss Fagen, and Manuel A. Garretón Merino. 1992. *Fear at the Edge—State Terror and Resistance in Latin America.* Berkeley: University of California Press.

Corrigan, Richard, and Derek Sayer. 1985. *The Great Arch: English State Formation as Cultural Revolution.* Oxford: Blackwell.

Deleuze, Gilles. 2005. *Foucault.* Barcelona: Paidós.

Desmond, Enrique, and Daniel Goldstein. 2010. *Violent Democracies in Latin America.* Durham, NC: Duke University Press.

Foucault, Michel. 2002. *The Archaeology of Knowledge.* Translated by A. M. Sheridan Smith. London: Routledge.

Gal, Susan. 1989. "Language and Political Economy." *Annual Review of Anthropology* 18: 346–367.

Gramsci, Antonio. 1972. *Selections from the Prison Notebooks of Antonio Gramsci.* Edited and translated by Quintin Hoare and Geoffrey Nowell-Smith. New York: International.

Gutierrez, Francisco, and Richard Stoller. 2001. "The Courtroom and the Bivouac: Reflections on Law and Violence in Colombia." *Latin American Perspectives* 28 (1): 56–72.

Hinton, Alexander. 2010. *Transitional Justice: Global Mechanisms and Local Realities after Genocide and Mass Violence.* New Brunswick, NJ: Rutgers University Press.

Jimeno, Myriam. 2004. *Crimen pasional: Contribución a una antropología de las emociones.* Bogotá: Universidad Nacional de Colombia, Facultad de Ciencias Humanas, Departamento de Antropología, Centro de Estudios Sociales.

————. 2007. "Cuerpo personal y cuerpo político: Violencia, cultura y ciudadanía neoliberal." In *Cultura y neoliberalismo,* edited by Alejandro Grimson, 195–211. Buenos Aires: CLACSO.

Kristeva, Julia. 1982. *Powers of Horror: An Essay on Abjection.* New York: Columbia University Press.

Kulick, Don, and Bambi Schieffelin. 2004. "Language Socialization." In *Companion to Linguistic Anthropology,* edited by Alessandro Duranti, 349–368. Malden, MA: Wiley-Blackwell.

Linke, Uli. 2006. "Contact Zones." *Anthropological Theory* 6 (2): 205–225.

Martinez, Catalina. 2012. "Memorialización y políticas públicas de la memoria en Bogotá: Centro del Bicentenario Memoria Paz y Reconciliación." Senior thesis, Javeriana University, Bogotá, Colombia.

Merry, Sally Engle. 2006. *Human Rights and Gender Violence: Translating International Law into Local Justice.* Chicago: University of Chicago Press.

Mertz, Elizabeth. 1994. "Legal Language: Pragmatics, Poetics and Social Power." *Annual Review of Anthropology* 23: 435–495.

Ochs, Elinor, and Lisa Capps. 2001. *Living Narrative: Creating Lives in Everyday Storytelling.* Cambridge, MA: Harvard University Press.

Ortner, Sherry, ed. 2006. "Power and Projects: Reflections on Agency." In *Anthropology and Social Theory: Culture, Power and the Acting Subject.* Durham, NC: Duke University Press.

Panourgiá, Neni. 2009. *Dangerous Citizens: The Greek Left and the Terror of the State*. New York: Fordham University Press.

Payne, Leigh A. 2008. *Unsettling Accounts: Neither Truth nor Reconciliation in Confessions of State Violence*. Durham, NC: Duke University Press.

Ramírez, María Clemencia. 2011. *Between the Guerrillas and the State: The Cocalero Movement, Citizenship, and Identity in the Colombian Amazon*. Durham, NC: Duke University Press.

Romero, Mauricio. 2003. *Paramilitares y autodefensas, 1982–2003*. Bogotá: Universidad. Bogotá, Universidad Nacional de Colombia, Instituto de Estudios Políticos y Relaciones Internacionales (IEPRI).

Ronderos, Maria. 2014. *Guerras recicladas: Una historia periodística del paramilitarismo en Colombia*. Bogotá: Aguilar.

Sánchez, Gonzalo G., and Donny Meertens. 2001. *Bandits, Peasants, and Politics: The Case of "La Violencia" in Colombia*. Austin: University of Texas Press.

Sanford, Victoria. 2004. "Contesting Displacement in Colombia: Citizenship and State Sovereignty at the Margins." In *Anthropology in the Margins of the State*, edited by Veena Das and Deborah Poole, 253–277. Santa Fe, NM: School of American Research Press.

Scott, James. 1990. *Domination and the Arts of Resistance: Hidden Transcripts*. New Haven, CT: Yale University Press.

———. 1998. "Cities, People and Language." In *The Anthropology of the State: A Reader*, edited by Aradhana Sharma and Akhil Gupta, 247–269. London: Blackwell.

Tate, Winifred. 2007. *Counting the Dead: The Culture and Politics of Human Rights Activism in Colombia*. Berkeley: University of California Press.

Taussig, Michael. 1987. "Espacios de miedo y cultura del terror." In *Chamanismo, colonialismo y el hombre salvaje: Un estudio sobre el terror y la curación*. Bogotá: Grupo Editorial Norma.

———. 1992. *The Nervous System*. New York: Routledge.

———. 2006. "Terror as Usual: Walter Benjamin's Theory of History as a State of Siege." *Globalization and Violence* 2: 172–192.

Theidon, Kimberly. 2007. "Transitional Subjects: The Disarmament, Demobilization and Reintegration of Former Combatants in Colombia." *International Journal of Transitional Justice* 1 (1): 66–90.

Transnational Institute. 2001. "Europe and Plan Colombia." http://www.tni.org/drugs/reports/debate1.htm.

Uprimny, Rodrigo, et al. 2006. *Justicia transicional sin transición? Verdad, justicia y reparación en Colombia*. Bogotá: Dejusticia Colección Ensayos y Propuestas.

Vera, Juan Pablo. 2015. "Memorias emergentes: Las consecuencias inesperadas de la Ley de Justicia y Paz en Colombia (2005–2011)." *Estudios Socio-Jurídicos* 17 (2): 13–44.

Williams, Raymond. 1977. *Marxism and Literature*. Oxford: Oxford University Press.

Wilson, Richard. 2001. *The Politics of Truth and Reconciliation in South Africa*. Cambridge: Cambridge University Press.

2   PURSUING JUSTICE IN JEWISH BUENOS AIRES

Karen Ann Faulk

INTRODUCTION

In July 2014, Argentines commemorated the twentieth anniversary of the attack on the Asociación Mutual Israelita Argentina (Argentine Jewish Mutual Aid Association). The attack, which occurred on July 18, 1994, struck the AMIA's main building, killing 85 people and wounding hundreds of others. To date, no one has been tried in court for direct participation in the planning or execution of the attack. In one of the many events held in remembrance of that destructive and tragic day, psychologist Natan Sonis gave a speech in which he said, "I was taught that people construct societies and societies construct people. In these 20 years, what kind of people have been built, those who have never seen justice function? . . . These new subjects no longer trust in a regulatory order, the rule of law isn't seen as an organizing principle, but as a theater piece, a work of fiction." He goes on to say that "insecurity"—the much-debated and oft-bantered buzzword of contemporary Latin American politics[1]—is in reality found not in the overemphasized acts of criminality themselves but in the ineffective and at times complicit justice system and the resultant impunity that defends the perpetrators and leaves society unprotected. "Demanding justice," he concludes, "is a necessary component to a dignified life."[2]

This chapter explores the history of activism surrounding the 1994 bombing of this Jewish community center in Buenos Aires, Argentina. It considers three foundational moments of this history as windows into the multiple meanings that justice holds for those most directly involved. I argue that while each of the four original factions within this body of activism (Memoria Activa, Familiares, APEMIA, and Ciudadanos de la Plaza) share basic fundamental principles over what constitutes justice, the relative ranking that they assign each priority directs their understanding of appropriate and necessary action, or how "justice" can and should be achieved. Specifically, this chapter suggests that justice for this event, which left 85 dead and hundreds wounded, is seen to necessarily include

(1) a legal reckoning of events, condemnation of the perpetrators, and the assignation of the corresponding punishment within a fair and impartial judicial process; (2) full disclosure and understanding of what occurred; (3) the preservation and continual invocation of the memory of the event, those who lost their lives, and its effects on the community; and (4) the maintenance and strengthening of community institutions in facing such attacks. However, it is the relative emphasis given to each of these factors that influences what is seen as appropriate action in working to secure justice.

Debates over the meaning and methods for achieving justice have been central to Argentine social, political, and legal life since the end of the most recent military dictatorship (1976–1983) (Payne 2003). Even as Argentines increasingly utilized the local court system to articulate and advocate for their demands (Smulovitz 2010), political and practical obstacles to achieving justice through juridical means during the 1980s and 1990s led movements to adopt an innovative variety of alternative or complementary tactics. Organizations like HIJOS popularized the use of public spaces to bring social condemnation on known perpetrators though escraches (Vaisman 2015), while others sought recourse through appeals to international human rights agencies and institutions (Huneeus 2010).

How activists, participants, and their allies position themselves in relation to one another and to the state, community, and international bodies to which they make their appeals also reveals a multiplicity of ways within which authoritative knowledge about the attacks and the investigations that followed it are constructed, debated, accepted, or rejected. These differing interpretations of what constitutes authoritative knowledge, and the elements necessary for its procurement and acceptance, lie at the heart of many of the debates that have emerged among those most involved in the search for justice, for the AMIA bombing and for struggles for justice more generally. This chapter suggests that the difficulty in achieving a sense of closure following dramatic and tragic events of this type is directly related to these debates over authoritative knowledge. Other works have shown how a sense of justice and closure following tragic events is often felt as lacking or incomplete when it fails to attend to the root causes of the issue or to adequately address a need for remembrance, commemoration, and recognition (Collins 2010; Hinton 2010; Lundy and McGovern 2008; Shaw and Waldorf 2010; Theidon 2012; Wilson 2001). Drawing on Jacques Derrida's formulation, Noa Vaisman (2015) argues that "justice," unlike legal resolution, "does not have a concrete future, a moment of materialization following which we could claim it has been done or achieved. Instead, justice . . . is forever an open project, a desire or an ethical aspiration that by its very nature cannot be and will never be complete." While justice may ultimately be elusive, it provides a very real rationale for action and an orienting principle for those affected by acts of violence. As Vaisman notes, the "tears in the social tissue" are felt as mendable only through achieving some sense (or senses) of justice or, as Sonis phrased it in that July 2014 speech, "these social traumas will not be healed within the four walls of a psychiatrist's office. . . . Expressing our resistance (to injustice) is also an act of mental health."[3] Through an ethnographic exploration of the search for justice after the AMIA bombing, this chapter links the desire to award justice in the fullest sense of the term to the disconnects that occur and can linger when what constitutes authoritative knowledge remains in dispute.

EVENT

The 1994 explosion that ripped through the AMIA/DAIA building on Pasteur Street was preceded by one in 1992 that had destroyed the Israeli Embassy in the *porteño* neighborhood of Recoleta. To date, no one has been prosecuted for the planning or execution of either attack, and the details and sequencing of events that led to the 1994 explosion, especially, remain shrouded in doubt and uncertainty.[4] The four groups discussed in this chapter are each comprised of those intimately concerned with achieving justice in the aftermath of this dramatic moment. For some, their lives were torn apart through the loss of direct family members. Others lost friends, neighbors, or acquaintances, or they felt an intimate connection to the events through their active or implicit association to the major organizations of the Jewish collectivity.

The destruction of the AMIA building deeply impacted the Argentine Jewish community.[5] The building housed the offices of the AMIA and the DAIA (Delegación de Asociaciones Israelitas Argentinas, or Delegation of Argentine Jewish Associations), the cornerstones of organized collective Jewish life. Each organization had formed in response to specific needs of the community, and they have continued to fulfill these roles throughout the vagaries of Argentine history. Importantly, each has played a role in mediating the relationship between the community and the state.[6] While the attack on these institutions was felt collectively by many within the Argentine Jewish community, the official response to the attacks by their successive leaderships has been contentious.

Key Moment 1: The Leadership "Goes to the Other Side"

The AMIA bombing was both literally and figuratively a ground-shaking moment for members of the Argentine Jewish community and its collective representation. The long years that have followed this disruptive event have revealed and given rise to a pronounced heterogeneity of opinions among individuals and groups within the community, particularly concerning the means of pursuing justice. Almost immediately after the AMIA bombing, members of the Jewish collectivity began to meet in order to decide how best to confront the tragedy. The leadership and managing members of the AMIA/DAIA came together to consider the immediate future and location of these badly damaged institutions and how they should react publicly.

Beginning the Monday after the attack, some family members of the victims held gatherings in the Plaza Lavalle. For those whose lives had been changed so irreparably, these weekly public assemblies served as not only a source of solace but also as a way to place pressure on the government and to draw attention to the ensuing events as they unfolded. The organizers of these weekly Monday gatherings in front of the Justice Building Tribunales (Palacio de Justicia) formed the nonprofit association Memoria Activa (Active Memory). Through their physical presence, this space, they argued, served as a site of remembrance of those who had been lost, as well as a form of public pressure to insist on a full investigation into the attack and justice for its perpetrators. They adopted as their rallying call the biblical line "Tze·dek tze·dek, tir·dof" (Justice, justice, you will seek) (Deuteronomy 16:20). For over 500 consecutive Mondays, these protest/memorial events or *actos* served as a ritualized public forum to remember those lost and, increasingly, to denounce the lack of adequate investigation into the attack and continuing impunity for those responsible in the planning, execution, and subsequent cover-up of the bombing.

When Memoria Activa first formed, it represented family members of victims, other members of the Jewish community, and their allies and supporters. Indeed, although the meetings convened in the wake of the attack were diverse in composition of participants and their positions in the collectivity (in postdictatorship Argentina, "family member of victim" has become an important subject position that holds considerable social and symbolic power), those involved acted largely in concert and without significant antagonism. Memoria Activa initially followed the official representation of the collectivity, centered in the AMIA/DAIA, as it worked tirelessly to reorganize and rebuild following the massive destruction to its physical infrastructure. However, as time went on, divisions between those most directly affected by the AMIA bombing (or those who chose to accept this role, either as a family member of a victim, a survivor, or an institutional representative of the AMIA or the DAIA) became acute and led to visible ruptures. Struggles began to emerge among those involved, mainly as to what the nature and role of Memoria Activa should be in achieving, according to Clarke and Goodale (2010), that "ever-receding and ever-shrouded social ideal": justice (10). Beatriz Gurevich (2005) argued that for the AMIA/DAIA, as well as for some of the initial members

of Memoria Activa, this group was to be "the symbolic representation of the destruction, and DAIA should remain as the sole formal and legal negotiator in the
name of the victims and the Jewish organizations vis-à-vis the national authorities, and also as the sole Jewish political representation within mainstream society"
(15–16). However, a number of family members, including the four women who
formed the core of Memoria Activa's leadership, were increasingly critical of the
stances taken by the collectivity's institutional leadership, accusing the DAIA of
being concerned with maintaining its close ties to the ruling political powers, even
when those powers were seen to act against the interests of the community. These
women felt that Memoria Activa should be willing to foster social mobilization
as well as publicly condemn irregularities or omissions in the actuation of government officials concerning the investigation, regardless of the position taken
by the AMIA and DAIA. On the other hand, some family members of victims,
who would have preferred that the organization serve "as the symbolic memory
of destruction and the space of solidarity, and not as a collective political actor"
(Gurevich 2005: 17), began to distance themselves from Memoria Activa.

   These divisions became increasingly acute. By 1996, Memoria Activa had begun to publically denounce problems they observed in the investigation being carried out by Judge Galeano, even though the magistrate maintained the support
of the AMIA/DAIA. The event that participants in Memoria Activa most often
cite as the incident that clearly marks the split between Memoria Activa and the
AMIA/DAIA leadership, and the first key event discussed in this chapter, came
during the acto organized for the third anniversary of the attack in July 1997. During this event, Laura Ginsberg, acting at that time on behalf of Memoria Activa,
read a speech that directly accused then president Carlos Menem, Buenos Aires
Province governor Eduardo Duhalde, and interior minister Carlos Corach of ob-
structing the investigation into the attack. In her words, "I accuse the administrations of Menem and Duhalde of giving sanction to impunity, of permitting the
indifference of those that know something and yet stay silent, of giving license to
insecurity, inexperience, and ineptitude. I accuse the Menem and Duhalde administrations of covering up the local connection (into the attack) that served to kill
our family members."[7] Immediately following the acto, the president of the DAIA,
Rubén Beraja, went (cruzó la vereda) to the House of Government and personally
apologized to President Menem for her statements. For Memoria Activa, this response by the DAIA gave priority to Beraja's relationship with those in power over
the interest of the Jewish community in the success of the investigation.[8] After this
divisive incident, Memoria Activa began to hold independent anniversary memorials and increasingly charged the AMIA/DAIA of complicity in the covering up
of the attack.

The estrangement that arose between Memoria Activa and the leadership of the collectivity led to some of the victims' family members forming a new group, Familiares y Amigos de las Víctimas del Atentado a la AMIA (Relatives and Friends of the Victims of the AMIA Massacre, henceforth Familiares).[9] This group initially stayed close to the AMIA/DAIA, holding their monthly memorials to the victims in front of the newly reconstructed AMIA building and sharing legal representation with the AMIA/DAIA (Figure 2.1). Memoria Activa, on the other hand, argued for and won the right to serve as an independent plaintiff in the case that was slowly mounted against a number of alleged accomplices in the attack (Figure 2.2).

FIGURE 2.1   A focal point for monthly Familiares/AMIA/DAIA actos, in front of reconstructed AMIA building. Photo by the author.

FIGURE 2.2   Independent protest/memorial event by Memoria Activa, in the Plaza Lavalle. Photo from 2004, by the author.

Familiares also often spoke out against members of the ruling elite and current members of government that they saw as complicit in the lack of justice, and in many ways, their criticisms echoed those of Memoria Activa. However, Familiares avoided direct criticism of these organizations and their former or actual leaders and acted in conjunction with them. Many of those who regularly attended the actos of Memoria Activa also frequented those of Familiares. As such, the division between the groups, at least for many of their supporters, was recognizable but not exclusionary.

Beatriz Gurevich has argued that the difference between Memoria Activa and Familiares is in the ethics guiding their actions (Gurevich 2005). She divides these into the "traditionalists identified with 'communitarianism' and respectful of what is known in the Argentine Jewry as 'communitarian responsibility,'" and contrasts this with the "liberals who think that a legitimate defense of individual rights does not interfere with a positive identification with a collective entity" (26). Although I would add further nuance into Gurevich's analysis of the workings of the gender dynamics among the different groups, in which she contends that the women of Familiares subscribe to a "care ethics," while those of Memoria Activa adopt a "rights ethic," I find great value in her attention to the ethos of responsibility operative among different groups of family members.[10] Many members of the Jewish community are supportive of the ethos of community as espoused by the organization and its many and consistent efforts in the promotion and defense of the welfare of the collectivity as a whole. However, while members of Memoria Activa base their demands and appeals for justice within a language of individual rights, I argue that they are also equally though differently concerned with the issue of collective well-being (Faulk 2013). The members of Familiares tend to support the AMIA/DAIA at least in part for their continued dedication to fostering community well-being. Memoria Activa, on the other hand, locates collective well-being in the strengthening of local and national institutions by forcing them to confront what is seen as the endemic corruption and impunity they engender. As mentioned above, at various moments in the organization's history, the DAIA has often been criticized for interpreting its responsibility to the community to the detriment of the best interests of certain individuals. Nonetheless, for the leadership of the AMIA/DAIA, at least part of this promotion of well-being has been interpreted as being served through the maintenance of a positive relationship and set of alliances with economic and political powers, including the government. For Memoria Activa, collective well-being is predicated on an efficient system of justice, one that is provided, organized, and enforced by the state.

These divisions over how to pursue and what constitutes justice for the AMIA and Embassy attacks have continued and multiplied. In 2002, Laura Ginsberg left Memoria Activa and formed a new movement, APEMIA (Agrupación por el Esclarecimiento de la Masacre Impune de la AMIA, or the Association for the Clarification of the Unpunished AMIA Massacre), which has since taken more radical and oppositional stances on the issues that have confronted the victims' relatives.[11] APEMIA's position was different from both Memoria Activa and Familiares. The founder and leader, Laura Ginsberg, was one of the four women who solidified the stance of Memoria Activa and was for years a key member and referent of this organization. Yet, the definitive split between the two came at the end of December 2001. After the convulsive political and social events of December 19 and 20, 2001, when popular protest forced the resignation of President de la Rúa, Argentina went through a difficult process of political reorganization, with the naming of four new presidents in a span of two weeks. During one of these ephemeral "administrations," that of Adolfo Rodríguez Saá, one of Memoria Activa's lawyers, Alberto Zuppi, was named Minister of Justice. Memoria Activa approved this move, hoping that his designation would lead to concrete advances in the AMIA investigation. However, Ginsberg was strongly opposed, concerned that it would compromise Memoria Activa's independence from government forces. As a result, she left Memoria Activa and founded APEMIA in early 2002.

Key Moment 2: The Last Acto

On May 25, 2003, Néstor Kirchner was sworn in as president of Argentina. With his administration came renewed hope for significant changes in the structure and practical workings of the judicial system, as well as a discursive shift on the need for legal prosecution, a functioning and fair judiciary, and a full investigation into the AMIA attack. For Memoria Activa and other human rights organizations, the change in political climates brought about at this time had significant effects. Most important, it came at a time when many saw reason for hope in achieving advances on legal aspects of the AMIA bombing cases. The Kirchner administration was successful in inculcating in many people a renewed faith in the legal system by paving the way for prosecutions of Dirty War offenders in Argentina and for a number of other high-profile corruption cases (see Chapter 4).

These legal developments changed the situation in which Memoria Activa operated and influenced concrete transformations in the group's tactics. Key among these was the decision to end the weekly protests in December 2005. This was done, according to the directive board, in order to focus their energies more directly toward the legal sphere.[12] Their decision must be understood within the context of a renewed, if still skeptical, faith in the legal system, advances in the international realm, and initial assessments of the politics of memory of the Kirchner administration.[13] These conditions are essential for understanding why Memoria Activa was able to consider this move toward a more focused approach on legal aspects.[14] This is not to say that preserving and maintaining the memory of the attack or its victims became unimportant but that meaningful recognition of the need for justice from the national government somewhat abated the fear that the memory of the events would be adulterated or dismissed. This made it possible for the leaders of Memoria Activa to direct their necessarily limited energies in other ways, rather than investing time and effort in their weekly presence in the plaza.[15] However, it was immediately evident that this tactical move on the part of Memoria Activa was not satisfactory to a large percentage of their base of supporters who had turned out in the plaza on Monday mornings over a span of more than ten years.

In December 2004, Memoria Activa invited its supporters to two open meetings, to discuss ending the weekly protests/memorials. I attended these meetings, and the intensity of the emotions that came out seemed to take everyone by surprise. The response was overwhelmingly against the cessation, but the decision of the organizers was clear: their energies would from now on be devoted elsewhere. There was a deep sense of betrayal among many of the supporters, who with this decision were being effectively excluded from all active participation in the group. Although Memoria Activa relied upon the support of those who devoted their time and efforts to attending the weekly events, all decision-making power was concentrated in the hands of the directive board, comprised mainly of a handful of family members of victims. Few of Memoria Activa's supporters were direct relatives of anyone killed in the attack. The majority of victims' relatives who maintained a level of activism were nucleated in Familiares, although a number of other relatives of victims approved of or supported at least some of Memoria Activa's actions. Nonetheless, these partial supporters were not willing to share legal counsel with the group or join them as a unified plaintiff in any of the national or international legal cases. Thus, the "inner circle" of the movement was a limited number of individuals, and their decision-making practices, while including all of its active supporters though events like the open meetings, were ultimately determined by the directive board.

The base of Memoria Activa's supporters, which by this time numbered around 50 regular or semiregular participants, were mostly among those in the Argentine Jewish community who felt deeply affected by the attacks and felt themselves committed to the principal of the need for justice as a moral right and a means of protection against future injustice. Many frequently cited feeling a sense of responsibility as Jews and/or as citizens for their active participation. Making the effort to come to the plaza early Monday mornings was their way of contributing to what they saw as the struggle against impunity and preservation of memory. Learning that this avenue for action was no longer available to them was difficult. The thought of the Plaza Lavalle and the memorial to the victims remaining vacant and unaccompanied even one Monday morning was clearly painful to many. One woman, T.,[16] a former *detenida*[17] and long-standing participant in the weekly *actos* of the Madres de Plaza de Mayo,[18] was especially vehement about the importance of "not losing the plaza" and "not abandoning the plaza." She spoke forcefully, drawing on her age to point out that she was old enough to be the mother or grandmother of most of them, and emphasizing the debt that Memoria Activa owed them. She detailed how whenever someone failed to come to the plaza twice in a row, they would call and check on the individual, and how whenever someone was sick, they would visit the person, all in name of Memoria Activa, and in this way maintain the case of support for the group and its presence in the plaza for ten years.[19]

On December 27, 2004, Memoria Activa held its last official weekly act. It was publicized as a big event, the major newspapers covered it, and ten orators instead of the usual one to three were in attendance. Taking a picture with some friends afterward, one faithful supporter of the group, B., wryly commented, "So that we have the memory, even if it's no longer active." He brought along a banner that read "Todos somos Memoria Activa" (We Are All Memoria Activa), but instead of holding it up to show the crowd, he draped it over the monument to the victims. He was not alone in voicing his feelings of exclusion, saying openly, "We are no longer all Memoria Activa."[20]

The first Monday following Memoria Activa's final weekly event, no less than half of their usual supporters gathered around the monument to the victims and improvised their own protest/memorial. None were direct relatives of victims, but all were committed to the idea of "not losing this space." As one woman, C., said, "The plaza is the soul. To be in the plaza is like a drop of water rubbing away at a rock. There are those who are arguing that the judicial struggle is the most important, or the political struggle, or being in the plaza, but these things cannot be separated."[21]

There were initial attempts by some to push this new splinter group in one direction or the other, but over time they slowly consolidated into a cohesive though diverse group of some 25 individuals, all committed to "preserving the space" of the plaza and maintaining, through their presence, the memory of the victims and the demand for justice.[22] They decided to call themselves Citizens of the Plaza (Ciudadanos de la Plaza), highlighting the centrality of the space they occupy. T. explains her commitment like this: "I am here for the dead. I will accompany the dead here in the plaza every Monday until I die, just as I accompany the Mothers of the Plaza de Mayo every Thursday."[23]

One feature that remains constant with the group is their lamentation that their gatherings have not managed to attract any direct family members of victims. This lack is mentioned repeatedly, and attempts are frequently made to convince one family member or another to come to the plaza. Nonetheless, they do not hesitate to take on the responsibility for remembering the dead. During the weekly gatherings, they often take up a collection in order to tip the city sanitation employee engaged in cleaning the space around the monument to the AMIA victims. (I couldn't help but notice how he quickly learned to time his rounds through the plaza to coincide with their presence.) They also pooled their resources and purchased a replacement for the stolen plaque that accompanied the monument in honor of the AMIA victims (Figures 2.3 and 2.4).

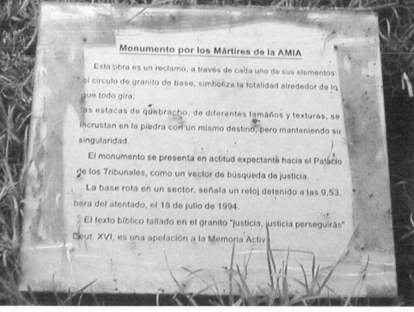

Monumento por los Mártires de la AMIA

Esta obra es un reclamo, a través de cada uno de sus elementos:
el círculo de granito de base, simboliza la totalidad alrededor de lo que todo gira;
las estacas de quebracho, de diferentes tamaños y texturas, se incrustan en la piedra con un mismo destino, pero manteniendo su singularidad.
El monumento se presenta en actitud expectante hacia el Palacio de los Tribunales, como un vector de búsqueda de justicia.
La base rota en un sector, señala un reloj detenido a las 9,53. hora del atentado, el 18 de julio de 1994.
El texto bíblico tallado en el granito "justicia, justicia perseguirás" Deut. XVI, es una apelación a la Memoria Activa.

FIGURES 2.3 AND 2.4   Monument in the Plaza Lavalle with a close-up showing the new commemorative plaque installed by Ciudadanos de la Plaza. Photos from 2006, by the author.

Lambek and Antze (1996) argue that the idea of memory has become individualized in Western societies. They say that memory, while increasingly recognized as collective and socially patterned, is nonetheless, through psychoanalytic and popular discourses, progressively located within the individual as the ultimate legitimate receptor and container of memory (xiii–xiv). The actions of Citizens of the Plaza both conform to and dispute this notion in particular ways. By lamenting the lack of participation of direct family members of victims, they are following a more general idea present throughout the Argentine counterimpunity community that privileges the place of those most directly affected by the repression in controlling the form that the public memory of the events can take (see Jelin 1995). Yet, by maintaining their protest/memorials even without this presence, they are performing a kind of collective and socialized memory in honor of the victims that is not dependent on individual experience.

Keeping the space. For Ciudadanos de la Plaza, their enactment of memory through public ritual is an essential feature of the search for justice.[24] Justice, in their eyes, cannot be achieved if the dead are not actively remembered. The events themselves were simple: after several minutes of casual chatting in small groups, they gathered in a circle in front of the monument to the victims.[25] Following the end of Memoria Activa's acts, B., mentioned above, took it upon himself to buy and learn to play the shofar (a gesture greatly appreciated by many of those present). Someone, usually chosen from one of three individuals who are seen as particularly gifted at speaking, would open the act with a reminder of why they were there and provide information about the AMIA case(s) or other events. In this sense, it was interesting to note what was considered appropriate and important information. The group defined and maintained its focus on what it considered as the central features of its act through an informal but highly effective democratic process of selection. Overall, this focus quickly became defined as concerning the preservation of memory and a visible performance of the struggle for justice. Thus, anything surrounding any of the many court cases surrounding the AMIA or its investigation was noted. Acts of anti-Semitism in Argentina or abroad were often mentioned, as were a wide range of events and activities relating to the memory and struggles against impunity around the Dirty War, particularly those related to people or places that directly involved some members of the group. Other cases generally considered under the rubric of impunity were also frequently discussed, such as cases of police brutality and the tragedy of the 2004 discothèque fire in Cromañón, when 194 young people died. These cases were considered nonpolemical, with all members sharing the same general assessment of the situation (and demonstrating the force that the broader discourses of impunity and human rights had among the participants). However, in an unspoken but collective agreement to avoid conflict, political or violent events in Israel were not typically mentioned at this point in the acts, nor were news items surrounding political topics in Argentina. When such issues would be mentioned, the speaker would be shushed or the topic quickly changed. Once the initial speaker had finished, they would invite anyone from the group who wished to speak to do so. At this point, contentious topics did often come up and were debated openly, as were historical items considered of interest or relevance. In this way, the group maintained a centralized focus on its purpose, while still allowing space for open debate among the widely varying spectrum of beliefs and opinions of those present.

The act would then be closed with one member leading the call for justice, with all turning to face Tribunales and the stone tablets that symbolized justice atop its neoclassical façade, though, as frequently mentioned by Citizens of the Plaza, these sculptures had not been seen for some eight years, having been covered "while undergoing repairs" that never seemed to occur, much less be completed. (They have since been uncovered.) Patterned off a format previously used by Memoria Activa, the unvarying call insisted:

> For the 30,000 disappeared at the hands of the military dictatorship, we demand JUSTICE
> For the dead in the Israeli Embassy bombing, we demand JUSTICE
> For the dead in the AMIA massacre, we demand JUSTICE
> Justice, justice, we shall seek[26]

Like Memoria Activa, Citizens of the Plaza is dedicated to the practice of citizenship through the struggle for justice in society. Unlike Memoria Activa, they refuse to give up their physical occupation of public space and visible presence as a key feature of this practice. Many no longer believe that any legal justice will be achieved surrounding the attack and its purposefully flawed investigation, but they continue to seek another kind of justice through publicly keeping alive the memory of what happened. Memoria Activa has vowed to continue working for institutional reform in Argentina through legal means. Citizens of the Plaza continue to insist on the preservation of memory as a practice of citizenship through direct physical occupation of what has become, for them, a sacred space of remembrance.

Key Moment 3: The IACHR Decision

In 1999, Memoria Activa took a case before the Inter-American Commission on Human Rights (IACHR), in which they accused the Argentine State of lack of justice and state protection following the AMIA attack five years earlier.[27] As a third key moment, the appeal by Memoria Activa to the IACHR has been a source of discord and conflicting sentiments for those involved and further exemplifies the divergent evaluations of the meanings of justice among those most deeply affected.

The IACHR and the Inter-American Court of Human Rights are the organs within the Organization of American States (OAS) for the promotion and protection of human rights. Functioning since 1979, they operate according to legal instruments, principally pacts or conventions, as well as a small but significant set of established precedents. Memoria Activa brought two major counts against the state of Argentina, each for violating the state's obligations as a signatory of the American Convention on Human Rights, or the Pact of San José, which Argentina ratified in September 1984 upon the official return to democracy. The first accusation concerned the right to life and physical integrity of the victims of the AMIA, as guaranteed under Articles 4 and 5 of this convention. Memoria Activa argued that after the 1992 bombing of the Israeli Embassy, the Argentine state had the obligation to foresee the possibility of another attack and respond appropriately in order to prevent such an occurrence. It contended that the Argentine state "failed to adopt the necessary measures to prevent the attack," charging that the police protection of local Jewish institutions was inadequate and noting the intelligence services' lack of attention to indications and warnings of a second attack.

The second count concerned the violation of the rights of both the victims and their families to obtain justice through local tribunals, as guaranteed by Articles 8 and 25. It denounced numerous irregularities in the investigation carried out by the investigating judge, Juan José Galeano, and his office (*juzgado*), claiming that the Argentine state had "violated to the detriment of the relatives of the victims the right to the judicial guarantees that assure that the causes of the events that produced the damage be effectively investigated, the right that a regular process be followed against those responsible for having produced the damage, and that as part of this process *the guilty be sanctioned and the victims compensated*."[28]

President Menem's reaction to Memoria Activa's accusation in 1999 had been to dismiss their claims, asserting that the State's performance in carrying out the investigation had been of "exemplary energy and promptness."[29] In 2000, the first audience of the case was held in Washington, D.C. At that time, the Argentine State under President de la Rúa argued that any decision in the case should be postponed until after the trial of a local man and several police officers accused of having possessed or conditioned the vehicle allegedly used in the bombings. Furthermore, they proposed that the IACHR appoint an observer to report on its proceedings. This was accepted. Chilean lawyer Claudio Grossman was designated as this observer in August 2001, and the trial began the following month.

This trial (*juicio oral y público*) took place in front of the Tribunal Oral en lo Criminal Federal n°3 (TOF3). It lasted nearly three years, one of the longest trials in Argentine history, and heard testimony from over 1,500 witnesses. When it finally concluded in 2004, all of the defendants were acquitted, and the case and the investigation were annulled and denounced part of an elaborate framework designed to falsely incriminate the accused. The verdict severely criticized the behavior of the investigating judge in the case, Galeano, and pointed to high-level government complicity in constructing a false hypothesis concerning the attack and failing to carry out a serious investigation.[30] The TOF3 called for an investigation into the investigation, which would examine the actions of Galeano and the prosecutors who worked for his office and look into the role played by, among others, former interior minister Carlos Corach; members of the Secretaría de Inteligencia del Estado (SIDE), including former head Hugo Anzorreguy; the federal judges who had received (and failed to act upon) expedients denouncing the behavior of Galeano; and ex-president of the DAIA Rubén Beraja; and DAIA lawyers Marta Nercellas and Roberto Zaidemberg. It also stated that the "distancing from the truth" that had occurred had involved different sectors from all three branches of state power, either in offering political support or directly covering the "illegal or irregular" actions of Galeano (verdict TOF3, case n487/00). Grossman presented his report to the IACHR on February 25, 2005. He supported the actuation of the TOF3, and he recommended that the IACHR accept Memoria Activa's accusations.

Memoria Activa applauded the work of the TOF3, and while they maintained that the principal accused should have been found guilty of the many crimes the trial revealed he had committed, they announced that they would not appeal the verdict. This is in keeping with their position, as the verdict concurred with many of the claims that Memoria Activa had been making for years and represented, in their eyes, a "rupture in the political-judicial pact."[31] In addition, the conclusion of the trial would allow their case against the Argentine State to proceed. Familiares and APEMIA, however, condemned the absolution of the defendants and organized demonstrations in rejection of the verdict, though each for different reasons. Familiares and the AMIA/DAIA contended that the defendants should have been found guilty and rejected the discrediting of Galeano's investigation. APEMIA, on the other hand, argued that the verdict was yet another stone in the wall of impunity that blocked the families from the truth, and it denounced what it saw as further manipulations and concealment of evidence by the three powers of state.[32]

The plaintiff unit formed by AMIA/DAIA/Familiares and that of the federal prosecutors appealed the verdict.[33] This, however, jeopardized the case that

Memoria Activa brought before the IACHR. For the case to be successful, there had to be, according to the IACHR, an "exhaustion of internal recourses," and an appeal was still a possibility for the conviction of individuals with alleged involvement in the attack. However, the *Grossman Report* recommended that the IACHR admit the petition regardless of an appeal, saying, "The IACHR has a solid jurisprudence establishing that slowness in investigations and the lack of results clearly generate an unjustified delay in the administration of justice, which implies a negation of such by not permitting the resolution of the events" (*Grossman Report* 2005: 97).

After the presentation of the *Grossman Report*, a new audience was scheduled to appear before the full IACHR on March 4, 2005. Shortly before that, the government announced that it would assume responsibility for the privation of justice following the AMIA bombing. This extraordinary announcement marked an absolute change in the position of the State in the AMIA case. Instead of denials and claims of good management that previous administrations had maintained, Néstor Kirchner's administration, when faced with almost certain condemnation by the IACHR, chose to publicly admit the State's guilt. In their declaration in front of the IACHR on March 4, 2005, the representatives of the State accepted the terms of Memoria Activa's original denouncement, saying:

> The government recognizes the responsibility of the Argentine State for the violation of human rights as denounced by the petitioners . . . as there existed a failure to fulfill the function of prevention for not having adopted the necessary and effective measures to avoid the attack . . . there existed a covering up of the facts, due to a serious and deliberate failure to fulfill the function of investigation . . . and because this failure to follow through with regards to an adequate investigation produced a clear privation of justice.[34]

The government went even further, formally asking Memoria Activa and all family members of AMIA and Embassy victims for forgiveness.[35]

This extraordinary declaration by the Argentine State, personified by Kirchner and transmitted through his official representation, was highly publicized across all major news media. This put the AMIA/DAIA in the uncomfortable position of having to reconcile their estrangement from Memoria Activa with this clear and popular advance in the State's treatment of the bombing. The more conservative publications, historical and/or economic allies of the official leadership of the collectivity, minimized or simply ignored the role of Memoria Activa in bringing about this sea change in government policy. For example, the newspaper *INFOBAE* published a photo of Alejandro Rúa (then head of the AMIA Unit of the Federal Ministry of Justice and Human Rights) with Abraham Kaúl, the charismatic and influential president of the AMIA at the time, and couched the events in terms of the reaction of the "Jewish community" and omitted all mention of how the audience before the IACHR came to exist.

APEMIA, however, was quick to denounce Kirchner's declaration. This group saw the admission of guilt as just another attempt, like all of the previous administrations, to portray the Argentine State as the victim of the bombing. Playing on the notion of institutional continuity, Kirchner's admission of State guilt is seen in this way as designed to achieve precisely the opposite: as an opportunity to present the State as a victim, having been subjected to the corrupt and "unscrupulous" practices of previous administrations, now vindicated under the new president. APEMIA's condemnation of the actions that the other organizations have taken as positive rests precisely on what they see as self-interested moves that divert rather than direct attention to the continuation of failed institutional practices.[36]

The idea that the problem of the AMIA attack and its cover-up, as the result of a failed state institutional structure, cannot be separated from the rights and needs of all Argentines is echoed in the following statements from a speech given at the APEMIA commemoration of the twelfth anniversary of the attack:

> Violations of human rights are of the State and not of persons. . . . The possibility to advance in the AMIA case will not exist if we do not manage to unite our demand for trial and punishment for those responsible for the AMIA attack with the struggle against the impunity that our people suffer, with the policies of misery, hunger, and repression that are in place today and that we see applied to us on a daily basis.[37]

In expressing its position, the group has forged alliances with traditional leftist political organizations and maintains an oppositional stance to the government. APEMIA chose to hold its initial demonstrations in the Plaza de Mayo instead of the Plaza Lavalle.[38] By choosing to make their public appearance in the historically resonant space for public manifestation, APEMIA highlighted the AMIA case as one affecting all Argentines and launched their criticisms not primarily at the justice system as with Memoria Activa but against the government as a whole. The vision of the state as proposed by Memoria Activa rests on the idea of the *estado de derecho*, or the rule of law. However, this notion is disputed by APEMIA, which argues that the incongruencies between the rhetorical use of this idea and the actual practices of government officials belie its status as a deceptive and manipulative mask. The group has expressed their position in this way:

> Memoria Activa guides their actions in name of an abstraction: the defense
> of (a State based on) the "Rule of Law"—of whom they demand that it "acts"

as it should—and not in defense of our rights, including that against the decomposition of this same "State." They end up disguising the (real) function of the judicial apparatus and the State itself: to uphold impunity. The reality of the "Rule of Law" is very different. If its essence were the provision of justice or rights and guarantees, how can do they explain that, of 20 years of "democracy," the last 12 (have seen) the explosion of the Israeli Embassy, of the AMIA, and the Military Munitions Factory at Río III, not to mention the laws of Full Stop and Due Obedience (that prevented the prosecution of Dirty War repressors)? How can they explain the 1,500 unpunished assassinations by *gatillo fácil* (easy trigger) or the criminalization of social protest and the new political prisoners of the K(irchner) era?[39]

APEMIA takes the provocative step of accusing the State itself of being responsible for the attack on the AMIA. This argument derives from the evidence that members of different branches of the State were complicit in the execution and covering up of the attack. In making this argument, they point to evidence that (1) the SIDE and the Ministry of the Interior had word of the attack before it happened and failed to prevent it; (2) members of the security and intelligence forces contributed in the carrying out of the attack; and (3) elements from all three branches of government worked in a coordinated manner in covering up what happened.[40] Given this position, for APEMIA, Memoria Activa's case against Argentina in front of the IACHR becomes ineffectual in the attempt to achieve justice. In addressing only specific claims of violations, within an established structure based upon individualized notions of retribution, the case fails to attend to what APEMIA sees as the need to reform the entire political system in ways that attend to the needs of all Argentines. In insisting on the establishment of an independent, non-governmental commission to investigate the attack and the irregularities of the investigation, including the opening and handing over of all classified and secret archives and documents, they seek to circumvent a state seen as corrupt and ineffectual and place their faith instead in an open and transparent process conducted by members of civil society.

RESOLUTION? THE PURSUIT OF JUSTICE

Each of these four groups—Memoria Activa, APEMIA, Familiares, and Citizens of the Plaza—is concerned with achieving "justice" for the AMIA attack. But what justice is and, especially, through what means it should be pursued have been contentious topics. Here, I identify four different visions of what "justice" entails as held and pursued by each of these groups. However, on a broader level, the difference between the visions of justice advanced by each lies, in my opinion, in the focus and chosen course of action. That is, each chose to make one aspect the main focus of their attention and actions, either because the group considered that aspect the most important or the one that most corresponded to the group's role. However, these four aspects form part of a broader vision that is in fact shared among all four groups. Justice itself is therefore defined as the conjunction of these features, rather than as one to the exclusion of the others. Nevertheless, each of these groups chose, to varying degrees, to define one or another of these aspects as the primary focus of their attention and constructed their course of action accordingly.

For the Citizens of the Plaza, the most important feature of their pursuit was a form of democracy in action, enacted by their own experiential weekly practice. Justice, in this sense, is concerned primarily with maintaining memory and keeping alive and active remembrance of the victims and the weekly visible reminder of their struggle through its physical presence in a public space. Knowledge about the attack and the means of resolution are intimately tied to the multiple expressions of memory that they enact and embody. For APEMIA, there is a fundamental need for citizen involvement in the investigation and in the justice-making process. The state, in their view, cannot be charged with investigating itself, especially when there is a continuation of personnel or political interests in power-holding positions. Therefore, the perceived need is focused on the establishment of the truth through an independent commission that has access to all pertinent information. Justice, for this group, is most directly concerned with full disclosure of information and the construction of independently verified authoritative knowledge about the attack. Neither of these groups expects or believes in justice as bestowed by the state; rather, justice for this case is seen as only possible through the continuous (Citizens of the Plaza) or punctual (APEMIA) actions of nonstate actors.

For Memoria Activa, legal justice and institutional change are the ultimate goals, and their pursuit is best realized by working with the government, even if this requires recourse to external pressure to gain their cooperation. Justice for the attack is most directly tied to legal condemnation for those responsible, both in the planning and execution of the attack as well as in its subsequent mismanagement and deliberate obfuscation. For Memoria Activa, authoritative knowledge about the attack can be constructed by and within the government, under the workings of a fair and impartial judiciary.[41] The need for such legal institutions thus becomes one of their primary demands on the state itself, and their ultimately successful struggle to remove the investigating judge reflects this concern. Familiares was also concerned with achieving legal justice. However, it can be seen as highlighting the perceived need to maintain the institutionality of the community representation.[12] Justice, in many ways, is intimately tied to strong and representative community institutions. Authoritative knowledge about the events and their resolution still needs to come from the state, but for Familiares, it was essential that community institutions accept, validate, and advocate for this information, rather than individual victims and their families taking on this role.

In cases like this one where a sense of reckoning or closure is lacking over a prolonged period of time, how to gain a sense of justice can be a point of division and of common ground for those involved. The three moments described in this chapter exemplify the currents of division as well as the underlying similarities in the ideals of justice as held and pursued by the members of these four groups comprised of those affected by the AMIA bombing. These four elements are the cornerstone of the concept of "justice" held by each. Each group focused on one of these elements, although all would agree that full justice necessarily includes the achievement of all. For those most directly concerned with achieving resolution for this case, their chosen focus affects their definition of their goals and plan of action, their interactions with state and community institutions, their relationship with the other groups of stakeholders, and their understanding of the validity and possibility for achieving legitimate and credible forms of knowledge in the aftermath of tragedy. Achieving "justice" for the AMIA bombing will ultimately require attention to all four levels of meaning embedded in the term. Careful consideration of the multiple meanings of justice and of its manifestations in the lived experiences of those affected is an essential part of achieving social reconstruction following this kind of tragic and destructive event, and it draws attention to the deep and multiple meanings that "justice" can and does take.

NOTES

I would like to thank the members of these organizations for their openness and generosity in sharing their time and thoughts for this research. I am also grateful to Noa Vaisman, Leticia Barrera, Sarah Muir, Sian Lazar, and Felipe Gómez for being stimulating and constructive interlocutors on the themes discussed in this chapter, and to my friends, colleagues, and students at Carnegie Mellon for many engaging conversations on the nature and meaning of justice.

1. Daniel Goldstein has written extensively on the discourse of "security" and on security and rights in Latin America. For a cogent analysis, see Goldstein (2007, 2012) and Desmond Arias and Goldstein (2010).

2. Natan Sonis, spoken at the commemorative event organized by Memoria Activa on July 18, 2014, Plaza Lavalle. Recorded and translated by the author.

3. Sonis, July 18, 2014, Plaza Lavalle.

4. Several high-level Iranian officials have been identified by the Argentine Justice System as allegedly involved in planning the AMIA attack. The suspects remain, as of this writing, on Interpol's "red alert" list for capture and questioning. In January 2013, Argentina and

Iran, or, more exactly, the Cristina Kirchner administration, represented by foreign minister Héctor Timerman, and Ali Akbar Salehi on behalf of the Ahmadinejad administration signed an agreement that would allow representatives of the Argentine Justice System to interview the suspects in Tehran. As of this writing, the agreement never went into effect, due in part to procedural obstacles in both countries and a changing geopolitical scene with regards to Iran. In January 2015, lead prosecutor and head of the Unidad AMIA (the federal body charged with investigating the attack) Alberto Nisman was found dead after he publicly accused President Fernández of using the agreement as part of an alleged economic deal with Iran. The Memorandum, the possibilities it theoretically opened for the questioning and prosecution of the accused, and interpretations of Nisman's death have been contentious within the Argentine Jewish community (see Faulk 2015), and this dissention follows in many ways the lines laid out in the analysis provided by this chapter. While Memoria Activa was cautiously optimistic about the possibility of such an agreement leading to some advancement in the case, the AMIA/DAIA opposed the government's actions and have attempted to have the Memorandum declared unconstitutional. APEMIA continues to insist on the formation of an Independent Investigative Commission. With the election of Mauricio Macri in late 2015, the Memorandum was shelved (http://www.info bae.com/2015/12/11/1775950-el-nuevo-gobierno-dejara-efecto-el-memorandum-iran-la -causa-amia).

5. I have adopted the common practice within Argentina of using the word *collectivity* (*colectividad*) in regard to Argentine Jews. This term is generally used to denote the diverse organized Jewish religious, social, and political organizations and their members, while at the same time recognizing the differences in attitudes and perceptions that exist among these. I have chosen to use the word *community* to refer to the broader set of all self-identifying Argentines of Jewish descent, whether or not these have any participation in organized Jewish life. In Argentina, what I call *community* is often referred to as the *calle judía*, or the Jewish street.

6. See Feierstein (1999) for a concise and insightful history.

7. Full text of this speech is available at http://memoriaactiva.com/, and an English translation can be found in Nouzeilles and Montaldo (2002).

8. Another of the most complicated and notorious of issues concerned the alleged participation of former DAIA president Rubén Beraja and the DAIA's legal counsel, Marta Nercellas, in falsely accusing members of the Buenos Aires Police Force during the only case to have come to trial. Allegations that Beraja and Nercellas were aware of the payment made to Telleldín and complicit in the attempt to close the investigation of the "local connection" in the bombing with the trial that ended in their acquittal further exacerbated these tensions. Beraja was subsequently imprisoned for his role in the bankruptcy and corruption scandal surrounding the Banco de Mayo, which resulted in the loss of the savings of many community members.

9. While all four of these groups have undergone changes over the years, Familiares has perhaps seen the greatest shifting in terms of active members and adopted stances. By 2014, there was also a new organization, 18J Asociación, which held its own independent protest memorial event in the Plaza de Mayo. The positions attributed to the different groups in this chapter should be understood as operating at the times mentioned, while recognizing that all continue to develop in new directions.

10. The various perceptions of appropriate gender roles, their role in Argentine social movements, and in particular their application in the case of the family members of AMIA

victims are all important topics that unfortunately lie beyond the scope of this chapter. See, for example, Jelin (1995).

11. As with Familiares, it is important to note that these divisions, no matter how contentious, are neither complete nor entirely exclusive. There are still aspects of cooperation and overlap between the different groups, especially among their base of supporters, who often participate in the demonstrations of more than one or even all of the different groups.

12. Author's field notes and interviews with board members, November–December 2005.

13. The Kirchner administrations embraced a radically different politics of memory, particularly concerning the acts and policies of state terrorism leading up to and during the last military dictatorship (1976–1983). Rather than encouraging forgetting and suppressing discussion of the era, the Kirchners opened the way for concrete legal and legislative action to prosecute those responsible for the violence, as well as engaging in numerous symbolic and practical acts condemning the repression.

14. Couso, Huneeus, and Sieder (2010) discuss this kind of increased willingness for legal activism across many groups in Latin America as part of a trend toward the "judicialization" of political action.

15. Some detractors of this decision related to me their suspicion that the decision was due to Memoria Activa's leadership wanting or agreeing to remove this pressure from the Kirchner administration in exchange for concessions in the IACHR case (an agreement was signed between the parties in March 2005). Whether or not this impending meeting held any influence in the determinations made at the end of 2004, Memoria Activa has since made strong public statements criticizing the failure of the administration to make concrete advances on the promises assumed in front of the Commission.

16. All names have been abbreviated.

17. Political prisoner, held (often clandestinely) by the de facto military government during the 1976–1983 dictatorship.

18. The iconic Madres de Plaza de Mayo have also undergone similar organizational splits, as have other human rights organizations, such as Hijos por la Identidad y la Justicia contra el Olvido y el Silencio (HIJOS, Sons and Daughters for Identity and Justice against Oblivion and Silence). While an analysis of these groups is outside of the scope of this chapter, in my view the multiple and layered meanings of justice and the means for its fulfillment are at least part of what is at stake in the points of contention between these and other victims' rights groups. See the Introduction.

19. Author's field notes, January 20, 2005.

20. Author's field notes, December 27, 2004.

21. Author's field notes, January 3, 2005.

22. The importance placed on the use of public space here is not surprising. From political rallies and symbolic events to social protest and calls for justice, the Argentine public sphere is continuously and dramatically (re)created in the streets. See Goddard (2006), James (1988), Lazar (2015), and Sabato (2004).

23. Author's field notes, January 10, 2005.

24. Ciudadanos de Plaza is also discussed in Zaretsky (2008).

25. I write in the past tense here, though, at least as of July 2015, the group continues to meet.

26. Por los 30,000 desaparecidos en manos de la dictadura militar, exigimos JUSTICIA / Por los muertos en la masacre de la Embajada de Israel, exigimos JUSTICIA / Por los muertos en la masacre de la AMIA, exigimos, JUSTICIA / Justicia, justicia, perseguimos

27. Coverage of this case (12.204) and documents relating to it can be found on the IACHR website: http://www.oas.org/en/iachr/default.asp.

28. From the presentation by Memoria Activa in front of the IACHR, case 12.204, AMIA-Argentina. Emphasis added.

29. Cited in Kiernan (2001).

30. Galeano was subsequently disrobed and faces criminal and civil charges.

31. Declaration by Memoria Activa, September 6, 2004.

32. APEMIA, Boletín 6, September 2004, and author's interviews.

33. APEMIA had not held a role as plaintiff in the trial and therefore could not have filed an appeal. The Cámara de Casación ruled in May 2006 to uphold the verdict of the TOF3 and sent a copy of their findings to Ariel Lijo, the federal judge in charge of investigating the irregularities of Galeano's investigation. Action remained stalled for many years. The trial, which has six separate plaintiff groups (APEMIA, Memoria Activa, 18J, and others) and whose defendants include ex-president Carlos Menem, Beraja, and Galeano is began in August 2015. http://www.pagina12.com.ar/diario/elpais/1-276220-2015-07-02.html.

34. Acta CIDH (IACHR Record), March 4, 2005, case 12.204.

35. Presentation in front of the IACHR by Alejandro Rúa, in representation of the Argentine State, March 4, 2005.

36. This position can be seen expressed in a set of communiqués issued by the organization during the first months of 2005, available at http://apemiacomisioninvestigadora.blogspot.com.ar/.

37. From a speech given by Graciela Rosenblum, of the Liga Argentina por los Derechos del Hombre (LADH) (Argentine League for the Rights of Man), July 18, 2007, corner of Corrientes and Pasteur.

38. Later events were held down the street from the AMIA building.

39. Cruzaron la vereda, APEMIA Boletín 6, September 2004. The information presented on APEMIA in this chapter comes primarily from the author's interviews with members of the organization and attendance at organizational meetings and public events. The quotes are taken from speeches given by members or from printed materials provided to the author by Laura Ginsberg.

40. "Salen los fiscales del juicio . . . ¿y ahora qué?," APEMIA Boletín 4, May 2004.

41. Their faith in the TOF3 is reaffirmed through their acceptance of its determination that the explosion in the AMIA building was due to a car bomb. The means of the explosion was a hotly debated topic for many years, and several competing theories on the location of the explosives and their means of delivery were based on available evidence. However, Memoria Activa accepted the TOF3's findings on this issue and has affirmed the same since that verdict.

42. This was the case during the era most directly discussed here, roughly 2004 to 2006. As mentioned, the Familiares organization has adopted differing stances at different points in time, in part in response to changing leadership administrations within the AMIA/DAIA.

WORKS CITED

Clarke, Kamari Maxine, and Mark Goodale, eds. 2010. *Mirrors of Justice: Law and Power in the Post–Cold War Era*. Cambridge: Cambridge University Press.

Collins, Cath. 2010. *Post-Transitional Justice: Human Rights in Chile and El Salvador*. University Park: Pennsylvania State University Press.

Couso, Javier, Alexandra Huneeus, and Rachel Sieder, eds. 2010. *Cultures of Legality: Judicialization and Political Activism in Latin America*. Cambridge: Cambridge University Press.

Desmond Arias, Enrique, and Daniel Goldstein, eds. 2010. *Violent Democracies in Latin America*. Durham, NC: Duke University Press.

Faulk, Karen Ann. 2013. *In the Wake of Neoliberalism: Citizenship and Human Rights in Argentina*. Stanford, CA: Stanford University Press.

———. 2015. "Truth and Meaning-Making in Liminal Politics: Unraveling the Death of Argentine Prosecutor Alberto Nisman." Paper presented at the Latin American Studies Association Annual Congress, May 29, San Juan, Puerto Rico.

Feierstein, Ricardo. 1999. *Historia de los judíos argentinos*. Buenos Aires: Ameghino.

Goddard, Victoria. 2006. "'This Is History': Nation and Experience in Times of Crisis—Argentina 2001." *History and Anthropology* 17 (3): 267–286.

Goldstein, Daniel M. 2007. "The Violence of Rights—Human Rights as Culprit, Human Rights as Victim." In *The Practice of Human Rights: Tracking Law between the Global and the Local*, edited by Mark Goodale and Sally Engle Merry, 49–77. Cambridge: Cambridge University Press.

———. 2012. *Outlawed: Between Security and Rights in a Bolivian City*. Durham, NC: Duke University Press.

Gurevich, Beatriz. 2005. *Passion, Politics, and Identity: Jewish Women in the Wake of the AMIA Bombing in Argentina*. Buenos Aires: Universidad del CEMA.

Hinton, Alexander Laban, ed. 2010. *Transitional Justice: Global Mechanisms and Local Realities after Genocide and Mass Violence*. New Brunswick, NJ: Rutgers University Press.

Huneeus, Alexandra. 2010. "Rejecting the Inter-American Court: Judicialization, National Courts, and Regional Human Rights." In *Cultures of Legality: Judicialization and Political Activism in Latin America*, edited by Javier A. Couso, Alexandra Huneeus, and Rachel Sieder, 112–138. Cambridge: Cambridge University Press.

James, Daniel. 1988. "October 17th and 18th, 1945: Mass Protest, Peronism, and the Argentine Working Class." *Journal of Social History* 21 (3): 441–461.

Jelin, Elizabeth. 1995. "La política de la memoria: El movimiento de derechos humanos y la construcción democrática en la Argentina." In *Juicio, castigo y memorias: Derechos humanos y justicia en la política argentina*, edited by Carlos Acuña, Inés González Bombal, Elizabeth Jelín, Oscar Landi, Luis Alberto Quevedo, Catalina Smulovitz, and Adriana Vacchieri, 29–38. Buenos Aires: Nueva Visión.

Kiernan, Sergio. 2001. *Seeking the Truth: The AMIA Bombing Goes to Trial*. New York: American Jewish Committee.

Lambek, Michael, and Paul Antze. 1996. "Introduction: Forecasting Memory." In *Tense Past: Cultural Essays in Trauma and Memory*, edited by Michael Lambek and Paul Antze, xi–xxxviii. New York: Routledge.

Lazar, Sian. 2015. "'This Is Not a Parade, It's a Protest March': Intertextuality, Citation, and Political Action on the Streets of Bolivia and Argentina." *American Anthropologist* 117 (2): 242–256.

Lundy, Patricia, and Mark McGovern. 2008. "Whose Justice? Rethinking Transitional Justice from the Bottom Up." *Journal of Law and Society* 35 (2): 265–292.

Nouzeilles, Gabriela, and Graciela R. Montaldo, eds. 2002. *The Argentina Reader: History, Culture, Politics*. Durham, NC: Duke University Press.

Payne, Leigh A. 2003. "Perpetrators' Confessions: Truth, Reconciliation, and Justice in Argentina." In *What Justice? Whose Justice? Fighting for Fairness in Latin America*, edited by Susan Eckstein and Timothy P. Wickham-Crowley, 158–184.

Sábato, Hilda. 2004. *La política en las calles: Entre el voto y la movilización, Buenos Aires, 1862–1880*. Bernal, Argentina: Universidad Nacional de Quilmes.

Shaw, Rosalind, and Lars Waldorf, eds. 2010. *Localizing Transitional Justice: Interventions and Priorities after Mass Violence*. Stanford, CA: Stanford University Press.

Smulovitz, Catalina. "Judicialization in Argentina: Legal Culture or Opportunities and Support Structures." In *Cultures of Legality: Judicialization and Political Activism in Latin America*, edited by Javier A. Couso, Alexandra Huneeus, and Rachel Sieder, 234–253. Cambridge: Cambridge University Press.

Theidon, Kimberly. 2012. *Intimate Enemies: Violence and Reconciliation in Peru*. Philadelphia: University of Pennsylvania Press.

Vaisman, Noa. 2015. "Variations on Justice: Argentina's Pre- and Post-Transitional Justice and the Justice to Come." *Ethnos*. DOI: 10.1080/00141844.2015.1080746.

Wilson, Richard A. 2001. *The Politics of Truth and Reconciliation in South Africa: Legitimizing the Post-Apartheid State*. Cambridge: Cambridge University Press.

Zaretsky, Natasha. 2008. "Singing for Social Change: Nostalgic Memory and the Struggle for Belonging in a Buenos Aires Yiddish Chorus." In *Rethinking Jewish-Latin Americans*, edited by Jeffrey Lesser and Raanan Rein, 231–256. Albuquerque: University of New Mexico Press.

PART TWO   THE SPACES OF LEGALITY

3 JUSTICE, RIGHTS, AND DISCRETIONARY SPACE IN BRAZILIAN POLICING

Graham Denyer Willis

INTRODUCTION

In May 2006, an organized armed group, the Primeiro Comando da Capital (PCC), unleashed a series of violent attacks on the city of São Paulo. In the attacks, the PCC explicitly targeted low-level state security agents in retribution for the rough transfer of the organization's incarcerated leader, Marcos Willians Herbas Camacho, known as "Marcola," to a higher-security prison in the interior of the state. During the week-long attacks, 8 prison guards and 31 police officers were killed, many of them close to their homes far away from their workplaces (Pereira 2008). In many periphery areas of the city, buses were burned and police precincts were attacked, creating a media firestorm throughout the world. The deaths of police officers and prison agents were swiftly avenged by shadowy figures at arm's length, or closer, to the public security system. Low estimates suggest that the Military and Civil Police reacted by killing 124 individuals suspected of being PCC members. High-end estimates set the number of dead at 493 (Cavallaro and Dodge 2007: 53). After the violence, the city became an increasingly divided space. Protests decrying the human rights abuses of police grew amidst the funerals of suspected PCC members. This sparked newspaper editorials and reactionary movements, and even some in the academic community, to claim that the discourse of human rights had been co-opted by "criminals," whose claim "We only want our rights" was disingenuous (Holston 2007, 2009). For police, more starkly, there seemed to be no right to rights. But for all of the claims for rights-based justice, something was missing: *any* sense of justice. How was this violence shaped by the everyday, and largely fruitless, pursuit of "justice" by police? Why should rights matter as a conceptual platform, a prescription, or a panacea, especially when it comes to *police work*? Why does the discourse of human and citizens' rights fail to resonate with Brazilian police officers? This chapter illustrates some of the distance between street-level logics and practices and the meanings of "justice" among those charged with working to enable it.

For decades, and again following the 2006 violence, Brazilian police have been the paragon of violence against citizens (Cavallaro 1997; Chevigny 1987; Human Rights Watch 2009; Penglase 1994; Serbin 1998). In the postauthoritarian period in particular, Brazilian police have provided a shopping list of severe abuses, such as Candelária (1993: 8 dead), Vigário Geral (1993: 26 dead), Carandiru (1991: 111 dead), and the Baixada Fluminense (2005: 29 dead). These incidents, and many other similar cases, are quickly (and understandably) picked up by Brazilian civil society and international human rights organizations and publicized nationally and internationally, garnering widespread attention and shock.

Civil society responses to police killings have doubled down on rights language to accentuate and position the gravity of police violence among citizens and policy makers. For those who adopt this discourse, there is no sense of justice here, not in the killing of (alleged or presumed) criminals nor for the victims of police violence. Human rights language provides a formal framework for criticism and response, serving as a key vehicle for citizenship claims (see Chapter 6). Consequently, rights-based assertions have shaped a reform agenda that seeks to transform the way Brazilian policing is done and are eschewed as *the* means to bring police into a democratic system of checks and balances. These prescriptions have taken many forms. Some have called for human rights training for police officers as a means to incrementally change corrupt behavior and violence (Chevigny 1987). Others advocate for broader rights-based overhauls of policing mandates to be more tightly connected with human rights ideals (Pinheiro 1997). Still others suggest that human rights, through the strength of regional rights tribunals, are integral for a wholesale reshaping of citizen security (Chillier and Varela 2009). The right-based approach to reform has drawn no shortage of attention from funding sources, ranging from private foundations such as Ford and Open Societies, international government bodies such as the World Bank and the European Union, and bilateral donors such as the governments of Canada, Britain, and the United States (Leeds 1996).

Yet, most of these efforts have struggled to make inroads or to make police organizations markedly more accountable, efficient, and democratically congruent. Explanations for this have differed, ranging from pervasive corruption and clientelistic politics (Hinton 2006), coordinated resistance (Holston 2007), and political inclination for hard-line policies (Caldeira 2000) to authoritarian legacies (Zaverucha 2000). Few analyses, if any, however, have emphasized the centrality of organizational weakness or the pragmatic and problematic influence that nonstate armed groups have on police in Brazil's major cities.

Proposals for rights-based reforms, which necessarily see police organizations as homogeneous, well organized, and driven by organizational cultures of violence and corruption, overlook the empirical patterns and challenges of police work. This chapter includes examples from the day-to-day functioning of Brazilian police work and its paradigm of constraint and agency. Based on these examples, I suggest that although police are routinely and roundly conceptualized as violent and abusive of rights, a rights-based response is antithetic to most explanatory ends. Rather, the evidence presented herein shows that police officers are distrustful of the discourse of rights because this discourse ignores the larger problem: organizational weakness, and its concordant consequences, especially the lack of technology and police vulnerability. Theoretically, and according to prominent concepts of what "good" police officers are, these actors are the gatekeepers of justice and the enforcers of the rule of law. However, where policing organizations are particularly weak, the empirical outlook of justice that police officers have is heavily influenced by the security challenges that individual police officers face. A police officer's idea of "justice" becomes reflective of the ways he or she must act in spite of those larger ideals.

We will see how police use discretionary space in ways that transcend and nullify justice on the books. These activities include discretionary negotiations with real or perceived "criminals" and police pragmatism in decision making on the job. Because the public security systems of São Paulo and other cities are weak in terms of hierarchical structure, police come into distinctly close and prolonged contact with powerful nonstate armed groups, both by choice and by occupational consequence. Lower-level police officers often need to navigate a "balance" with nonstate armed groups.

Recent research argues that this has resulted in "illegal networks" that span the divide between police and organized armed groups, wherein police coerce, extort, and use violence as a means of influence over criminality. But police are not the only group doing the coercing. In the face of the extreme violence of armed groups—violence that often directly targets public security agents—police must find ways to cope with the threat, and opportunity, of working alongside criminal organizations and influences. Because police can be coerced as much by these forces as by their own organizational hierarchy, they draw heavily on discretionary space. Justice, and particularly what police understand to be "just" given their own needs, cannot be disentangled from a police officer's use of discretion.

This chapter has five sections. The first reviews some perspectives on policing and rights-based reforms in Brazil. The second introduces the nature of contemporary policing in urban Brazil. Building on this, the third section details the scope and characteristics of discretionary practices and networks that cross the licit/illicit boundary of the books. The fourth section draws upon ethnographic research undertaken in Civil Police Precincts in São Paulo and Rio de Janeiro, detailing the operational environment of police, including the parameters of discretion. The fifth section provides an empirical example of pragmatic navigation of discretionary space by police, with regards to the threat of violence, personal security, and the demands of the job. Overall, the chapter explores these "translegal" spaces, showing why a discourse of human and citizens' rights fails to resonate with Brazilian police officers, for whom ideas about "justice" are deeply impacted by the challenges of inadequate pay and lack of protection from the violence they are meant to control.

NONSTATE ARMED GROUPS AND POLICING

Rashes of extreme violence in Brazil, like that which occurred in May 2006, underscore the challenge of policing in what is a pluralistic security environment (Arias and Goldstein 2010). Nonstate forms of governance—that is, alternative regimes imposed by organized armed criminal groups over a particular space—have become common throughout Latin America and in other countries in transition (Davis 2009). Since the early 1990s, Brazil has witnessed the mass emergence of these nonstate forms of order and security within its marginalized urban spaces. Rio de Janeiro provides a poignant contrast between police control of the streets and the criminal organizations' monopoly over shantytown hillside favelas (Arias 2006b; Dowdney 2005; Goldstein 2003; Penglase 1994; Perlman 2006; Zaluar 1996).

The city of São Paulo suffers from its own taxonomy of criminal governance. Here, expansive spaces of periurban sprawl have become central to the city's preeminent nonstate armed group, the Primeiro Comando da Capital (PCC). In these spaces and with networks to the prison system, the PCC has morphed into an organization with more than 400,000 members that systematically controls swathes of the urban periphery (Denyer Willis 2009; Feltran 2010, 2011). The PCC's imposition of law and order seemingly operates independent of the state, being upheld by the statute of the organization, a written document explicitly detailing a code of conduct for members, affiliates, and, often, the community. Residents and members of the organization are subject to these rules—no theft, no adultery, no lying or deception—with punishment for these transgressions including removal from the organization and, exceptionally, death. This alternative security structure has had a decisive impact. In one community controlled by the PCC, the homicide rate has declined by more than 75 percent (SEADE 2007). Although subject to an extreme and imposed form of order, most residents believe the new regime is better than the one provided by the police and the public security system (Denyer Willis 2009). While this type of "law and order" may seem distinct from the state, the PCC and similar armed groups connect with the state in unexceptional ways. This is the focus of ongoing research (see Denyer Willis 2014a, 2015).

In the mid-1990s, Elizabeth Leeds (1996) noted the existence of "parallel powers" at work in the drug trade within Rio de Janeiro's favelas. Leeds observed that these organized criminal groups operated outside the scope of public security, having sprouted up in areas neglected by police and other state services. These groups often clashed with police in struggles related to the drug trade, but they existed independently of one another. Recently, this portrayal has been challenged. How power, the influence of the state, and political processes are at play in this relationship have become hot topics, recast as relationships of "interpenetration" (Pereira 2008), "illegal networks" (Arias 2006a), and "symbiosis" (Mingardi 2007). Research has shown that such major and contentious groups do not operate alongside the state as sovereign authorities. These groups, such as the Comando Vermelho and Amigos dos Amigos of Rio de Janeiro, do not exist outside the realm of the state. Rather, they subsist based on the weakness and permeability of agents of the state in "illegal networks" that allow police, criminal organizations, and civil society groups to consistently negotiate a mutually beneficial equilibrium. These networks arise "when groups need to maintain trust and cultivate enduring stable contacts but where it is impossible or inconvenient to form strict hierarchical structures" (Arias 2006a: 40). In other words, illegal networks—a self-consuming paradox because they can only be deemed illegal by the same institutions they pervade—occur in translegal space and encompass the regular but informal horizontal, reciprocal, and voluntary sublegal engagements that occur back and forth between state bureaucrats, politicians, police, and armed groups.

It is clear that the arrangement between the police and criminal organizations is evocative of a violence-mitigating equilibrium. This relationship, where criminal organizations go about their business and police are coerced or incentivized to look the other way, has become the preeminent challenge to policing and public security in many of the major urban centers of Brazil. Yet, the existence of two major but interconnected poles of violence speaks to an erosion of the state's monopoly on violence. Where a definitive state monopoly on violence does not exist, there is a propensity for regular intervals of violence. And when the balance of power between these two poles of violence is tipped—as in the 2006 attacks—extreme outbreaks of violence are likely to occur.

DISCRETIONARY SPACE: STREET-LEVEL BUREAUCRATS AMIDST VIOLENCE

A well-established body of scholarship has examined how bureaucrats use discretion in their everyday work. Much of this perspective, which values the agency of local-level bureaucrats, follows the seminal work of Lipsky (1980) in his book

Street-Level Bureaucracy. Lipsky believes that the decision-making processes and constraints of frontline workers shape the delivery of public policies in meaningful ways. How they utilize their discretion, how much discretion they have, and what institutional guidelines shape each pattern alter what the public receives in terms of service.

Discretionary space is a useful way to analyze how police work in locations where the law-on-the-books holds little sway. Indeed, there is a remarkable dearth of discussion about how police in violent situations constitute a particular category of street-level bureaucrat. The idea of discretionary space clarifies how street-level decisions police are forced to make in the midst of violence routinely span both the "legal" and the "illegal," even as these bureaucrats are believed to be guardians of what is legal and, by consequence, are defenders of public-facing rights and justice.

Although police officers work in shifts, they are never really off the job. They must make decisions that cut across personal livelihood, job success, and public demands, as well as personal and security needs. Their advantageous use of discretionary space reflects this. The notion of a discretionary space also addresses the conceptual flaws of the illegal (or illicit) "network" analogy that has been used to analyze the connectedness of the police, civil society, and nonstate armed groups in Latin America (for an overview, see Andreas 2004). The network's idea emphasizes a perceived weakness of the Weberian state; the role of regular relationships across the legal, illegal, and malfeasance compared to the laws on the books; and the regular nature of exchange and negotiation occurring between state and nonstate armed actors. The analogy, prominently advanced by Arias (2006a, 2006b), borrows from Powell's (2003) widely referenced definition:

> [The police–armed group illegal network consists of] voluntary, reciprocal,
> and horizontal (though not exclusively equal) patterns of communication and
> exchange that can be contrasted with both markets (short-term contract-based
> horizontal exchanges) and hierarchies (long-term vertical systems of control). As
> institutions, networks are based on flexible links among component parts that
> work to achieve mutual interests. (39)

The armed group–police relationship, however, does not fit the theoretical mold of hierarchies or markets. The way we currently use the illegal network nomenclature does not adequately reflect the nuances of power that bind police and armed groups. It struggles to encompass the nature of informality and the reasons why state and nonstate actors are compelled to engage. In this regard, there are three important factors to consider. How does the transfer of a concept from a world where the law on the books appears legitimate suit an environment of apparent lawlessness and nonofficial rules—a space regulated primarily by the threat or reality of violence? How does the way in which we currently use the illegal network nomenclature fail to adequately express what is happening in the real world? What does it mean when network participation is obligatory and not voluntary in everyday decision making and is made under threat of pain or death?

The network definition proposed by Powell (2003) and borrowed for the "illicit" network analogy has typically been used to analyze business linkages and social relationships that exist in spaces with a strong sense of law and clear, if not codified, regulation. How networked groups interact typically rests upon the basic presumption of an existing rule of law that can be used by police to regulate the egregiously illegal actions of one party or another. A set of mutually understood legal norms that are largely defined by written law and enforced by a perceived neutral party—the police and the criminal justice system—serve as both deterrents and consequences for participants. In these "legal" networks, for example, where one business chooses to steal the intellectual property of another, the offended business has formal recourse. It may seek out the police or a legal representative to get its property back and decide to press criminal charges. Informally, it may seek to inform peer firms within the network and/or could withdraw from its arrangement with the offending business and seek a replacement partner. In networks with these options, it is uncommon for one party to strike back with identical tactics or violence. This is true despite the flexible, informal, and plastic nature of network relationships. Though the legitimacy of law may not be a regular and guiding factor in networks arrangements, which are premised on concord, cooperation, and mutual beneficence, it serves an important deterrent role.

When the laws on the books hold little legitimacy, concord, voluntarism, and cooperation are much less central factors to network dynamics. This is particularly true when the offending party *is* the police and the offended party is an armed drug-trafficking organization. Alternative forms of influence fill the void, and coercion and the threat of violence emerge as the key punitive and deterrent tools. Typically, network definitions carry assumptions that cannot reconcile with this dynamic: relationships across the legal and illegal are entrenched, by definition, *within* a relationship between armed and powerful groups. Such empirically existing networks are more than just conceptual networks that happen to have an "illegal" actor. Such networks need to be seen as entirely conceptually distinct, stripped of deep normative assumptions about the legal and the illegal. Both of the parties involved *and* the ties that bind them act outside the bounds of the law on the books. These relationships occur in a space that transcends (and sometimes avoids) formal law in such a way that it redefines the practices, allegiances, and raison d'être of policing as a whole, making a conceptual distinction that hinges upon the letter of the law almost entirely useless.

The second difficulty with the illicit network conception is the nature of exchange and the chronic presence of coercive activities. What are the key processes that make illegal networks bind? Who is doing the binding? These network relationships are governed by coercion, but directionality is hard to define. Violent activity, or the threat of it, is a two-way mechanism that retains and assures membership. For their part, police and other state actors hold legal license to coerce but often resort to informal means of coercion. Extortion, kidnapping, beatings, and summary killings have been common tools of policing (Barcellos 1992; Cavallaro 1997; Chevigny 1987). On the other hand, criminal organizations also coerce police and other state agents. With massive arsenals, an absence of public accountability, and a need to strongly defend interests in the drugs trade, these groups are willing and able to use extreme violence. Killings, intimidation, and even sexual violence against state agents like police and prison guards have been common, and all occur in a social sphere beyond law as the state formally defines it.

Discretionary space amidst violence is a more appropriate way to think about the problem of policing, nonstate armed groups, and insecurity. The autonomous and exposed nature of low-level police is indicative of both a great deal of discretion, especially within an organization unable or unwilling to contain crime and violence. In this context, nonstate armed groups have grown with little concerted state response. In fact, the most obvious form of state regulation exerting itself over armed groups is that which occurs not according to the laws on the books but as a mode of *law in practice*. What exists is a tentative noncompete agreement that governs police relations with criminal organizations. In what is often described as an *acordo*, parties accept nominal levels of coercion and violence in order to maintain and safeguard their most central interests. Such an accord provides a basic, if often unspoken, degree of understanding upon which other relationships are based. One ongoing example of this occurred in São Paulo between the PCC and the Civil and Military Police. During a closed Federal Parliamentary Inquiry (Comissão Parlamentar de Inquérito) following the PCC's 2006 attack on São Paulo, the imprisoned leader of the PCC, Marcola, was questioned about his relationship with police (Câmara dos Deputados 2006):

CONGRESSMAN NEUCIMAR FRAGA: You went to another country with a lot of money. This would have allowed you to live the rest of your life with money without any problems.

MARCOLA: I had to pay. No, I had to pay.

FRAGA: Why did you come back?

MARCOLA: Because they went to my place and held my wife. So I had to give 200,000 . . . 300,000. They knew she was innocent, but they also knew . . . I'm not saying in this case, now, that they have my girlfriend, the one who visits me, but I'm saying that . . . they went there before and kidnapped my daughter. They went there . . . All they want is money.

FRAGA: They who?

MARCOLA: The São Paulo police, the Civil Police.

FRAGA: They actually kidnapped your daughter?

MARCOLA: Well, at the time she wasn't my daughter. She was the daughter of my girlfriend, Ana, and I had to pay $300,000.

FRAGA: To police?

MARCOLA: Yes, to police.

FRAGA: Did you identify who they were?

MARCOLA: Yes, I did.

FRAGA: Can you give their names?

MARCOLA: These names, no, because I think that . . . I'll have to . . . I won't talk about this.

FRAGA: You paid how much? You said $300,000.

MARCOLA: Three hundred thousand.

FRAGA: Are these police still alive?

MARCOLA: They are still alive.

FRAGA: Are they active in the police, or have they moved on?

MARCOLA: They are alive and active.

FRAGA: Are you maintaining any . . .

MARCOLA: They must be really fearful. But they are alive and active.

FRAGA: Do you maintain . . . Are you giving them payments to maintain a good relationship, like . . . How does it work? Is it a Mensalão[1] of the police, like you've said?

MARCOLA: It isn't quite like that, okay, sir? But, for example, if you are a policeman, you find some proof against me. Instead of arresting me, which will amount to nothing, you know that I'll be just another guy in that system, which is totally rotten, and you come to me and say, "I want this much to get rid of this."

With this last statement, which underscores the police-PCC arrangement as a whole, the congressman switches to a different topic. Yet, this short dialogue is indicative of the conditions and the organizational constraints of the police that underscore how discretionary space can be used. The PCC is accustomed to responding to these affronts by police and has an ongoing knowledge of the police officers who have sought them out in the past.

It is not a stretch, however, to question the other side of the coin. Police are also coerced by the PCC. That leading members of the PCC recognize their identity but may not have sought retribution indicates that they may be important assets. This is indicative of an ongoing balance between the PCC and the state, where the PCC gains influence within the state via the possibility of violence, blackmail, and targeted killings. This is part of a larger systemic "consensus" between the two, which is stable enough to decrease homicides in the city (Denyer Willis 2015).

When that relationship is tipped and one party exerts too much pressure or coercive force on the other, violence can take more serious forms. Unwilling partners, "righteous" police, or other insurgent actors may cause one of the parties to become particularly violent to defend its interests. In 2003, a judge from the São Paulo city of Presidente Prudente, who was in charge of hearing many PCC cases, including PCC complaints of mistreatment in the prisons they control, was shot multiple times and killed on his way home from the courthouse. An investigation into the case, concluded in 2009, found Marcola and his PCC deputy guilty of ordering the killing, which had been carried out by PCC members.

Violent coercion, or the threat of it, is a central feature of relationships across legal-illegal bounds. It compels participants to act, while governing their ability to resist. This speaks to a third important feature of "trans-legal" relationships in a police officer's discretionary space: its obligatory nature. Most do not participate wholly by choice but are obligated by assignment, place of residence, occupational demands, and their own personal safety. Typically, police are assigned certain routes or placements and must find a way to cope in that environment, navigating through constraints, challenges, and opportunities. In São Paulo, internal Civil Police politics often dictates the area of the city where a police officer will be stationed. Those with strong political connections, with more advanced tenure and with good track records are assigned to stable districts or *delegacias de luxo*. By contrast, police officers who have clashed with their superiors, who have resisted organizational politics, or who have been sanctioned for one reason or another are often relocated to peripheral areas of the city. In these spaces, the amount of discretionary space seems boundless compared to areas in more central areas of the city. One Civil Police officer working in the extreme *zona sul* of São Paulo once said to me, "O estado esqueceu da gente" (The state has forgotten us).

In the peripheral areas of São Paulo, police exist—and are placed— alongside or within urban spaces controlled by organized armed groups like the PCC. Their role as law enforcement is diluted in communities with allegiance to the nonstate forms of order created and enforced by armed groups. Policing as we know it is reduced to a reactive role, whether on the beat or in an investigation. Police do little preventative work and expend most of their efforts responding to egregious crimes—or those reported by superiors or power holders. These types of incidents often expose the long-running incapacities of the police, as in the May 2006 attacks, or are cases made severe because they confront the integrity and will of the police to do their job as many expect them to do it.[2] In the meantime, day-to-day policing is a tacit negotiation between police and criminal organizations, where police find nominal ways of conveying success on the job by making arrests or seizures, while criminal organizations continue with large-scale drug dealing and local control (Denyer Willis 2009).

For police and prison agents, this arrangement is complicated by concerns for personal security. In Brazil, many state agents work in the station or prison during the day and return to their homes in another area of the urban periphery at night. Low salaries have meant that police must often negotiate these tricky relationships both on the job and in their own neighborhoods. Indeed, and ominously, in his testimony to the Parliamentary Inquiry, Marcola noted that police and state agents "come from the same favela" as the PCC (Câmara dos Deputados 2006: 130). Although Hinton (2006) has correctly suggested that police work in the urban "first world" and sleep in the "third world," the truth is that many police officers rarely leave the "third world," even for work.

It should come as little surprise that the May attacks disproportionally targeted prison agents, a group that is most tightly interconnected with members of the PCC. In large part, prison agents serve at the pleasure of the PCC, who control most of the prisons in São Paulo state and who can reach outside the prisons to engage in violence or carry out killings (Denyer Willis 2009). When prison agents and police are dealing with the PCC, they are cognizant of this threat, recognizing the weaknesses of their own organizations to protect them. It is unavoidable, then, that the decisions they make place their own personal security at the forefront, shaping why discretionary activities often carry a particularly intimate quality.

WEAKNESS AND DISCRETION IN THE CIVIL POLICE

Although reformist plans for police have often sought to remake the organizational culture, it is clear that public security in São Paulo and other major Brazilian cities is in a severe state of disrepair and dysfunction (Caldeira 2002; Chevigny 1987; Hinton 2006; Mendez, O'Donnell, and Pinheiro 2000). Police are manifestly unable to uphold the law as many expect and to provide security for much of society. Discretionary space, a sphere largely outside of formal legal accountability, has become an eminent challenge for policing in urban Brazil, especially as it has come to legitimate certain off-duty activities. Yet, recent research on police in Brazil has been scant on this point, drawing in method and epistemology from actors affected by the police but not, in large part, from the police themselves (Hinton 2006). Other noteworthy research has examined the weakness of police vis-à-vis society (Caldeira 2000; Holston 2007). Yet, little is known about how great discretion alters the larger rationales of public security, especially as it is delivered to citizens (Macaulay 2007). Except in a couple of cases, rarely has research on police been carried out within police organizations (Kant de Lima 1986; Mingardi 1992). Such an approach is central to understanding what weakness looks like in practice, even if it is comparatively rare.

After the end of the dictatorship period, and as public services were impacted by neoliberal reforms, the size of the Brazilian police force decreased. Budgetary shortfalls and lack of political will to reinvest in an organization associated with repressive politics eroded the capacity of police to provide basic security under democratic conditions. As resources declined and barriers to effective policing grew, new challenges arose for police. With urban violence and criminality on the rise in a nascent democracy, police were expected to do more work with fewer resources, while simultaneously upholding a complex and increasingly scrutinized rule of law.

STREET-LEVEL SOLUTIONS

Police are cognizant of the conditions of organizational weakness in which they work. Foremost in the minds of many police officers who interact with powerful criminal groups is ensuring their personal security. Police recognize the degree to which they are exposed to the violence of these groups and often address their exposure by using trans-legal space to make concessions. These concessions often involve a trade-off between illegal activity and personal security.

One Civil Police officer, Samuel, described this problem to me one afternoon in a Rio police station. While I watched a video of him and other police officers during a police operation in a Rio favela, he pointed out each officer and told me where he was now. "That guy there, he died last year. Outside a little bar while walking down the street. They shot him." "Who?" I asked, knowing that *they* usually refers to *bandidos*. "We don't know. They didn't take money. He tried to react and pulled his gun to shoot, but they came up behind him in a car. No chance . . . No one knows if it was random or an *acerto de conta* (payback). Only him." The chances that this killing was random are slim. Nothing was taken, and the victim was clearly targeted.

Perhaps more telling, however, is that these kinds of killings of police officers are so common that police talk about them as very likely *acertos de conta*. Police officers consider the fact that their colleagues are buried in networked space as just part of the job. This same pattern is also apparent for police forces that manage Brazil's jails and prisons. One day in the precinct, I asked Antonia, a Civil Police Inspector, about what positions she had held previously. Antonia had been many places within the organization, from case investigation (*cartório*) to station reception (*plantão*) in many different precincts. Most recently, though, she had been working in one of the centralized jails:

> It was an interesting job. I worked with Marco [pointing to a colleague smoking a cigarette in the corner]. We had about 500 prisoners, most of whom had been there for some time and hadn't gone to trial yet. The prisoners liked me there, and I tried hard to make things a bit easier for them.

Antonia spent a few years managing the prison, which was one of the "neutral" buildings—not controlled by any criminal gang or housing any convicted police.

> They say the neutral places were the worst. Ours wasn't too bad. The prisons controlled by the [drug] factions are a bit safer. Still, we had to be careful. There were two or three of us for all of them, and we had to make sure things didn't get out of hand. They liked me, though, so it was okay. I tried to respect them by treating them nicely and by giving them things like books to make it a bit easier. It can be really dangerous otherwise because of riots if they want to cause trouble.

Navigating this awkward power imbalance in this way was a strategic move for Antonia, and she recognized the need to develop more personal relationships with prisoners in order to protect herself and to ensure continuity in her work. Her only effective means of coercion for misbehaving prisoners was based on the informal power structure in the prison system. Transferring a prisoner to a different unit means recognizing who controls which prisons, whether gangs, ex-police, or no one in particular. Transferring a gang member to a prison controlled by another gang is sure death, while transferring a prisoner to a neutral prison means subjecting him to free-for-all violence in a disordered space. "They didn't like it if we told them we would move them," she said. Developing more personal relationships with prisoners and "career criminals" was one way to mitigate her insecurity and to find a solution for her inability to call on greater resources.

In the Civil Police *delegacia* of Santa Clara, a police precinct in a middle-class neighborhood of the city of São Paulo where I conducted ethnographic research, police face myriad organizational weaknesses that obstruct their ability to ensure due process, do diligent criminal investigations, and avoid corruption. Street-level constraints can be summarized as technology, human resource, pay, and physical security related. Additionally, there are many challenges of interorganizational coordination between the street-based Military and investigative Civil Police. Civil Police lack many of the basic tools necessary to grapple with complex questions of organized crime and chronic urban violence, making it difficult to make ends meet without exploiting discretionary space.

Technologically speaking, the Civil Police have a limited repertoire of criminological tools at their disposal. For common day-to-day work, police rely heavily on fingerprinting suspects and pulling basic data from the Secretary for Public Security intranet database of criminal records, addresses, and personal details. Crime scene investigations are uncommon or severely delayed, as are ballistics tests and the comprehensive collection of evidence, except in very egregious or high-profile cases. The ability of police to manage complex cases is limited as a result. Difficulties and delays in figuring out the identities of suspects— fingerprints must be sent to a central headquarters, taking days to process—clash with a generalized lack of physical evidence in which to base criminal charges. Where technology is unavailable and investigative due diligence is severely delayed or does not occur, cases may not stand up to the rigor of evaluation in court. As routine requires, completing cases that are backed up by sound police work and physical and other evidence with sufficiently sophisticated technological tools is not possible.

The technological challenges of policing are certainly less significant, however, than the lack of police available to do the job. Delays between the filing of crime reports and the moment they reach an investigator's desk are weeks long, effectively nullifying the quality and extent of evidence or other key information that can be collected. This is the case even in the more secure areas of the city, such as Santa Clara, where levels of crime still vastly exceed the number of police officers available to respond. Most crime reports go uninvestigated, accepted as minor incidents that do not merit the limited time of police investigators. In an environment of chronic violence, the inability to respond to burdensome levels of crime becomes normalized and internalized by police as beyond their scope and ability to address.

Not only are the Civil Police understaffed, but those who are currently on the job are barely surviving because salaries hardly cover the cost of living. The result has been police officers who must moonlight or find alternative means to make money, including in ways that use police weapons and borrow state authority, as in private security. At Santa Clara, it was common for police officers to work multiple jobs and to talk openly about their jobs outside the force. Police, by consequence, do not have a unique allegiance to the state, but they often are also attentive to the demands of other employment in private security as entrepreneurs or, in some circumstances, as members of vigilante groups (Cano 2008; Huggins 1991, 1997). There are other important consequences. The latent demand for financial security has not only driven a "brotherly" acceptance for second jobs, but it has become fertile ground for illicit activity, extortion, and troubling relationships. The result is that police officers are more likely to seek out extortion opportunities and to accept unsolicited or coerced opportunities when their basic needs are unfulfilled.

Even where this collection of organizational constraints may not be prevalent, police officers must consider the chronic exposure of their own personal security. The safety of police officers is not minimally guaranteed. As in the 2006 attacks, police officers have been killed or threatened for how they have done their work. In the last five years, roughly ten police officers have died per month in Rio de Janeiro. As individuals in a weak system, they are not capable of responding and are not adequately sheltered from violence. As a result, in cases where police officers may be confronting powerful political or illegal groups, they may be inclined to make concessions in order to ensure a degree of security for themselves.

For street-level police officers, the extent to which they can exert the authority of the law is diminished by the relative impotence of the organization and the system. Endemic gaps between the capacity of police officers and expanding public expectations for a universal, effective, and accountable police force create an environment of police pragmatism and a dependence on discretion. The persistence of constraints has fostered a quantitative and qualitative difference in the kinds of cases that Civil Police are able to successfully handle. Unable to close cases that require compiling comprehensive evidence through hours of work, technological evidence gathering, and diligent crime scene investigations, police concentrate on in flagrante delicto crimes. Flagrante crimes fit within a specific legal space as incidents in which a criminal suspect is picked up during a crime or within 24 hours after the crime has been committed. Here, police are given greater leeway and bureaucratic discretion to temporarily detain suspects as they collect information from the Military Police, witnesses, victims, and the suspects themselves. Most of this information is precompiled by the Military Police, who conduct flagrante arrests, making these cases much easier to complete (Denyer Willis 2014b). In São Paulo in 2008, 68 percent of the individuals arrested by police were involved in flagrante crimes (SSP 2008).

Yet, the persistence of constraints has meant that police must innovate to avoid failure, even in their work on flagrante crimes. This often makes them resort to illegal strategies to ensure that criminals caught red-handed are tried successfully before the courts. These strategies include finding somewhat underhanded solutions for a chronic lack of (or contradictory) evidence by manufacturing information, omitting witnesses, and using "creative" license and language to obscure ambiguity in criminal statements and cases. The response of police to the incapacity of public security has been to pragmatically cut corners in order to ensure some semblance of "justice," or at least that called for by the law on the books. Without the innovation and entrepreneurship of police to ensure that individuals caught committing a crime are successfully prosecuted, the nascent fragments of the rule of law that currently exist would dissolve entirely.

Police continue to operate within a large discretionary space that allows them to exercise many strategies. Well-consolidated, capable, and presumed channels of police accountability do not exist. The ombudsman (*ouvidoria*), internal affairs (*corregedoria*), and public prosecutor (*ministério público*) are all important services that are increasing their depth and significance to hold police accountable. Yet, lawyers are only present in cases involving suspects who are able to pay. Public defenders are available for few cases, and they usually come later in the process. The operations of internal affairs, as well as police ombudsmen, are maturing and slowly becoming internalized among police, who are less frequently engaging in torture, extortion, and violence as routine tools of everyday police work (Mingardi 1992). Still, police, particularly those situated in peripheral areas, have a great deal of space in which to make ends meet.

In the context of Santa Clara, policing is not purely about ensuring law and order. For police, it is a complex process of negotiation among the constraints of an untrustworthy organization, the demands of one's personal life—security, pay, and family—and the need to fulfill, at least in part, the mandate of public security. This negotiation is a persistent challenge that exacts compromise from each of these worlds. A weak and underfunded police organization undermines the ability of police to respond to crimes and bring criminals "to justice." Police officers are concerned more for their personal livelihoods than for the provision of security. Public security becomes a function of pragmatism and innovation that must dip into informality in order to make ends meet. The kinds of justice demanded by human rights activists, either in the form of top-down international norms enforced by prosecutors or as performance goals reviewed by police reformists, and that highlight elements like due process for the accused and swift resolution of crimes for victims are far from the minds of street-level police.

REFOCUSING ON REFORM

Contemporary Brazilian policing is, in large part, a tale of street-level police agency. Neoliberal reforms, politicians distancing themselves from an organization of (perceived) authoritarian politics, and a state-level division of policing have compounded the problem of underfunding for police and distance between top and street. Much discretionary space, which stems from such an environment of weakness and a set of complex demands in the midst of violence, further in-flames public perception and distrust in police. Justice, in such a context, is what you make of it.

Human rights are widely understood as an inclusive and broad framework for social movements and individuals to make claims upon the state. With internationally created and nationally ratified agreements in place in Brazil, rights principles enable great exposure and wide publication of police violence. However, in a society with consistent and chronic human rights challenges of the most egregious varieties, for many in the police force, human rights seem a fruitless normative and prescriptive approach—especially when it comes to "making" justice. Acutely, applying rights-based concerns directly to police reform plans carries presumptions of organizational integrity, hierarchy, and ability, and assumes that, at present, police are unwilling to act in accordance with human rights. By consequence, rights-based reforms perceive police as structuralist agents, subdued and entrenched in an organizational culture in which corruption, violence, and resistance to human rights are intrinsic. In other words, rights reforms see police violence as ordered or mandated from above and, as such, call for a change in police culture via an institutionalization of human rights ideals.

This assertion is challenged by the empirical world of street-level police. The right/wrong dichotomy of rights eliminates the subtlety and nuance evident in the street-level negotiations of Brazilian police. The empirical situation appears to be more complex. Brazilian police struggle with capacity. They are mired in a weak hierarchy with a notable absence of a unitary organizational culture. A certain degree of police incapacity can paralyze top-down culture-change reforms. Public security suffers from a dramatic lack of capacity for police to carry out the most menial criminal justice tasks. When police are unable to perform their duties because of a lack of organizational capacity, they often find solutions in trans-legal spaces, as in illegal "networks." Rights-based reforms struggle to cope with this reality; that trans-legal space is not only the primary obstacle to reform but also the day-to-day front line of state weakness in Brazilian cities. Attending to how members of the public security forces conceive of justice and the kinds of justice they are able to ensure exposes these disconnects and opens new lines of exploration for improving urban security in Brazil and beyond.

The vertiginous rise of major nonstate armed groups in cities is the preeminent challenge for public security actors, existing as a central threat to the security of citizens and the state's monopoly on violence. The rapid growth of nonstate armed groups cannot be seen in separate from the state of Brazilian public security. In thinking about human rights and police in Brazil, a broader consideration of the contemporary challenges of police work is needed. Unlike advanced liberal democracies, where police functions are carried out through strong organizational channels and in social spheres of Foucaultesque government, police work—and the practice of sovereignty—in Brazil are very different (Denyer Willis 2015). This stands in contrast to scholarly portrayals of the police as a coordinated and monolithic organization swayed by top-down policy and with a well-defined and recognizable culture (Caldeira 2000; Hinton 2006; Holston 2007). The reality of urban violence and policing in Brazil are much better viewed through agency and discretion than through perceptions about how bureaucratic hierarchies shape everyday police practice.

The troubled state of public security in São Paulo and Rio de Janeiro both exposes police to criticism and provides them with broad discretionary space in which to carry out their mandate and negotiate solutions. For the Civil Police, the state of public security leaves police wanting for both security and financial stability. Police cannot count on the organization to ensure their security, nor can they carry out diligent police work because of a series of organizational constraints related to technology, human resources, and pay. As such, police use their discretionary space to find solutions for these exposures, often settling into arrangements—moonlighting, predation, exchanges with nonstate armed groups—that further weaken public security. Justice, in this case, is what can be made in discretionary space.

NOTES

1. *Mensalão* refers to a political scandal that was occurring at the same time involving President Lula's party, the Partido dos Trabalhadores (PT), in which monthly payments were allegedly made to congressmen (*deputados*) for voting in favor of PT bills.
2. In 2003, a video of a public party organized by the PCC in the streets of a favela in Greater São Paulo was broadcasted by BAND, a major television network. The video showed hundreds of attendees openly using cocaine arranged in the shape of the letters "PCC" and members of the PCC taunting the police and politicians for their absence and inability to control the illegal activities taking place at the party.

WORKS CITED

Andreas, Peter. 2004. "Illicit Political Economy." *Review of International Political Economy* 11 (3): 641–652.

Arias, Enrique Desmond. 2006a. *Drugs and Democracy in Rio de Janeiro: Trafficking, Social Networks and Public Security*. Chapel Hill: University of North Carolina Press.

———. 2006b. "The Dynamics of Criminal Governance: Networks and Social Order in Rio de Janeiro." *Journal of Latin American Studies* 38 (2): 293–325.

Arias, Enrique Desmond, and Goldstein Daniel. 2010. *Violent Democracies in Latin America*. Durham, NC: Duke University Press.

Barcellos, Caco. 1992. *Rota 66: A história da polícia que mata*. São Paulo: Editora Globo.

Caldeira, Teresa. 2000. *City of Walls: Crime Segregation and Citizenship in São Paulo.* Berkeley: University of California Press.

———. 2002. "The Paradox of Police Violence in Brazil." *Ethnography* 3 (3): 235–263.

Câmara dos Deputados. 2006. *Transcrição ipsis verbis: Depoente Marcos Willians Herbas Camacho, CPI—Tráfico de armas.* http://www1.folha.uol.com.br/folha/cotidiano/20060708-marcos_camacho.pdf.

Cano, Ignacio. 2008. "Seis por Meia Dúzia? Um estudo exploratório do fenômeno das chamadas 'Milícias' no Rio de Janeiro." In *Segurança, tráfico e milícias no Rio de Janeiro,* 50–85. Rio de Janeiro: Fundação Heinrich Böll/Justiça Global.

Cavallaro, James. 1997. *Police Brutality in Urban Brazil.* New York: Human Rights Watch.

Cavallaro, James, and Raquel Dodge. 2007. "Understanding the São Paulo Attacks." *ReVista* 6 (3): 53–55.

Chevigny, Paul. 1987. *Police Abuse in Brazil: Summary Executions and Torture in São Paulo and Rio de Janeiro.* New York: Americas Watch.

Chillier, George, and Silvia Varela. 2009. "Violence (in) Security and Human Rights in Latin America." *IDS Bulletin* 40 (2): 70–78.

Davis, Diane E. 2006. "Undermining the Rule of Law: Democratization and the Dark Side of Police Reform in Mexico." *Latin American Politics and Society* 48 (1): 55–86.

———. 2009. "Non-State Actors, New Imagined Communities, and Shifting Patterns of Sovereignty and Insecurity in the Modern World." *Contemporary Security Policy* 30 (2): 221–245.

Denyer Willis, Graham. 2009. "Deadly Symbiosis? The PCC, the State and the Institutionalization of Organized Crime in São Paulo." In *Youth Violence in Latin America,* edited by Gareth Jones and Dennis Rodgers, 167–189. New York: Palgrave.

———. 2014a. "The Gun Library." *Boston Review.* http://www.bostonreview.net/world/graham-denyer-willis-pcc-gun-library-sao-paulo-prisons-crime.

———. 2014b. "Antagonistic Authorities and the Civil Police in São Paulo." *Latin American Research Review* 49 (1): 3–22.

———. 2015. *The Killing Consensus: Police, Organized Crime and the Regulation of Life and Death in Urban Brazil.* Berkeley: University of California Press.

Dowdney, Luke. 2005. *Neither War nor Peace: International Comparisons of Children and Youth in Organized Armed Violence.* Rio de Janeiro: COAV.

Feltran, Gabriel. 2010. "Crime e castigo na cidade: Os repertórios da justiça e a questão do homicídio nas periferias de São Paulo." *Caderno CRH* 23 (58): 59–73.

———. 2011. *Fronteiras de tensão: Política e violência nas periferias de São Paulo.* São Paulo: UNESP.

Goldstein, Donna. 2003. *Laughter Out of Place: Race, Class, Violence and Sexuality in a Rio Favela.* Berkeley: University of California Press.

Hinton, Mercedes. 2006. *The State on the Streets: Police and Politics in Argentina and Brazil.* Boulder, CO: Lynne Rienner.

Holston, James. 2007. *Insurgent Citizenship: Disjunctions of Democracy and Modernity in Brazil.* Princeton, NJ: Princeton University Press.

———. 2009. "Dangerous Spaces of Citizenship: Gang Talk, Rights Talk and Rule of Law in Brazil." *Planning Theory* 8: 12–31.

Huggins, Martha, ed. 1991. *Vigilantism and the State in Modern Latin America: Essays on Trans-legal Violence.* New York: Praeger.

———. 1997. "From Bureaucratic Consolidation to Structural Devolution: Police Death Squads in Brazil." *Policing and Society* 7 (4): 221–234.

Human Rights Watch. 2009. *Lethal Force: Police Violence and Public Insecurity in Rio de Janeiro and São Paulo*. New York: Human Rights Watch.

Kant de Lima, Roberto. 1986. "Legal Theory and Judicial Practice: Paradoxes of Police Work in Rio de Janeiro City." PhD Diss., Harvard University.

Leeds, Elizabeth. 1996. "Cocaine and Parallel Polities on the Brazilian Urban Periphery: Constraints on Local Level Democratization." *Latin American Research Review* 31 (3): 47–83.

Lipsky, Michael. 1980. *Street-Level Bureaucracy: Dilemmas of the Individual in Public Services*. New York: Russell Sage.

Macaulay, Fiona. 2007. "Knowledge Production, Framing and Criminal Justice Reform in Latin America." *Journal of Latin American Studies* 39 (4): 621–657.

Mendez, Juan E., Guillermo O'Donnell, and Paulo Sérgio Pinheiro, eds. 1999. *The (Un)Rule of Law and the Underprivileged in Latin America*. Notre Dame, IN: University of Notre Dame Press.

Mesquita Neto, Paulo. 2006. "Public-Private Partnerships for Police Reform in Brazil." In *Public Security and Police Reform in the Americas*, edited by John Dammert and Lucia Dammert, 44–57. Pittsburgh: University of Pittsburgh Press.

Mingardi, Guaracy. 1992. *Tiros, gansos e trutas: Coitidiano e reforma na polícia civil*. São Paulo: Scritta.

———. 2007. "O trabalho da inteligência no controle do crime organizado." *Estudos Avançados* 21 (61): 51–69.

Penglase, Benjamin. 1994. *Final Justice: Police and Death Squad Homicides of Adolescents in Brazil*. New York: Human Rights Watch/Americas.

Pereira, Anthony. 2008. "Public Security, Private Interests, and Police Reform in Brazil." In *Democratic Brazil Revisited*, edited by Peter Kingstone and Timothy Power, 185–208. Pittsburgh: University of Pittsburgh Press.

Perlman, Janice. 2006. "The Metamorphosis of Marginality: Four Generations in the Favelas of Rio de Janeiro." *Annals of the American Academy of Political and Social Science* 606: 154–177.

Pinheiro, Paulo. 1997. "Violência, crime e sistemas policiais em países de novas democracias." *Tempo Social* 9 (1): 43–52.

Powell, Walter. 2003. "Neither Market nor Hierarchy." In *The Sociology of Organizations: Classic, Contemporary, and Critical Readings*, edited by Michael Handel, 104–117. New York: Sage.

SEADE—Fundação Sistema Estadual de Análise de Dados. 2007. *Informações dos distritos da capital*. http://www.seade.gov.br/produtos/imp/distritos/.

Secretaria de Segurança de São Paulo (SSP). 2008. *Estatísticas trimestrais*. http://www.ssp.sp.gov.br/novaestatistica/Trimestrais.aspx.

Serbin, Kenneth. 1998. "The Anatomy of a Death: Repression, Human Rights and the Case of Alexandre Vannucchi Leme in Authoritarian Brazil." *Journal of Latin American Studies* 30 (1): 1–33.

Tilly, Charles. 1990. *Coercion, Capital and European States, AD 990–1990*. Cambridge: Basil Blackwell.

Zaluar, Alba. 1996. *Da revolta ao crime S.A.* São Paulo: Moderna.

Zaverucha, Jorge. 2000. "Fragile Democracy and the Militarization of Public Safety in Brazil." *Latin American Perspectives* 27 (3): 8–31.

4 IMAGINARIES OF JUDICIAL PRACTICE AMONG LEGAL EXPERTS IN ARGENTINA

Leticia Barrera

INTRODUCTION

By the end of 2001, an economic and financial breakdown in Argentina had led the country to a profound political crisis, one that impacted upon the credibility of political and legal institutions, the Supreme Court of Justice among them. The crisis turned the Court into a recurrent target of massive public demonstrations—in particular by middle-class bank depositors whose savings had been "frozen" by the de la Rúa administration's (1999–2001) restrictions on cash withdrawals in December 2001 and converted into Argentine pesos at an unfavorable exchange rate in January 2002 during the Duhalde administration (2002–2003). Many people believed that the Court shared responsibility for the country's debacle due to its unconditional backing of the ten-year-long monetary policy of convertibility (*convertibilidad*)[1] that had been implemented by the Menem administrations (1989–1999) and that, according to many experts, had triggered the crisis.

Notwithstanding the sharp criticism of the Court's workings triggered by the 2001–2002 crisis, the discrediting of the tribunal dated from 1990, when President Menem promoted its enlargement from five to nine members, which allowed him to appoint six new Justices.[2] The crisis also paved the way to a unique opportunity for non-governmental organizations (NGOs) in their advocacy for transparency, accountability, and practices of good governance of public institutions. In the legal field, NGO activism spawned newspaper articles, public reports, campaigns, debates, conferences, judicial reform projects, and justice watchdog programs aimed at changing the Supreme Court's practices that, according to these organizations, undermined the legitimacy and prestige of the judicial institution in Argentina.[3]

This chapter elaborates on the disparate and even contradictory understandings and perceptions of the Supreme Court's workings in the field of judicial practice in Argentina, as well as of the tensions that arose as a result. I draw on ethnographic material collected through long-term fieldwork (from August 2005 to June 2008) on the forms and practices of knowledge formation and circulation within the Argentine Supreme Court of Justice (Barrera 2012a). In examining the different views of the Court's workings and judicial practice, we learn more about the relationships among the subjects' conceptualizations, experiences, and perceptions of justice and their positions vis-à-vis the judicial apparatus. This association, in turn, points toward a phenomenon that can be frequently appreciated in the legal field in general, not just in the particular case of Argentina. It reflects the mode in which legal experts tend to apprehend law. For instance, scholars scrutinize the workings of courts through the content of legal decisions; lawyers, for their part, interpret these documents as the mode to advance (or not) their clients' interests. Consequently, legal knowledge tends to be apprehended through its visible *ends* and not by its *means* (Riles 2005; Vismann 2008). Notably, this mode of understanding law's workings as a *result* contradicts representations of the judiciary as a *process* that come from within, which became apparent from the ethnographic analysis of the Court's internal workings. However, as we will see, in one instance, my subjects' divergences would seem to collapse: it is in their evocations of a missing social order of relationships within the Court—a social order that for many of interlocutors has not been achieved yet.

Finally, the chapter recounts briefly a series of historical, political, and legal events that, in my opinion, inform the representations and popular perceptions of the judicial field in Argentina as a site of contingency, unpredictability, and even illegality. Under these rubrics, the workings of legal institutions such as the Supreme Court are cast as the distorted image of what they *should* be. Notions of what constitutes "justice" are thus reflected through assertions of how it should be produced in the workings of the Court. I do not seek to question such representations, but rather, I use them as the basis to reflect on the mode in which knowledge of law and legal institutions is constructed. In doing so, this chapter ultimately tries to advance different analytical possibilities to approach the workings of the judiciary in the native legal field seeking to move beyond dichotomies such as modern/premodern, objective/subjective, stable/erratic to which those workings are often reduced.

A FIELD OF CONTRADICTIONS

In 2005, an Argentine Supreme Court Justice said to me, "There are so many ideas *here* about what the law is." With his assertion, he was trying to point out to me different and even conflicting notions of law that, according to him, coexisted within the (Argentine) Court, and even within the small circle of his Supreme Court colleagues. His comment came in response to my query about the possibility of finding a correlation between the Court's discursive practices and an established idea of law, republic, and democracy within the legal field in Argentina. I based my question on a likely correlation between a native idea of law and judicial decision making from the observations made by legal scholar Mitchel Lasser (2005) in his comparative study of different Supreme Courts' modes of judicial adjudication: the U.S. Supreme Court, the French Cour de Cassation, and the European Court of Justice. In this work, Lasser built his comparison on the analysis of the conceptual structure of each Court's judgment and thus elaborated on its mode of adjudication and production of judicial authority. His conclusions encouraged me in my study of a juridical field (Bourdieu 1987) such as the Argentine one where legal experts are often eager to compare the workings of the Argentine Court and those of the U.S. Supreme Court (Barrera 2012a). However, my interest in Lasser's work was more methodological than theoretical: as my approach to judicial practice prioritized ethnography over textual theory, his findings appeared to me an interesting tool to provoke my informants' reactions.

The judge's assertion about people's different appreciations of law resembles divergent and even contradictory understandings of how the judiciary and the Court in particular work in Argentina. The different points of view about the Court and the judiciary in general that I encountered—as well as about the workings of judicial actors—exemplify a "dialectic of binaries" (Hoag 2011) through which the analysis of the institution and its subjects is usually framed. Accordingly, judicial practice tends to be inscribed with a logic of objective-subjective, stable-erratic, and actual-ideal behavior, according to the interpreter's point of view and her position vis-à-vis the judicial apparatus. Those binary representations of judicial practice are found not just in scholarly analysis, media communications, newspaper articles, or NGO statements but are also enacted in mundane interactions among legal experts within the judicial arena. Yet, these experts' encounters can be seen as themselves instantiations of a literal and symbolic divide between the inside and the outside of the judicial apparatus—a *gap* that not only accounts for competing notions of judicial-making but also for the actors' "deferral on seeing the other's point of view," to quote Rolland Munro from another context (1997: 15).

My point is that the actors' position regarding the judicial apparatus influences their appreciations of the making of the law and the workings of the judiciary. My informants in the Court (mostly law clerks) used to recreate the institution's workings through accounts of enduring everyday and mundane practices inscribed in a scheme of labor division and bureaucratic and formal (though not necessarily written) procedures (Barrera 2008, 2012b). These subjects' perspective matter-of-factly derives from an inward connection: they are themselves part of the judicial apparatus, even when many of them may reflect critically on their workings. The legal experts I met outside the Court (mostly progressive legal scholars and civil rights activists), however, tended to point out to me the Court's erratic behavior manifested, in their view, in the tribunal's different rulings on similar issues along a short period of time. Thus, the Court's inability to follow its own precedents[4] was representative of the tribunal's readiness to change its decisions according to the political interests at play, as in the 1990s during the Menem administration. In general, these actors engaged the Court's actions from a space outside the tribunal (civil rights advocacy and litigation, scholarly work, and pedagogy) and situated themselves from a standpoint that scrutinizes and criticizes the workings of the judiciary. Yet, many of them, in particular progressive NGOs representatives, had a voice in the political debate on judicial reform and changes to the Supreme Court that spawned after the crisis. To illustrate my point, the next sections present ethnographic data gathered from my interactions with legal experts and observation of the process of legal knowledge construction in a classroom. I selected these examples because they reveal, through the intersubjective exchange, the interplay of different authoritative legal knowledges, senses, and understandings about judicial practice and how they are permeated by the actors' subjectivities.

A PROBLEM OF SCALE, AND A PROBLEM OF LEGITIMACY

I met Lawyer García[5] in the fall of 2005. At that time, he worked part-time as a law professor at a top private law school in the city of Buenos Aires and as a civil rights advocate in an NGO. I had gotten his name from a legal scholar who thought he could be a great help to my research due to his background not just as a legal scholar and a civil rights activist but also because he had clerked for a Supreme Court Justice. At our first meeting, I told him that I was also interested in getting insights about the Court's workings from legal scholars and civil rights activists who were involved in legal change and judicial reform. He told me a lot about his experiences in the Court and his current positions as both a law professor and civil rights activist. The next time we met, after a year of fieldwork, I told him that in moving from inside the Court to outside, and vice versa, I had gotten some very different perceptions and interpretations about the Court's practices. I found having to elaborate on contradictory understandings of the subject or the Court's contemporary modes of knowledge production very challenging.

He said he was not surprised and that, in his view, I should expect to encounter disparate representations of Court between insiders and outsiders and that the reason for such varied opinions was rooted in a "problem of scale." He explained, "In general, a law clerk draws on a micro-perspective, which is her/his own perspective. That is the view of somebody who is used to doing her or his work, and hence does not see beyond her or his job obligations." In other words, in Lawyer García's opinion, the Court's bureaucrats worked on a micro (personal) scale, whereas legal scholars and professionals (like himself at the time of our meeting), the media, and public opinion in general build upon a macro (social) scale. Two weeks after meeting Lawyer García, I interviewed a Supreme Court Justice who had worked many years in the judiciary before she was appointed to the Supreme Court. I asked her about contrasting conceptualizations of the Argentine judiciary that one could encounter inside and outside the Court. She replied, "This is not true. It depends on whom you ask." Moreover, to support her assertion, she argued that several of the ongoing reforms to the judicial system—in particular, to the Court's procedures—had come from "inside" (the judiciary). She explained that they are the result of an internal consensus and pointed out that in 2002, during the crisis "when the country was falling down" (*cuando se caía el país*),[6] judicial functionaries (judges, secretaries, and other legal professionals) joined the Mesa del Diálogo Argentino, which had been created by the United Nations Development Programme (UNDP) to discuss and propose amendments to the Argentine federal judicial system. She believed that the committee on judicial reforms of the Mesa del Diálogo was the only group still in operation that revealed the ongoing commitment of judicial agents to improve the workings of the judiciary.

I told her that I had come to my conclusions based on my own interactions with NGOs representatives, mostly progressive legal scholars and activists who ran judicial reform and access to justice programs at their institutions and who devoted their time to closely monitoring the Court's operations. Again, she insisted that I was incorrect. She pointed out a cluster of NGOs that had been working closely to the judiciary "from within." That was possible because many of their members were also judicial functionaries, in sharp contrast to my interlocutors who were "outsiders." The NGOs' rhetoric of reform may be one thing, she said, but "reforms must be consensual." She went on to explain that "some people have the wrong idea about how judges work." She emphasized the widespread concept in the Court—and in the judiciary in general—that changes are more "legitimate" (and even more likely to be successful) when they are grounded in inner accounts—that is, when they come from "within" the institution.

Noticeably, the judge's account focused on legal change and judicial reform—topics that I did not expect to be the main subjects of our conversation. Her concern about reform, however, could be understood in the context of new internal regulations on transparency that the tribunal had been adopting in past years, after the 2001–2002 crisis. Those regulations were welcomed by NGOs, legal scholars, and the media. Moreover, a few NGO representatives whom I interviewed pointed out to me that the new Court's rules were a response to their (or their organizations') advocacy for transparency in judicial procedures. However, in contrast to the opinions about transparency regulations as the result of external pressures, all my informants at the Court asserted that the new by-laws on transparency were the consequence of the then Court's president's long-standing concern about opening up the tribunal's lawmaking practices.

Also interestingly, by referring to the group of NGOs most closely tied to the judiciary, the Justice not only sought to rebut my comment about conflicting representations of the judicial system but also gave me a very important insight: "Judges are reluctant to engage in reforms that bring about dramatic changes in the judiciary, though they are less reluctant when changes come from inside, when reforms are consensual, and when they involved judges' participation."

"IS" VERSUS "OUGHT TO BE"

Another situation when I observed tension between different and contrasting opinions about judicial practice was during a seminar on "judicial reasoning" taught at the Judicial School of the Argentine Magistracy Council (Escuela Judicial del Consejo de la Magistratura), in which I participated from May to July 2006. The Judicial School offers courses for judges, judicial bureaucrats (civil servants), judiciary staff member, and any other lawyer who wants to pursue a career in the federal judiciary.[7] The school curricula are divided into three area of study: judicial function; direction, organization, and management of the judicial unit; and research and evaluation. The two former areas are in turn subdivided into different subjects. Accordingly, the judicial function area includes juridical logic and judicial decision; techniques of argumentation and oral and written communication; alternative dispute resolution; and interdisciplinary education and new juridical issues. The direction, organization, and management area includes the subjects institutional relations; case-handling, court administration, and management quality; and information technology.[8] This seminar in particular was taught by a constitutional law scholar and civil rights activist who was sympathetic to my research topic and gave me permission to audit his course. The seminar's audience was composed of only six students, all functionaries and employees of federal lower courts (first-instance civil, family, and criminal law courts) who were taking the seminar to gain credits to advance in their judicial careers. No high-ranking judicial functionaries or Court clerks attended the seminar. The weekly meetings of the course set up a stage for a subtle but strong confrontation of different interpretations about the role of the judicial power and judicial practice in Argentina: the seminar professor's perspective on the one hand and the students' perspective on the other.

The distance between the professor and the students was very noticeable from the beginning. By "distance" I do not mean the gap usually perceived in Argentine law schools' classrooms among those who play the role of students and of the professor, respectively, manifested in dress codes and social norms (for instance, professors teaching in business attire, students calling them "doctors" whether or not they hold a doctoral degree). On the contrary, if I had to describe this seminar professor's attitude toward the class in light of traditional professor-student dynamics, I would say that his attitude was intended to challenge those traditional codes, as suggested by his very casual outfit and body language. In a different venue with a different audience, I most likely would not have noticed how the professor addressed the students. However, in this particular locale, where students were drawn from a very formal field, like the judiciary,[9] and male students attended class in business attire, the professor's attitude toward the class was especially noticeable. Ironically, by working to bridge the teacher-professor distance that normally exists in law school classrooms, the professor demonstrated another type of division between himself and his audience.

The professor opened up the seminar with an explicit provocation. He described the course as a venue to discuss "what the judges do, what they do in practice, and the theoretical responses that have been given to those problems." By "theoretical responses," he explained, he meant the contributions of legal philosophy, political philosophy, and, to a lesser extent, legal sociology. The seminar, he continued, was aimed at discussing the role of judges in a constitutional democracy. "This is not a course about techniques or operative tools to make a good ruling," he stated, but rather, it "has been thought as a reunderstanding, as a critique of the judicial function." He then said, "I am here to provoke you." After his opening remarks and outlining of the seminar, he handed out two anonymous and consecutive surveys about the judicial behavior. He argued that the overall purpose of the exercise was to develop a "general proposal" and to reach a consensus among the participants regarding how the judiciary actually functioned. And that, he said, would allow them to move forward in their discussion from a common groundwork.

Before handing out the first survey, the professor warned his class that it was not about how judges' "ought to be" (*Esta no es una encuesta acerca del deber ser de los jueces*). Among other statements, the first survey included the following:

"Judges are permeable to political, economic, and moral influences."

"Judges know the political implications of their rulings and take them into account before reaching a decision."

"Judges have a more or less intuitive idea about the solution of the case based
on their personal ideas and construct the rationales that support their rulings afterward."

"Judges interpret the Constitution and statutes according to their own philosophical, moral, and political values."

"In Argentina, judges are strongly constrained by the political values of the
political branches of the government, in particular the Executive Power."

"Judges deliver decisions that require them to make only a neutral and almost
mechanical application of relevant legal norms."

"Judges are considered very important characters in the institutional and political system."

To respond to the survey questions, the students were asked to check "in general,"
"hardly ever," or "never" after each statement. Once they completed and returned
this first survey, the professor handed out the second one, which had the same
format as the first but, through a series of slight grammatical changes, had a completely different meaning. Among this second set of statements were the following:

"Judges should be permeable to political, economic, and moral influences."

"Judges should know the political implications of their rulings and should take
them into account before reaching a decision."

"Judges should have a more or less intuitive idea about the solution of the case
based on their personal ideas and construct the rationales that support their
holdings afterward."

Once again, students had to choose among "in general," "hardly ever," and "never."

I was not so much interested in the students' answers on these surveys but
rather in their feelings about having to take the surveys and then discuss their
answers in class. It was through this interaction that I was able to see the divide
between those who come from within the judiciary and those from outside it. One
student seemed reluctant to take the surveys. When she saw the first survey questions, she told the professor, "I can't answer the questions I am being asked here.
I was formed inside [the judiciary]," meaning she was trained within the judicial
body. "We are constrained by our workplace." Another student agreed with her.
She continued, "I would like to know the opinion of the people on the street."
A third student added, "We are in the trenches."[10] The professor addressed the
students' concerns by asking them to "depersonalize" their answers. He told them,
"Then respond according to the community of judges—the judicial community

where you have been formed." It was not the students who were under scrutiny but the legal tradition in which they had been educated, the professor explained.

Once both surveys were completed, the professor went through the answers and compared them. He said to me, "If I were doing research on legal anthropology, I would be happy to have this data." He then read the conclusions out loud, pointing out the differences between the results of both surveys. One student offered, "So, there are differences about the 'is' and the 'ought to be.'" The professor, who appeared pleased with the contradiction that arose from the answers to both surveys, pushed the discussion forward. He asked the students what the opposition between their responses about how judges *really act* on the one hand (according to the first survey) and those about how they *should behave* (second survey) on the other hand meant for them. He teased the audience: "Are we cynical? Are judges cynical?" He said that laypeople were likely to believe in the dissociation between the judges' actual behaviors and the judges' reasoning. "This cynicism is shared by laypeople, the press, and lawyers in general," the professor argued, indicating that the workings of the Argentine judicial system were perceived differently by laypeople and those inside the judiciary. The discussion then moved to questions about meaning and scope of statutory interpretation. The first class session finished with the professor's promise that the course would try to explore more complex responses to their cynicism and to discuss the students' understanding of—and the functioning of—judicial reasoning. "Our system might be demanding us to do more that we are now doing," he concluded.

Although the students appeared sympathetic to the professor's approach and willing to engage in discussions about the issues he proposed on the first day of class (the Supreme Court's legitimacy, the use of its precedents, the effects of Court's rulings, judges' use of discretionary powers, political influences upon the Court, among others), a series of interactions that unfolded in the course of the seminar between the professor and his class made palpable their different representations of judicial practice, as well as how their points of view are permeated by their positions vis-à-vis the judicial apparatus. Indeed, some of the professor's critical statements about the workings of the courts were rebutted by the students' recounts of episodes drawn from their workplaces. Actually, the students' concerns about judicial decision making seemed to contradict the professor's (and those of the legal theorists/scholars presented in the class readings). In their view, the actual cases they brought from the field provided a more "authoritative" basis for discussion than the hypothetical ones drawn from the scholarly texts assigned by the professor. On one occasion, the professor, who was disappointed by the students' apparent lack of interest in the theoretical discussions he intended to pursue in class, confided to me that it was as if the students were not interested ın removing themselves from the mundane and routine problems of their work-places. Interestingly, whereas for the students, legal theory appeared too abstract and too distant from their focus on everyday practices, for the professor, the mundane and routine courts' practices that mostly concerned the students sounded too procedural and too technical to discuss in class.

NOSTALGIA

In spite of their conflicting impressions, I could not help but notice that many of my informants' narratives about the workings of the judiciary converged at some point. Regardless of their workplaces (the Court, a law school, or an NGO), accounts of their practices often turned into nostalgic representations of the workings of the Argentine judicial system.

Nostalgia, however, worked differently inside and outside the Court. In most of the Court bureaucrats' statements, I was referred to some past version of the Court that my subjects evoked as better. Accordingly, my subjects cited the Court as a place where "we [the Court staff] knew each other" or was "like a little family" and a time "when we were only a few [in the Court] or "when [the Court] had more control of its docket" and yet "held more legitimacy" to explain why the social order of relationships had fallen apart. For most of them, the current Court's status was a consequence of President Menem's Court-packing plan that enlarged the Court in 1990. Those relationships still influence the law clerks' perceptions of the Court, not just of the senior ones who used to work at the Court before the enlargement but also of those who were appointed afterward. Among these latter law clerks, there are many who do not yearn for a lost social order. However, their narratives succeed in turning such an order into an imagined whole, as can be perceived in the following statement made by a junior law clerk:

> They [the older clerks] speak about the "Court of 5" (five justices), an elite Court, as the best Court ever, not because of its members' intellectual skills—actually they were better—but because of the Court's size; it was a small Court and they knew one another. (Barrera 2008: 9)

Anthropologist María José Sarrabayrouse Oliveira (2011: 1–2) accounts for a similar reaction to the effects of the "Menemism era" among her subjects in the federal judiciary in Buenos Aires:

> In all the interviews I conducted in the courts, I noticed a common denominator that linked them: a kind of constant lament about the operation of justice. Such lament was expressed in sentences like "this has not been the way it is now,"

"both employees' and functionaries' levels have been strongly deteriorated," "everyone can become a judge," "magistracy has lost its value and prestige." All the misfortunes seemed to have a common origin: the Menemist administration, which different sectors of the judiciary (from the most conservative side to the most progressive) held responsible for the problems that affected the judicial institution.

Nostalgia, as encountered in the Argentine Court, is bound up with the agents' perception of the end of face-to-face relations and the loss of status and tradition. However, in accounting for a break between the past and the present, the Court bureaucrats' narratives did not seem to entail resignation or defeat, feelings that are commonly associated with nostalgia. On the contrary, a certain sense of honor is perceivable in those subjects' discourses. As Michael Herzfeld (1997) explains, the idea of nostalgia may engender political motivations for present actions: "The static image of an unspoiled and irrecoverable past legitimizes deeds of the moment by investing them with the moral authority of eternal truth." In this sense, the nostalgic mood that permeates judicial actors' accounts also activates a prospective momentum in which the Court is reenacted in the eyes of the public by exercising its authority. Accordingly, parallel to their evocations of the tribunal's past glory, my informants at the Court also urged the institution to assert its role "as a real state power," to act as "a check of both the Congress and the Executive," to behave as a "co-governance body," and to "secure the rule of law,"[11] among other actions conducive to regaining authority and prestige after the crisis. I often heard comments like "The Court is the institution that traces the path through which the country should pass; it must be the real guarantee of the Constitution (*garante de la Constitución*)."

Anthropologist Debbora Battaglia (1995) distinguishes the synthetic and historically modern and willful nostalgia (understood as a moral and political order, or "Edenic," in Herzfeld's view) from what she defines as a practical or active nostalgia, the latter being a transformative action with a connective purpose. For Battaglia, rather than analyzing nostalgia as a disembodied idea, it can be in appreciated with a culturally specific historicity and a wholly contingent aesthetic efficacy. Accordingly, nostalgia "may be *practiced* in diverse ways" (1995: 77). "It is in this [practical, active] variety that nostalgic connection may also be imagined toward a past object without necessarily being the enemy of unformulated future relationships. Indeed, nostalgia is a sense of future—for an experience, however imaginary, of possessing the means of controlling the future—may function as a powerful force for social reconnection" (78).

Battaglia's view of nostalgia as a practice or an activity—and also as a "method" that enables both reconfigurations of the self and the ethnographer's knowledge—was helpful when it came to understanding my own subjects' nostalgic moments when I was in the field. As I said, my interlocutors both inside and outside the Court usually framed their accounts of the Court's workings through the instantiation of what is missing from the present. Like Court bureaucrats, many NGO officers and progressive scholars mourned for something lost. However, unlike Court agents, the latter did not draw on representations of past relations taken as exemplars. On the contrary, for the NGOs officers I spoke with, nostalgia mobilized a different way of embodying the past in the present. These actors' narratives used to point out an existing *gap* between reality (how the Court actually works) and (their) idea about justice, judicial adjudication, and lawmaking, among other institutional practices that for them have not yet been achieved. In inquiring about the ideas that moved these actors' actions and advocacy, the director of a civil rights organization explained to me that they were stated in the Argentine Constitution: "All our proposals are in the [Argentine] Constitution. . . . We are not importing any foreign legal system."

Consequently, for my informants outside the Court, what seems to be missing might be in the norm—that is, the "ought to be" that the present fails to realize. In this way, a nostalgia for the (legal) texts and the community and idea of nation that the actors interpret as imagined by drafters of the Constitution is more palpable outside the Court than inside it. In my opinion, the nostalgic narratives that I collected outside the "judicial space" (Barrera 2012b)—in particular among NGO people—account for a reality that, drawing on Miyazaki, "is still in a state of not-yet" (Miyazaki 2004: 9).[12] To put it another way, they do not mourn for a past and glorious order of relationships within the juridical field as many Court agents do. In fact, from the outside, that previous social order is often regarded as a conservative, backward-looking, even elitist paradigm of judicial practice and legal bureaucrats' behavior. It does not mean, however, that the legal text is taken at face value—that is, that a plain and literal interpretation of the norm guides activists' practices. It is the *ideals* embedded in it—rules, principles, purposes that, in turn, are interpreted, appropriated, and reconfigured by them—that directs the subjects' practices. These idealized rules seem to be always in deferral, which distances them from actual judicial practice. Such a gap between reality and the ideals seems to give these actors' present moment a future orientation (Levine 2004).

LAW AND POLITICS

Competing images of the Court are evoked in different spaces of legality in accordance with the actors' experiences in the field of judicial practice. The powerful, albeit unacknowledged, sense of nostalgia embedded in my subjects' accounts of the Court's workings helps elaborate on their mode of knowledge construction of a concrete object—the Supreme Court—and, also important, it speaks of the ways in which the field of judicial practice in Argentina is interpreted, questioned, reconfigured, and resisted in political terms by different actors.

Although a detailed analysis of Argentina's political history[13] is beyond the scope of this chapter, I should note here that the political process that the country underwent throughout the twentieth century necessarily influenced its contemporary legal history (Gargarella 2004; Oteiza 1994). The military coup of 1930—backed by the composition of the Supreme Court at that time—was a watershed moment in the country's institutional history as it gave way to the infamous practice of military interventionism in civil and political matters that extended to 1983. During such a period, dictatorships and democratic governments alternated in power. Therefore, military regimes selected judges who legitimized their seizure of power and their de facto governments. Likewise, each subsequent return of a democratic government brought the opportunity to appoint almost all new judges to the Supreme Court (Gargarella 2004; Nino 1996; Oteiza 1994). The political instability was reflected not only in changes to codes, statutes, and even the Constitutional text, but it also impacted upon the juridical field, affecting institutional practices and individuals' and groups' subjectivities. The brutality of the human rights violations carried out by the military juntas that ruled the country from 1976 to 1983 certainly was a turning point in Argentina's political and legal history, not only due to the significance of the crimes themselves (kidnapping, assassinations, torture, and child abductions, among others) perpetrated by the state but also because of their long-term effects on Argentina's legal system and judicial practice. They include, within 20 years, the trial and condemnation of the chiefs of the juntas in 1985, promoted by the democratically elected president Alfonsin (1983–1989); the passage of amnesty laws in 1986 and 1987 (also during the Alfonsin administration) that foreclosed criminal prosecution of human rights violators; presidential pardon to the chiefs of the juntas in 1989 and 1990 by Carlos Menem; and the Supreme Court's landmark decision in the *Poblete* case in June 2005, which overturned the "impunity" laws of 1986 and 1987, enabling criminal prosecution of perpetrators of human rights violations.[14]

Additionally, the 1994 amendment to Argentina's National Constitution was a very significant political event that modified the Argentine legal regime. In particular, the reform granted constitutional rank to international human rights treaties and incorporated collective rights such as environmental rights, consumer rights, the rights of indigenous peoples, the protection of personal data, and equal protection, which capitalized many decades of struggles for human rights by social organizations and paved the way to new rights advocacy. Moreover, the constitutional amendment allocated significant roles in judicial adjudication and rule-making to institutions other than the courts. Among these institutions are the Magistracy Council and the Judicial School, the Offices of the Public Prosecutor and the Public Defender, respectively, and the National Ombudsman.

These changes, among other sociopolitical factors and in addition to the negative impact on the prestige of legal and political institutions spawned by the 2001–2002 crisis, which affected in particular the physical composition of the Court,[15] have contributed to configure a very dynamic juridical field. Moreover, a series of laws on judicial reform (the so-called Reform toward the Democratization of Justice) that were promoted by President Cristina Fernández de Kirchner (2007–2015) were passed by Congress in April 2013. Originally, the laws regulated the management of the Supreme Court's budget, the number and selection process of the members of the Magistracy Council, the modes of appointment of law clerks and staff members at lower federal courts, restrictions on the time that a particular kind of judicial rulings (*medidas cautelares*) against the state can be enforced, and the federal judiciary organization and procedures through the creation of a new appeal instance before the Court in civil and commercial, social security, and administrative matters. The reform, as proposed by the Executive and backed by the ruling party at that time, had been contested in different venues—for instance, academic, professional, political, some non-governmental organizations, mass media, and the judiciary,[16] although in the last, it had found many supporters.[17] Finally, after the laws were passed, several lawsuits against their enforcement were filed in the courts based on the alleged unconstitutionality of some of the statutes, and the Supreme Court partially overturned the reform.[18]

In this context, the image of the Argentine legal field as the site of "indeterminacy" (Faulk 2013: 178), contingency, and even discontinuity—for example, perennial norms, practices, and proceedings can be changed according to political shifts, as many of my interlocutors argued—is often projected by experts who interpret those changes as contrary to predictability of legal institutions (*seguridad jurídica*) and, ultimately, against the rule of law.

In this context, perceptions about an increasing responsiveness by the courts to right-based public law litigation coexist, for instance, with accusations of lack of transparency of court workings. Or at the same time that many federal courts are praised for drawing on international human rights instruments to decide cases, they can also be seen as part of a judicial body dominated by patronage and kinship relations among its members (an idea that is epitomized in the widely propagated metaphor of the "judicial family"). Additionally, also in the last decades, Argentina and Latin America in general have experienced the advance of judicial power into policy domains formerly left to the executive and legislative branches

(Couso 2010: 142). For Huneeus, Couso, and Sieder (2010), a relevant aspect of such a phenomenon is "the growing use of law, legal discourse, and litigation by a range of political actors, including politicians, social movements, and individual actors" (8). These data necessarily question the traditional roles played by the courts in Argentina and the very act of judicial adjudication. In this sense, it is likely to find people both inside and outside the judiciary for whom adjudication is only the act of interpreting the legal text. From this point of view, judicial activism would be the interference of the judicial branch in political matters that are not the province of the courts.

A SITUATED PRACTICE

Drawing on the ambiguities she found in the Argentine judiciary, Sarrabayrouse Oliveira (2004: 211) described it as a "double-faced" body: on the one hand, a bureaucratic apparatus governed by universal and general rules and, on the other hand, a world of personal relations characterized by a pervading *clientelismo* (a clientele, patronage system), status, and hierarchy. Building upon Da Matta (1980), she makes an interesting argument about how these apparently contradictory "worlds" are related: they operate in a relationship of reciprocal reflexivity; they feed and complement each other. In some sense, Sarrabayrouse Oliveira's point about the Argentine judiciary recalls Colin Hoag's argument about the perils of studying bureaucracies if one approaches them from an empirical perspective. If the attention focuses on bureaucracies' policies and everyday practices, argues Hoag, it is most likely that they appear as rational and efficient bodies, while at the same time, they remain opaque, inscrutable, and illogical to both "insider" and "outsider" alike (Hoag 2011: 81–82). Bureaucratic ideals, therefore, tend to predetermine the analysis that is set up through binary categories that seek to explain how bureaucracies "should work" against how they actually work.

To engage in the study of bureaucracies "without allowing their idealizing self-frames to predetermine our analysis" (Hoag 2011: 84) means moving the analysis beyond the dialectic of binaries that it anticipates. Accordingly, to avoid the all-or-nothing extremism produced by the binary objective-subjective that dominates bureaucracy studies, Hoag appeals to Donna Haraway's (1988) insight about knowledges as situated practices: "vision as an embodied practice, reminding us that all gazes are from somewhere. . . . They are partial knowledges" (Hoag 2011: 84). Ultimately, this insight challenges the idea of a universal and powerful gaze to scrutinize social action.

Hoag's reflections about the study of bureaucracy apply to the examination of the Argentine judicial practice. I have noted, following Weber (1968), that "judicial decision making in Euro-American cultures is materialized in practices that resemble the modes of operation of a professional and depersonalized bureaucracy" (Barrera 2008: 5). In the field of sociolegal studies in Argentina, representations of the workings of judges and judicial bureaucrats tend to be extreme. They oscillate from descriptions that account for subjective, and even discretionary, practices to narratives of almost mechanical and emotionally disengaged behaviors. So rather than sticking to the contradictions and ambiguities that the field poses to the ethnographer, I argue that it is more worthy to pay attention to the modes in which knowledge about law and legal institutions is created, produced. Consequently, this chapter concentrates on the knowledge, or knowledges, of the Court that emerged from different and concrete spaces of legality. These knowledges are indexical of disparate indigenous modes of thinking, perceiving, experiencing, and imagining the workings of the courts. The subjects who inhabit those spaces embody different meanings and understandings of the Court and the field of judicial practice in Argentina—that is, different understandings of how the local judiciary works and how it should work.

In that scheme, the Court is instantiated both in semiotic and material domains through the actors' interactions and experiences with the judicial apparatus. Accordingly, as I said before, visions of the judiciary as a rational organization and a discretionary body are intertwined in the narratives and practices of the subjects. Rule-bounded bureaucratic action mixes up with appreciations of judicial decision making influenced by the subjects' affects. Between these two extreme worlds, a constellation of meanings about justice and judicial workings may emerge in the interplay of the actors and the judicial system. This is not something new. Different conceptual frameworks have been drawn to explore people's experiences and images of the law and justice. In this sense, categories such as legal consciousness (Ewick and Silbey 1998), cultures of legality (Huneeus, Couso, and Sieder 2010), or legal subjectivity (see Chapters 2 and 5 and the Introduction to this book by Faulk and Brunnegger) work to explain the meanings of legality to different actors in a plurality of settings.

The expert domains that I documented ethnographically during my research reflect the authoritative knowledge about judicial workings that precede the subjects and that they contribute to reproduce both materially and semantically. Needless to say, the subjects' immersion in a web of authoritative legal knowledge and legal and judicial practices (see Chapters 2 and 5) highlights the spatialized character of their practices and their process of legal-knowledge production, even though they can be just as critical of those processes as a few of my informants inside the judiciary were. This does not mean that judicial practice is delimited to a site in particular—namely, a courtroom or the Supreme Court's facilities. On the contrary, it suggests that disparate individual and institutional knowledges and practices may compete to create and shape the judicial body. In this light, the historical, legal, and political contexts in which native judicial institutions have developed in Argentina are likely to be interpreted as manifestations of a contingent and unpredictable legal field.

NOTES

Field research for this article was supported by Cornell University. Thanks to all the legal experts inside and outside the Argentine Supreme Court for sharing their time and knowledge, in particular to the law professor at the Judicial School who generously granted me permission to attend his seminar. Conversations with Amy Levine, José Antonio Sánchez Román, and Noa Vaisman a few years ago encouraged me to take on nostalgia as both an ethnographic and analytical category. This piece benefited from lively discussions held at the workshop críticas: Argentinean Legal Theory in the Twenty-First Century, organized by José Bellido and Hannah Franzki at Birkbeck College on April 5, 2014. I am also grateful to editors Sandra Brunnegger and Karen Faulk and two anonymous reviewers for their comments.

1. Unless otherwise noted, all translations are mine. The monetary policy of convertibility implied the tying of the Argentine peso to the U.S. dollar at a 1:1 rate, regardless of the dollar's fluctuations.

2. The post-enlargement Justices ended up grouping themselves into an "automatic majority" that was partial to the Menem administration's position in every pressing political issue decided by the Court. See Helmke (2005) for an analysis of the Supreme Court Justices' behavior from a political science perspective.

3. See, for instance, the 2002 and 2003 reports by a group of NGOs that formed the Una Corte para la Democracia (A Court for Democracy) coalition. These documents became very popular among different audiences—the legal academia, the media, and even legislators, government officers, and members of the judiciary—to the extent that some NGO directors and representatives whom I met in the field interpreted the regulations of transparency that the Court implemented afterward as the result of their successful advocacy of transparency in judicial procedures. See "Una Corte para la democracia I" at http://www.pensamientopenal.org.ar/una-corte-para-la-democracia-i/; and "Una Corte para la democracia II" at http://www.cels.org.ar/common/documentos/corte_II.pdf.

4. The *stare decisis* doctrine, or the rule to follow the Supreme Court's precedents by lower courts, is not mandatory in Argentina's judicial regime.

5. All names have been replaced by pseudonyms.

6. Supreme Court Justice in an interview with the author, November 9, 2006. This metaphor was widely used to refer to the magnitude of the 2001–2002 crisis, in particular by judicial actors.

7. See Law 24937, Article 13, modified by Law 26080. This amendment established that the goal of the Judicial School is to educate functionaries and candidates for the magistracy. Additionally, the controversial reform changed—and "hierarchized"—the status of the school in the sense that the successful completion of the Judicial School's courses is now considered a part of the qualifications for the selection and promotion of justices. Before

the 2006 amendment, attendance was not mandatory for applicants for the judiciary or for candidates for promotions. See Argentina, Law 26080, *Boletín Oficial* 30854, 1.

8. See Argentina, Consejo de la Magistratura, Escuela Judicial, *Memoria Anual*, 2006.

9. The following experience shows how the solemnity of forms matters even outside the courthouse. In December 2006, I met an old acquaintance from my law school in the Province of Tucumán, Argentina, who told me he was designing the curriculum for the LLB degree at a new private law school. This school was being promoted as an innovative and liberal institution. He told me one of the courses offered would be on protocol and etiquette (*protocolo*). When I asked him why they would include such a course, he emphatically replied, "A lawyer has to know how to behave correctly in different social situations."

Along the same lines, in her work on criminal cases brought *ex oficio* by the police to the federal courts of Buenos Aires City, Eilbaum (2008) describes how the judicial world is characterized by the etiquette and social norms that accompany any social situation preoccupied with hierarchy. She argues that those norms do not draw necessarily on juridical rules but, among others, on the ways actors speak and interact, their modes of entertainment, how their offices are decorated, and so on.

10. It was common to hear this court-trench analogy in the field. Like this seminar student, other judicial bureaucrats I interviewed—in particular those who worked in first-instance courts—often drew on this analogy to describe their routine obligations in the workplace. Tribunals are seen as trenches from which judicial agents face the conflicts brought daily to the courts. As a Supreme Court Justice once told me, "To work in a first-instance criminal court is like being in the trenches; many people can't stand it."

11. Interviews with the author, March 23, 2006; November 9, 2006; and February 16, 2007.

12. Miyazaki (2004) elaborates on the idea of "not-yet" from Ernst Bloch's discussion of "not-yet" consciousness in his philosophy of hope.

13. See Faulk (2012) for an examination of the sociopolitical events that influenced the constitution of the legal field in Argentina. See also Dezalay and Garth (2002) for accounts of the changes that operated in the Argentine juridical field during the transition from the latest dictatorship to democracy. Additionally, for the long-term transformations that explain the increasing judicialization of conflicts and social interactions in the last years in Argentina, see Smulovitz (2010).

14. In the so-called *Poblete* case, the Court upheld the constitutionality of a law passed by Congress voiding—both retroactively and prospectively—the "due obedience" and "final stop" laws of 1986 and 1987 that precluded the prosecution of the crimes committed by the military. See *Simón, Julio Héctor y otros*, 328 *Fallos* 2056 (2005). Also, on July 13, 2007, the Court held unconstitutional the presidential pardon that then president Menem granted in 1990 to the chiefs of the military juntas and other high-ranking military officials who had been prosecuted and condemned for human rights violations during the last dictatorship. This meant that all the criminal prosecution procedures that had been closed and archived due to the presidential pardon resumed. See *Mazzeo, Julio L. y otros*, 330 *Fallos* 3248 (2007).

15. In 2006, Congress passed a law reducing the number of Supreme Court Justices to five. However, since the number of Justices was seven at the time the law was enacted, it was therefore statutorily established that the Tribunal would be composed provisionally of seven members—and that four (out of seven justices) would make majority. See Argentina, Law 26183, *Boletín Oficial* 31055, 1. In 2014, two Supreme Court Justices passed away, and a third resigned when he turned 75, as required by the 1994 constitutional amendment. In June 2015, the Supreme Court had only four Justices. President Cristina Fernández de

Kirchner had nominated a candidate to the Court in January 2015, but his file is still pending Senate review. It is unlikely that this nominee will be elected, however, because the senators from the opposition—whose votes would help to reach the two-thirds majority needed for the confirmation of Justices as required by the Constitution—signed a document in 2014 stating that they would not review the filing of any of President Kirchner's nominees. Representatives of the ruling party had been questioning Justice Carlos Fayt's capacity (both physically and intellectually) to sit on the bench because of his age (97 years old). In May 2015, the Impeachment Committee from Cámara de Diputados (Argentina's House of Representatives) approved a petition for Fayt to undergo a physical examination. Members of political opposition parties and other organizations, such as the Buenos Aires Bar Association, had protested this decision by denouncing the Executive's encroachment of judicial independence through a Court-packing plan. On September 15, 2015, however, Justice Fayt resigned, although in his letter of resignation to then president Cristina Kirchner, he stated that his last day would be December 10, 2015—the day President Kirchner would leave office and the winner of the October presidential election would be inaugurated. See "Fayt renunció y le dejó la renovación de la Corte Suprema al próximo gobierno," *La Nación* (http://www.lanacion.com.ar/1828226-fayt-renuncio-y-le-dejo-la-renovacion-de-la-corte-suprema-al-proximo-gobierno).

16. See, for instance, "Miles de personas marcharon contra la reforma judicial," *Clarín*, April 19, 2013 (http://www.clarin.com/edicion-impresa/Miles-personas-marcharon-Congreso-judicial_0_904109632.html); "Avance sobre la justicia," *La Nación*, April 19, 2013 (http://www.lanacion.com.ar/avance-sobre-la-justicia-t49250); "Guiso a la opositora," *Página 12*, April 19, 2013 (http://www.antelaley.com/2013/04/mucho-ruido-pocos-jueces-los-problemas.html; http://www.saberderecho.com/; http://poderciudadano.org/wp/wp-content/uploads/2013/04/20130416-Comunicado-Justicia-ONG.pdf); "Plataforma 2012: Una reforma judicial" (http://seminariogargarella.blogspot.com.ar/2013/04/plataforma-2012-una-reforma-judicial.html); "Se viene el downsizing" (http://todosobrelacorte.com/2013/04/10/se-viene-el-downsizing/).

17. See "Por una justicia legítima" (http://xunajusticialegitima.blogspot.com.ar/).

18. See *Rizzo, Jorge Gabriel (apod. lista 3 Gente de Derecho) s/acción de amparo /c Poder Ejecutivo Nacional Ley 26855 /s medida cautelar.* CSJN R. 369. XLIX. REX (2013).

WORKS CITED

Barrera, Leticia. 2008. "Files Circulation and the Forms of Legal Experts: Agency and Personhood in the Argentine Supreme Court." *Journal of Legal Anthropology* 1 (1): 3–24.

———. 2012a. *La Corte Suprema en escena: Una etnografía del mundo judicial.* Buenos Aires: Siglo XXI.

———. 2012b. "Relocalizing the Judicial Space: Place, Access and Mobilization in Judicial Practice in Post-Crisis Argentina." *Law, Culture and the Humanities* 8 (2): 350–373.

Battaglia, Debbora. 1995. "On Practical Nostalgia: Self-Prospecting among Urban Trobrianders." In *Rhetorics of Self-Making*, edited by Debbora Battaglia, 77–96. Berkeley: University of California Press.

Bourdieu, Pierre. 1987. "The Force of Law: Toward a Sociology of the Juridical Field." *Hastings Law Review* 38: 805–853.

Couso, Javier. 2010. "The Transformation of Constitutional Discourse and the Judicialization of Politics in Latin America." In *Cultures of Legality: Judicialization and*

Political Activism in Latin America, edited by Javier Couso, Alexandra Huneeus, and Rachel Sieder, 141–160. Cambridge: Cambridge University Press.

Da Matta, Roberto. 1980. *Carnavais, malandros e heróis*. Rio de Janeiro: Zahar. Quoted in María José Sarrabayrouse Oliveira, "La justicia penal y los universos coexistentes—Reglas universales y relaciones personales." In *Burocracias y violencia: Estudios de antropología jurídica*, edited by Sofia Tiscornia, 203–241. Buenos Aires: Antropofagia, 2004.

Dezalay, Yves, and Bryant Garth. 2002. *The Internationalization of Palace Wars—Lawyers, Economists and the Contest to Transform Latin American States*. Chicago: University of Chicago Press.

Eilbaum, Lucía. 2008. *Los "casos de policía" en la justicia federal en Buenos Aires: El pez por la boca muere*. Buenos Aires: Antropofagia/IDES.

Ewick, Patricia, and Susan Silbey.1998. *The Common Place of Law—Stories from Everyday Life*. Chicago: University of Chicago Press.

Faulk, Karen A. 2013. *In the Wake of Neoliberalism—Citizenship and Human Rights in Argentina*. Stanford, CA: Stanford University Press.

Gargarella, Roberto. 2004. "In Search of a Democratic Justice—What Courts Should Not Do: Argentina 1983–2002." In *Democratization and the Judiciary: The Accountability Function of Courts in New Democracies*, edited by Siri Gloppen, Roberto Gargarella, and Elin Skaar, 181–197. London: Frank Cass.

Haraway, Donna. 1988. "Situated Knowledges: The Science Question in Feminism and the Privilege of Partial Perspective." *Feminist Studies* 14 (3): 575–599.

Helmke, Gretchen. 2005. *Courts under Constraints—Judges, Generals and Presidents in Argentina*. Cambridge: Cambridge University Press.

Herzfeld, Michael. 1997. *Cultural Intimacy, Social Poetics in the Nation-State*. New York: Routledge.

Hoag, Colin. 2011. "Assembling Partial Perspectives: Thoughts on the Anthropology of Bureaucracy." *PoLAR: Political and Legal Anthropology Review* 34 (1): 81–94.

Huneeus, Alexandra, Javier Couso, and Rachel Sieder. 2010. "Cultures of Legality: Judicialization and Political Activism in Contemporary Latin America." In *Cultures of Legality: Judicialization and Political Activism in Latin America*, edited by Javier Couso, Alexandra Huneeus, and Rachel Sieder, 3–21. Cambridge: Cambridge University Press.

Lasser, Mitchel de S.-O.-L'E. 2005. *Judicial Deliberations: A Comparative Analysis of Transparency and Legitimacy*. Oxford: Oxford University Press.

Levine, Amy. 2004. "The Transparent Case of Virtuality." *PoLAR: Political and Legal Anthropology Review* 27 (1): 90–113.

Miyazaki, Hirokazu. 2004. *The Method of Hope: Anthropology, Philosophy, and Fijian Knowledge*. Stanford, CA: Stanford University Press.

Munro, Rolland. 1997. "Ideas of Difference: Stability, Social Spaces and the Labour of Division." In *Ideas of Difference*, edited by Kevin Hetherington and Rolland Munro, 3–24. Oxford: Blackwell.

Nino, Carlos S. 1996. *The Constitution of Deliberative Democracy*. New Haven, CT: Yale University Press.

Oteiza, Eduardo. 1994. *La Corte Suprema: Entre la justicia sin política y la política sin justicia*. Buenos Aires: Platense.

Riles, Annelise. 2005. "A New Agenda for the Cultural Study of Law: Taking on the Technicalities." *Buffalo Law Review* 53: 392–405.

Sarrabayrouse Oliveira, María José. 2004. "La justicia penal y los universos coexistentes—Reglas universales y relaciones personales." In *Burocracias y violencia: Estudios de antropología jurídica*, edited by Sofia Tiscornia, 203–241. Buenos Aires: Antropofagia.

———. 2011. *Poder judicial y dictadura—El caso de la morgue judicial*. Buenos Aires: Del Puerto.

Smulovitz, Catalina. 2010. "Judicialization in Argentina: Legal Culture or Opportunities and Support Structures?" In *Cultures of Legality: Judicialization and Political Activism in Latin America*, edited by Javier Couso, Alexandra Huneeus, and Rachel Sieder, 234–253. Cambridge: Cambridge University Press.

Vismann, Cornelia. 2008. *Files—Law and Media Technology*. Stanford, CA: Stanford University Press.

Weber, Max. 1968. "Bureaucracy." In *Max Weber on Charisma and Institution Building: Selected Papers*, edited by S. N. Eisenstadt, 66–77. Chicago: University of Chicago Press.

CASES CITED

Mazzeo, Julio L. y otros, 330 *Fallos* 3248 (2007).

Rizzo, Jorge Gabriel (apod. lista 3 Gente de Derecho) s/acción de amparo /c Poder Ejecutivo Nacional Ley 26855 /s medida cautelar, CSJN R. 369. XLIX. REX (2013).

Simón, Julio Héctor y otros, 328 *Fallos* 2056 (2005).

PART THREE

DIFFERING SCALES

OF JUSTICE

5 THE CRAFT OF JUSTICE-MAKING THROUGH THE PERMANENT PEOPLES' TRIBUNAL IN COLOMBIA

Sandra Brunnegger

For three days in July 2008, the Leon de Greiff auditorium of Colombia's National University in Bogotá thronged with people. They had come together to conclude a two-and-a-half-year-long fact-finding process convened by the international Permanent Peoples' Tribunal (hereafter PPT), a nonstate forum of international opinion that had taken upon itself to investigate the roles of transnational corporations in Colombia. Approximately 2,000 people listened to the words of an international jury (which included Nobel Peace Prize winner Adolfo Pérez Esquivel—who presided over the session—university professors, indigenous authorities, judges from different countries, and grassroots activists) as they handed down a ruling on multinationals' activities in the country (Paley 2008). This audience drew on the whole spectrum of those participating in the solidarity network. Attracting interest from the media as well as support from unions, international human rights organizations, and indigenous leaders, the jury's ruling cited a long list of violations of social, political, and labor rights and environmental standards carried out by more than 30 multinational companies; it further accused the Colombian and U.S. governments of complicity in this wrongdoing. The jury's ruling stated it is "essentially a moral and ethical denunciation," while participants themselves hailed the verdict as one of social justice (Final Session of Permanent Peoples' Tribunal in Bogotá 2008; Paley 2008).

Several months before this final session in spring 2008, Luis Fernando Arias Arias, who was then the advisor to ONIC (National Indigenous Organization of Colombia) and is currently this body's *consejero mayor* (elder councilor), invited me to attend the PPT's prehearings.[1] I took part in two of the five prehearing sessions dealing specifically with the topic of indigenous communities affected by transnational corporations' activities. These sessions addressed in particular companies' exploitation of natural resources (specifically mining and the extraction of petrocarbons) and the political, social, and environmental implications for communities living on or near the companies' sites of operation. At these localities,

FIGURE 5.1   Graffiti in Bogota announcing the final hearing of the PPT in Bogotá. Photo by Dawn Paley.

members of the affected communities and their organizations gave testimony, often in narrative form, to the prehearings' organizers. The general form of the tribunal process was to gather knowledge from individuals' narratives at prehearings and to make this amenable for political or legal use at the final session and ruling in Bogotá. ONIC itself convened the prehearings through liaisons with regional indigenous organizations and was backed by many other organizations active in the PPT initiative, including trade unions and non-governmental human rights organizations such as the José Alvear Restrepo Lawyers' Collective.

On the one hand, much of the scholarly work theorizing and ethnographically mapping indigenous activism has worked to unravel the forms taken by the intense networking between indigenous communities or organizations and other grassroots movements and international human rights organizations (e.g., Brysk 2000; Rodríguez-Garavito and Arenas 2005; Warren 1998). Scholars have also been concerned to present indigenous activism within a conceptual frame defined by neoliberalism and as a form of struggle or resistance to neoliberal states and transnational companies in Latin America (e.g., Fisher 2011; Postero 2005; Sawyer

2004). On the other hand, I read these practices of alliance building among indigenous communities and organizations, grassroots movements, and international human rights organizations as a form of knowledge-based activism, understanding movement-related activities as practices of knowledge-making shaping what is understood to be valid knowledge in the world (Casas-Cortés, Osterweil, and Powell 2008; Escobar 1992; Sousa Santos 2005).[2]

This chapter neither sets out to provide a comprehensive account of the multiple forces and processes that informs the tribunal and its prehearings nor to take an interest in the hearings' outcomes, per se. This chapter is concerned with demonstrating how the hearings seek to acquire legal and moral authority to reconceptualize the dynamics of the very practices that comprise knowledge-making in these justice-seeking processes. In this way, I highlight the efforts of activists to make certain knowledges visible and credible by translating often abstract political and moral visions of a just society in Colombia into on-the-ground actions such as hearings and public events.

I treat the workings of the tribunal as a political act in the sense that it seeks to invoke or summon authoritative knowledge about legal and moral wrongdoings. Conceived in this way, the appropriation of knowledge through hearings can be fashioned to serve various specific purposes, including political purposes such as producing legitimacy for the organizations involved; moral purposes such as locating accountability; and legal purposes such as authoritatively establishing the facts of rights violations. At the same time, tribunal processes are also generative processes, connecting and feeding into the "imaginative work" of fashioning a renewed public perception of a just society through a reinvigorated concept of justice in Colombia (Ross 2003: 326).

This chapter begins by introducing the broad history of the PPT and briefly describing some of the constitutive challenges it faces. The chapter then discusses two of the PPT's prehearings in depth, one held in Cúcuta and one in Cabo de la Vela, both located in northeast Colombia. The chapter's ethnographic settings provide the backdrop for the remainder of the discussion, which centers on the conception of justice, and of knowledge- and subject-making processes, including those of the dispossessed.

THE PPT, OR THE "PEOPLE'S COURTS FOR THE DISPOSSESSED"

The PPT sees itself as a "people's court for the dispossessed . . . for marginalized voices" (Klinghoffer and Klinghoffer 2002: 164). It exists to hear and to give voice (on their own terms) to groups that are affected by a lack of access to justice and are disregarded by their national governments and by the international community. The tribunal's website describes its mission as the "identificat[ion] and public[ation] of . . . cases of [the] systematic violation of fundamental rights, especially cases in which national and international legislation fails to defend people's rights" (Fondazione Lelio e Lisli Basso-Issoco n.d.).

Founded in 1979, the PPT took its inspiration from predecessor organizations, including civil society tribunals that existed to draw attention to injustice, most notably, the International War Crimes Tribunal, also known as the Russell Tribunal, an investigative nonstate body formed in 1966 by the British philosopher Bertrand Russell. The Russell Tribunal examined war crimes committed during the Vietnam War and later by Latin American dictatorships. The late Italian senator Lelio Basso, a Russell Tribunal member, founded the Lelio Basso Foundation (Fondazione Lelio e Lisli Basso-Issoco), which was the founding body of the PPT. The scope of the PPT's investigative function ranges from inquiries (e.g., "Industrial Hazards and Human Rights—Bhopal" [1992]) to reports (e.g., "Asylum in Europe" [1994], "Crimes against Humanity in Former Yugoslavia" [1995], "The Violation of Fundamental Rights of Children and Adolescents in Brazil" [1999], and "Sri Lanka and the Tamil People" [2010]). It has held 36 sessions to date.

Basso understood the legitimacy of the PPT as "emanat[ing] directly from the popular consciousness" (Fondazione Lelio e Lisli Basso-Issoco n.d.). The PPT's claim to moral authority also derives from its recognition and public support. Participants in the PPT are thus turned into politically conscious moral agents— agents whose assumed responsibility grounds any claim on the tribunal's part for moral authority. For Basso, "the needs of public conscience can become a recognized source of law" (Fondazione Lelio e Lisli Basso-Issoco n.d.). The mechanism envisaged by the tribunal for achieving this is to hand down "rulings . . . of a legal nature" against the state or nonstate actors accountable for violations (Fondazione Lelio e Lisli Basso-Issoco n.d.). While couched in a legal idiom,[3] the PPT's rulings do not have legal standing and are nonbinding. The political scientists Klinghoffer and Klinghoffer (2002: 190) take issue with the character of the tribunal's verdicts by highlighting its vocabulary: its "panelists" (not judges) "investigate" (rather than indict) countries, organizations, and individuals in order to arrive at "findings" (as opposed to verdicts). In the same vein, Richard Falk (2011), an international relations and international law scholar, raised the question on his blog: "[Which civil society] initiatives really qualify as 'law'?" He answers his own question by writing: "People are the ultimate source of legal authority and have the right to act on their own when governmental procedures, as in these situations, are so inhibited by geopolitics that they fail to address severe violations of international law" (ibid.). This reflects the PPT's approach in conceiving its legitimacy to emerge from a wellspring of support in civil society.

The PPT seems to derive its moral weight not merely from popular testimony and support but also from the standing of its own jury members. It understands the prominence of the jury as a tool for raising awareness and bringing the concerns excavated by its process to public attention. Since it seeks to influence public opinion, the PPT values "ideological pluralism" and sets out to embody this by ensuring that its leading figures represent different shades of political opinion (Fondazione Lelio e Lisli Basso-Issoco n.d.). In other words, the very same processes aimed at valuing ideological pluralism that underwrite the justice promoted by its investigations also buttress the tribunal's own claims to moral authority. This informs the institution's production of its own legitimacy. Nevertheless, the PPT has been accused of ideological bias, not least by Klinghoffer and Klinghoffer (2002), who state, "The PPT is firmly based on radical leftist ideology" (165). It may not come as a surprise, then, that the PPT has received other strong criticism, including allegations of having a "kangaroo court atmosphere" (190) and of presenting a spectacle akin to "'a circus,' [or] a theater piece with pre-assigned roles" (Falk 2011). Even a seemingly more sympathetic account describes it as "mock litigation" (Shivji 1996: 20). Others, such as Leary (1979: 207), have taken a different approach, praising PPT initiatives as an instance of non-governmental organizations working to further the development of international human rights law. In responding to repression, these initiatives are thus taken to move us toward a more fine-tuned formulation of international human rights standards. This has been said in particular with reference to the elaboration of the 1976 Universal Declaration on the Rights of Peoples, or the Algiers Declaration, which was adopted and proclaimed at a conference of non-governmental participants organized by the Lelio Basso Foundation (Leary 1979: 207).[4] As Leary (1979: 198) has observed, "Human rights organizations have been credited with much of the progress which has occurred in the international protection of human rights," often through their recording of violations and promotion of discussion about them. It is precisely this task of recording that the PPT undertook in Latin America from 2006 to 2010 in logging the activities of transnational corporations and reflecting on the role of the European Union in company misdeeds (Transnational Institute 2010: 7).

The session of the Permanent Peoples' Tribunal concerning itself with Colombia should be seen in the context of these wider investigations. This session was initiated in 2005 when the PPT received a petition from various social bodies requesting an investigation into the role of transnational corporations in the country. These bodies comprised a number of organizations, many grassroots, including indigenous communities, Afro-Colombian groups, peasant associations, trade unions, women's groups, and other organizations concerned with human rights in Colombia. In its six thematic hearings between 2006 and 2008, the tribunal addressed in turn the oil industry, the mining sector, food production, public services, and questions of biodiversity and indigenous peoples' rights. These hearings were located at specific relevant sites across Colombia; in addition, there were many more locally organized prehearings and associated events. Each public hearing was dedicated to considering alleged offenses committed by multinational companies as they were linked to the political and economic dynamics of Colombian society and its lived reality of conflict. People offered testimony naming individual companies and sometimes bringing forward documentary evidence of wrongs they or their friends or family had suffered. Prior to the hearings, some members of the international PPT jury toured the region, especially conflict zones, in the company of other national and international participants. These hearings, prehearings, and other smaller events all fed into the final hearing in Bogotá. At the final hearing in July 2008, the international jury handed down a final ruling on multinationals' activities based on findings from all six thematic hearings. The ruling of the PPT turned as much on political and moral arguments as on specifically legal questions. The ruling determined that the Colombian government and over 30 multinational companies had violated social, economic, and political rights. The cases considered by the tribunal reflected a broad array of legal, social, political, and economic inequalities that existed, and continue to exist, in Colombia.

Since the late 1980s, Latin American economies have been reshaped according to a neoliberal model, which has promoted different kinds of market reforms. Trade liberalization of the Colombian economy has brought with it privatization, deregulation, competition for foreign direct investment, the cutting or withdrawal of state services, and the commodification of public goods. Further, Coombe (2005) lists that the "conditions of neoliberalism" also include "the evisceration of labor rights, an acceleration of extractive industries, threats to subsistence livelihoods, and a concomitant loss of human security" (38). Above all, the PPT deliberations have drawn attention to the complexity of Colombia's intertwined military, political, and economic difficulties. The country has been shattered by several decades of armed conflict, during which state, paramilitary, and guerrilla parties have all been accused of human rights violations. Scholars (e.g., Escobar 2004; Gill 2009; Gledhill 1999) have suggested that economic neoliberal agendas (or a "high-growth capitalist development" agenda [Gledhill 1999: 217]) have aggravated economic insecurity and political violence, displacing and impoverishing rural communities through "the management of asymmetrical and spatialized violence, territorial control, sub-contracted massacres, and 'cruel little wars'"

(Escobar 2004: 18). Acts of resistance emerge in the context of struggles against inequalities, violence, and economic insecurity and, as such, against a so-called neoliberal paradigm. Alliances or networks of peasant cooperatives, indigenous populations, women activist groups, and trade unionists have all taken up different oppositional causes, yet it can be argued that they are waging similar struggles and share a desire to secure social justice (e.g., Gill 2007: 240; Keen and Haynes 2012: 288). These wider social and political struggles shape various initiatives invoking social justice in the country, including the PPT.

JUSTICE IN THE MAKING

The process of the tribunal hearings brought together the different movements and organizations mentioned earlier to share stories and cases.[5] In agitating for a just response to inequality, these organizations have the broader aim of accomplishing social transformation. Organizations entered the tribunal process in order to affirm the rights violations perpetrated by multinationals and thereby to contest the *impunidad* (impunity) felt by their members to characterize multinationals' actions. The forms of networking that constitute the tribunal events produce a discursive construction of social justice that, while not legally binding, rests on a moral foundation and aspires to be eventually realized in legal terms. These events release an abstract (or even utopian) vision in that they project an alternative conception of justice. In fact, one of the organizers of this "new solidarity network" suggested in her address to attendees in Cúcuta that the tribunal's ultimate goal was not to bring any prosecution against perpetrators but rather to set up a large-scale, symbolic, alternative justice system. This would be an alternative to the state system, which many saw as unable or unwilling to deliver justice. The vision of an alternative justice is grounded in a moral language (a sense of right or wrong) concerned to make multinationals accountable and revealing the Colombian government's role in this process. NGO members and indigenous leaders alike are using the process to envisage a new, more just Colombian society in which community members participate on a platform of *no impunidad* (no impunity), *no violencia* (no violence), and *justicia alternativa* (alternative justice). In encouraging participation in the prehearings, ONIC, the national indigenous organization, set out a vision of indigenous political autonomy for its communities, as this remains the summit of their political aspirations. In its brochure on the PPT, ONIC (2008) states that while it would be "necessary to convene an Indigenous Tribunal [session] to judge" purported crimes, members of indigenous groups should participate to the full in backing the tribunal's challenge to impunity and in giving its statement of the economic risks of multinationals' activity the greatest moral possible weight. ONIC (2008) envisions that by taking part in the process, indigenous peoples are committing to "the recovery of historical memory [and] the search for truth, justice . . . full reparation for victims, [and] the strengthening of social movements." They thereby, as proclaimed by ONIC, will lend their support to a progressive alliance of self-strengthening persecuted communities. The verdict of the tribunal, it seems, emerges as a by-product of these social processes.

The verdict as announced in Bogotá took the form of a 40-page written judgment listing rights that had been violated in terms of international law and citing legal precedents. The PPT verdict cites individual companies and indicates the failings of the government and its institutions; it then proceeds to spell out recommendations for various actors. The verdict also acknowledges that it possesses moral, but not legal, force. For the participants, it is important—as the text emphasizes—to attract the attention of the international community to wrongdoing in Colombia. The tribunal verdict expresses a belief in enhanced transparency and accountability, and it hopes to have acted so as to put these in place. In this way, the tribunal underwrites a legal, moral, and political notion of accountability in the sense of insisting that companies take responsibility for their wrongdoings. The tribunal is casting off companies' *impunidad* (impunity), especially as the perception of this impunity forms a fundamental part of tribunal participants' grievances. Here the tribunal frames "a model through which people could engage in the work of considering experience, reshaping their understandings, and seeking acknowledgment" (Ross 2003: 300). With this verdict, the PPT brought about an emphasis on articulating the voice of the "dispossessed" as a form of action.

The tribunal's events evince and showcase a particular conception of justice as a category of meaning and experience, fleshed out with the very real individual experiences of its attendees and participants. Victims' narratives were attended to and valued in the prehearings, where victims had the chance to tell their own stories. Community members overcame hesitations and fears to offer testimony on how multinationals infringe on their daily lives. In her work, Ross (2003) says on the process of testifying before the South African Truth and Reconciliation Commission: "The testimonial form became a means in the ongoing work of fashioning the self in relation to changing social circumstances" (300). However, in being collected, the prehearing stories then "became standardized and replicable" (328) as a certain kind of knowledge. Many scholars (e.g., Coxshall 2005; Theidon 2012; Winter 2009), who have studied the mechanisms of, for example, truth commissions, point out that problems may arise through this "testimony-giving" and "testimony-collating" process, including elevations, omissions, exclusions, distortions, and various appropriations of knowledges. In the case of the two PPT prehearings, attendees recognized the political nature of the tribunal and they un-derstood the limitation of it, underlined by the fact that the PPT is a nonbinding and a non-governmental initiative, while at the same time there was a clearly ex-pressed sentiment of being heard as a moment (albeit fleeting and hopeful rather than affirmative) of empowerment. While attendees at the PPT invested a hope of achieving justice through the PPT, the acknowledged political nature of these pre-hearings, where outrage at the behavior of these multinational companies was ex-pressed, came to characterize the PPT as an inherently political and politicized act, in the sense that the tribunal sought to invoke or summon authoritative knowl-edge about legal and moral wrongdoing.

In these terms, the appropriation of knowledge through hearings serves to mark various specific purposes: political (in producing, for instance, the legiti-macy of the organizations concerned); moral (in locating accountability); and legal (in authoritatively establishing the facts of rights violations). It is these processes of gathering knowledge through "testimony-giving" and "testimony-collating" that now merit further attention.

KNOWLEDGE IN THE MAKING, OR "CERREJÓN ES UN MAL VECINO" (CERREJÓN IS A BAD NEIGHBOR)

The prehearings, or sites of knowledge-making, that I attended in Colombia dealt specifically with how the indigenous communities, the Barí and the Wayúu, have been affected by the activities of transnational corporations operating in the de-partments of North Santander and La Guajira. Companies such as Cerrejón and Ecopetrol exploit natural resources through mining and petrocarbon extraction, activities with significant political, social, and environmental implications for the Barí and Wayúu communities living alongside these operations. The PPT prehear-ings explicitly invited members of these groups to contribute their knowledge to its process as agents of the PPT. As one member from a participating organization articulated in the Cabo de Vela prehearing in the department of La Guajira:

> The purpose here is precisely to generate discussion, to debate, to continue with the discussion, and to put together a strategy, to face up to all the problems caused by one mega project after another. . . . The invitation is then to continue in the process of resistance, in particular to participate in the two national events which culminates in the process of the permanent tribunal that is the indigenous hearing in the Sierra Nevada de Santa Marta and the final hearing in Bogota, where the legal opinion . . . of the international jury will be formed to evaluate all the cases filed against companies.

The prehearing in Cabo de Vela in the arid desert of the Guajira Peninsula[6] in June 2008 interrupted the mundane events of the daily lives of the village's inhabitants. Tourists have recently discovered the coastal area; its picturesque scenery, crystal blue water, and surrounding desert make it a relaxing paradise. The Wayúu, Colombia's largest indigenous group, mostly inhabit Cabo de la Vela. More than 100 people attended the prehearing, mostly from Cabo de Vela itself, with some Wayúu coming from different areas, as well as representatives from participating activist organizations (e.g., ONIC, the José Alvear Restrepo Lawyers' Collective, and labor unions) and local indigenous organizations (e.g., Wayúu Painwashi, Fuerza de Mujeres Wayúu [Wayúu Women's Force], and Asociación de Cabildos y Autoridades Indígenas Wayúu del Sur de La Guajira [Association of Wayúu Indigenous Councils and Authorities in the South of Guajira]).

The prehearing was next to the crystal Caribbean sea in a space normally used as a restaurant; it was a hut constructed of yotojoro cactus wood (the inner core of the yosú cactus), which is widely used in local construction. Three days had been set aside for participants to recall and narrate histories of their community's engagement with the multinationals. Taking as its subtitle ONIC's themes of *denuncia* and *visibilidad* (denunciation, visibility), it was concerned with collecting details of the area's experience with resource exploitation. The meeting began with attendees listening to the different organizations, which presented themselves and informed the participants about the tribunal, legal changes, and any political or other developments within their organizations. Then attendees, mostly residents of the village, took the floor to contribute stories in Spanish or in *Wayuunaiki* (the Wayúu language, which was then translated into Spanish), presenting their accounts to the other participants who now sat on plastic chairs on the beach. Over the microphone speakers described the wind farm project; tourist hotel projects launched by the government; the militarization of the region; and the health and ecosystem implications of the mines of the coal producer Cerrejón, a multinational corporation[7] with the largest open-pit mines in the world, sited on Wayúu territory.

One participant, a representative of the Wayúu regional organization, offered a historical overview of the area's militarization, adding that the conflict had cost many Wayúu their lives. His account suggested that the armed groups (paramilitary and state army) flowed into the area not so much as a consequence of struggles against guerrilla movements but as part of a push to appropriate land and natural resources. This speaker portrayed multinationals as pursuing social and political control strategies, and he saw various interests as having a hand in the displacement of Wayúu communities. In particular, communities were forced to resettle due to the expansion of the mine. This had happened over the course of a number of incidents, many of which were recalled at the meeting through the calling-out of a personal or place name. One Wayúu woman brought up the Bahía Portete massacre. In that case, a paramilitary group killed six people (four of them women), and two women were still unaccounted for (Grupo de Memoria Histórica 2010: 16). In consequence, some 500 Wayúu were forced to leave this area, an area that is also a private port that connects to Cerrejón via train and which is the disembarkation point of the mine's coal. The belief was that the women were attacked due to the plan to enlarge the port, a proposal opposed by the Wayúu living there. The community representative further suggested that the women were targeted intentionally because they were known spokespersons in this matrilineal society.

Another participant who belonged to Sincracarbón, the Cerrejón labor union, spoke of the working conditions in the mine, describing many workers' health problems caused by the coal dust. His testimony suggested that very few Wayúu worked for the company, and if they did, it was mostly as cleaners rather than in any technical roles. One woman in the audience said after his presentation, "So much for their promise of benefitting the community," which drew nods and also expressions of relief that only a few people were actually working in the mine. The suggestion was also made that the few indigenous people who did work for the mining company were motivated by economic necessity, given the scarcity of pastoral lands.

One participant also complained that there were no longer any fish because the government had allowed commercial fishing off the coast. Another participant reflected:

> When Cerrejón came, I was a child, my father was a fisherman, and our area was rich in animals and fishing. We were happy. But when the company arrived, my family sank into extreme poverty. We don't even have traditional housing. We live from the recycling of Cerrejón . . . with the things the company throws away. We make our homes [from recycled materials] . . . now you can't get yotojoro anymore, as they are all inside the mining zone. . . . The only work to be found for the Wayúu in Media Luna is collecting coal from under the docks. . . . Cerrejón has not come up with any sustainable solutions for communities. . . . Cerrejón is a bad neighbor![8]

More individuals from the villages came forward to share their own accounts of their dealings with Cerrejón in their daily lives. There was a moment of uneasiness on the first day when a man from the local army battalion came forward and sought to address the audience, but the participants sent him away on the grounds that he was probably a spy and informant. The soldier's knowledge and whatever insights he may have had were not welcome. By contrast, in the final hearing in Bogotá, organizers called on accused parties to attend, an offer that was rejected because these parties generally commented that the court lacked juridical competence (Dictámen Final Audiencia 2008: 4).

The other prehearing took place in the auditorium of the public library of Julio Pérez Ferrero in the city of Cúcuta, a city close to the border with Venezuela in the North Santander department. One of the few historic venues in the town, the library frequently holds cultural events. Cúcuta is a bustling border city with a thriving street market. The prehearing took place in the city rather than on Barí community territory, due both to easier access and safety concerns for participants gathering to discuss oil and mining on Barí land. This prehearing was convened with the participation of indigenous associations—those of the Motilón Barí communities (ASOCBARÍ [Motilón Barí Community Association of Colombia]) and ONIC, which called the hearing to consider the exploitation of oil and coal on Barí land. Human rights organizations and national, departmental, and municipal state authorities were invited to attend the session. The organizations in particular sent out an invitation to Barí communities living across state lines in Venezuela, and to U'wa communities, who are also settled in this region and who themselves have experienced decades of engagement with transnational companies on their land. The prehearing was given the subtitle *Inchiyi itan bayt satchridry* (We will speak up for our land). The auditorium was packed with over 150 people.

The event opened in the morning with a Barí singing performance, accompanied by an introduction to Barí culture delivered to the audience in a PowerPoint presentation. Next, all of the audience members introduced themselves. Each stated whether they were representatives of an NGO or of a state agency, such as the *defensoria del pueblo* (the government ombudsman), and in contrast to the previous event, even the state army was invited to attend. As with the Guajira event, the session proceeded to outline the history and anticipated end of the tribunal process, with emphasis placed on constituting a symbolic form of justice and an alternative to formal state processes. Arias, who was again present, spoke about the role of ONIC in convening tribunal prehearings, describing the session as a means of endorsing senses of history, rights, and justice held by those of the "comunidades de base" (base communities). As one Barí indigenous leader remarked:

> The Barí case is very concrete. . . . I know that it's in the hands of judges from
> different parts of the world. . . . They will get to know this [case]. We are going

to deliver documents, we will provide evidence, so that they can say that it's happening.

On the second day, Barí members and leaders gave testimony (spoken in Barí and translated into Spanish) on the continuing threats of open-cut coal mining (according to the tribunal documents, eight companies petitioned to mine coal in this area). Further testimonies recounted the historical trajectory of oil exploration activities on their land. Leaders told the audience that they have been subject to "oil exploitation colonization" since the first granting of a concession for their land in 1905, a concession that has yet to be taken up. One leader described the impact of aerial fumigation on Barí land. Aerial fumigation is a form of illicit crop eradication in Colombia, a strategy pushed by the Colombian government and backed by the U.S. government. Fumigation continues to serve to "encourage . . . drug cultivation and processing in remote areas that are relatively pristine, such as national parks and undeveloped forest areas . . ." (Marsh 2004, 31), such as in the Motilón-Barí National Park and the Motilón reserves, both Barí land, according to the Colombian government ombudsman. The practice of fumigation resulted in the cultivation of coca in the park and reserves. Fumigation practices ultimately cause the displacement of indigenous communities because of environmental damage to their lands, destroying their livelihoods, causing health concerns, and impacts due to the influx of coca farmers and drug traffickers on their land (Marsh 2004). A closely related concern aired at the prehearing was the militarization of Barí territories, with paramilitary, guerrilla, and state armies present in the area. Barí leaders and members at the prehearing argued that the violations committed by these groups included restricting their "ability to exercise their cultural practices"; their "right to autonomy"; their "right to use their own land" (a right made impossible by military activities); and their "inherent right to life and physical integrity," which was threatened by armed groups attacking Barí and others who were defending their own lands. The indigenous leaders insisted that the government was under an obligation to end these many militarized practices on Barí land, and to thereby uphold Barí human and indigenous rights.

The prehearings worked to collect people's pronouncements and individual or collective stories together; as events, they produced knowledge intersubjectively by facilitating the exchange of narratives. These sessions generated concrete knowledge in the form of notes and a *memoria* (memorandum) produced at the end of each event. At the Cabo de Vela event, for example, elders of the region were invited by ONIC to sit together and author a document to *denunciar la situación en Cabo de Vela* (denounce the situation in Cabo de Vela). The elders' text should be understood not only as a *memoria* but also as the basis for a legal deposition backed morally by these figures' authority. When taken up into the national and international arena of the PPT project, the very particularity of this local knowledge gathered in these prehearings lent the tribunal process as a whole a feeling of great moral force. It is worthwhile, therefore, to trace in greater detail the circuits in which knowledge moves in these hearings.

As referred to previously, these processes of knowledge-making are similar to that of truth commissions and the roles of testimony-giving in transitional societies. Ross (2003) argues it is a process "that rests on narrating specific kinds of experience [that] renders the individual scrutable in terms of that experience as translated into various public domains" (333). The tribunal's work of producing and recording spoken and written notes follows conventions in which individuals vocalize their experience, thus giving it a public voice (326). Tribunal hearings disseminate people's ways of knowing selectively, caring less to record, per se, than to appropriate collective social practices such as storytelling, sharing experiences, or passing on expertise. Most attendees treat the hearings as an open space in which members of the community can narrate to, and ask questions of, their peers and leaders. In particular, knowledge flows from community levels to regional representatives of indigenous, trade union, Afro-Colombian, or human rights organizations who inform themselves about a variety of separate but thematically connected cases. This level of storytelling and of sharing a "justice discourse" necessarily begins in individuals' communication of their own stories and experiences. A process like the tribunal "offers a way for the subjective to become social," as Ross (2003: 332) describes. In this vein, tribunal processes release the most local and personal forms of knowledge from their moorings. Narratives then become an artifact and, more specifically, a commodity (see Colvin 2002: 5), as value becomes attached to its particularity and moral force as local knowledge. This lends an interesting twist to Polanyi's (1944) term "commodity fiction," as here, knowledge turns into a fictitious commodity capable of creating and reproducing a network of social relations around the (legal and moral) acknowledgment of wrongdoing (Jessop 2007; Johnson and Lundvall 2003; Whitt 2009).

While knowledge is produced through these practices, knowledge is not only what comes to the table—what participants offer up for sharing—but it must be understood as itself "a product of appropriation" or the result of "a political act" (Lambek 1990: 24). Only specific kinds of knowledge are made visible: the kind that will serve certain purposes. Hearings are thus a site of knowledge recall, production, and negotiation (which, as we have seen in the case of the representative from the local army battalion, includes rejection). They comprise a "gathering of knowledge for social . . . [political and legal] use" (Strathern 2000: 284). Certain stories are selected for endorsement in this negotiated production of knowledge, which are then channeled, made accessible, and standardized, to be finally framed in terms of legal prerogatives.

In the PPT final ruling, the participants' collected experiences and narratives, which amounted to more than 40 pages, were turned into *hechos probados* (proven facts) and categorized into four sections of violations: civil and political rights; economic, social, and cultural rights; the right to environment; and the collective rights of indigenous peoples. These collected facts cite (sometimes in very specific terms) events recounted at the hearings. From the two prehearings at issue here, the Bahía Portete massacre (listed under the civil and political rights section) is given a prominent place in the subsection dealing with the rights of women. The section dealing with economic, social, and cultural rights claims that the owner of Cerrejón appointed an army battalion commander to take charge of the mine's security.[9] The way in which people's testimonies are transformed into facts for the PPT is not in the form of unmediated transcription but through an editing process, which generalizes them and arranges them together with similar cases. Thus, in the subsection dealing with the right of communities to collective ownership of land (under the section about collective rights of indigenous peoples), we read of the militarization of various regions, including La Guajira, a process associated with the presence of multinationals. The ruling reads like a legal document, citing articles from various human rights documents and decisions of the Colombian and other international courts. It is also scattered with numbers and percentages, as these underline a narrative of establishing "the truth" of the wrongdoings of multinationals in Colombia. However, important as it is to first grasp how the tribunal process is, in fact, a form of "truth production" (see Wilson 2001), what I want to highlight is the importance of these truth-claims for the PPT's political legitimacy.

LEGITIMACY IN THE MAKING

The PPT is an institution and conglomerate of organizations working with a broad common aim of highlighting multinationals' wrongdoing. The process is collaborative in the sense of pulling together the testimony of a range of local communities and NGOs. In enfolding participants in its process, the tribunal conscripts them to a language of (public) participation and justice to which they are all taken to consent. At the same time, the process rests on a plural sociopolitical setting in which the meanings of justice and legitimacy vary according to the identities of interlocutors (ranging from individuals, to indigenous leaders, to regional organizational representatives, to international NGO representatives) and according to their specific interactions. A "productive confusion" (Tsing 2005: 247) characterizes the tribunal processes in that different participating individuals and organizations, from trade unions to indigenous and Afro-Colombian movements, each have their own agendas upon which they take part. Liu (2006: 76–77) notes that social actions draw on "multiple sources of legitimacy," and this is certainly the case here, as the meaning of the tribunal is being continually refashioned by its leaders and organizations to mirror their own requirements and desires. This is evident in the way each organization, in designating certain cases for the attention of the PPT, aims to push its own agenda forward. ONIC, for instance, wants to concentrate on the various threats that indigenous communities are facing or, in their terms, as noted in its brochure on the PPT, "the imminent danger of physical and cultural extinction faced by some indigenous communities" (ONIC 2008), choosing examples from different regions to convey the seriousness and breadth of the threat.

These diverse and contesting narratives are also tangled up in the processes of producing legitimacy in which the various organizations are locally enmeshed. Most of the organizers see that a lack of denunciation of wrongs at a community or local level would undermine the (moral) force (and legitimacy) of the case made in any wider arena by umbrella groups. They actively look for support for their endeavors and for an affirmation of their legitimacy in representing communities from the tribunal. Arias, as representative of ONIC, explained to the audiences in Cúcuta and Cabo de Vela how the PPT and ONIC were set up to present a broad front. Informing the Wayúu and Barí communities about ONIC's new plans, Arias made the following assertions at the Cabo de Vela meeting:

> For the national indigenous organization in Colombia, it is very important. . . .
> We have always emphasized generating this kind of space, [being on] a stage with
> the *comunidades de base*, with my people in communities, with men, with women
> who every day face many difficulties in indigenous territories . . . the indigenous
> tribunal precisely responds a little to this situation.

Through this statement, Arias envisioned a broad-scale collective agency orchestrated by ONIC. He reached out to individual members of the indigenous communities who presented themselves as the marginalized and dispossessed, and thus as differently positioned and differently entitled subjects (see Aparicio and Blaser 2008: 81). Arias thus positions ONIC as an interlocutor between the grassroots indigenous communities and the international players, here exemplified by the PPT's international NGOs backers. His statement can also be seen against the backdrop of a broader political conception of ONIC's role in general. In fact,

ONIC has been criticized by local bodies as being out of touch with many communities and unconnected to their "history and their own authority structures" (M. Jackson 2002: 102). The question of to what extent and on what basis ONIC can represent indigenous peoples in Colombia became more significant after the 1991 Constitution bestowed significant rights of legal autonomy on "local indigenous authorities" (M. Jackson 2002).[10] In this respect, a leader of the Wayúu community emphasized the value of working with ONIC and other grassroots NGOs at the meeting in Cabo de Vela, speaking after the ONIC representatives. To this delegate, the local community's participation in the tribunal processes ensured they were heard by national or international organizations.

The action of representing a community's stories imparts a certain legitimacy: it constructs a legal testimony or object. The umbrella organization's analyses were forged in this social context, or rather made informed or relative, by the tangible moral authority of narratives, shaped by the experience of subjects telling their stories (Casas-Cortés, Osterweil, and Powell 2008: 31). The collecting of stories plays into each umbrella organization's own legitimacy production, as already noted for ONIC, but it also serves as a form of knowledge exchange, which likewise feeds the process of legitimacy production of these umbrella organizations. Umbrella organizations in turn use the tribunal process to tell community members about recent legal or political changes. For example, a lawyer from the José Alvear Restrepo Lawyers' Collective—the Colombian non-governmental human rights organization mentioned earlier—informed the community at Cabo de Vela of the 2001 Codex on mines; another speaker gave a historical overview of the digging of coal in Latin America; and ONIC representatives used the tribunals to speak about their events and future plans to advocate the cause of indigenous peoples in Colombia. In other words, knowledge is being exchanged, and serves different purposes in each of the contexts where it has been received; yet, only a certain kind of knowledge is being appropriated here. Upon this analysis, it becomes clear that in making knowledge and circulating discourse, the tribunal both displays and produces power relations, while at the same time enables social relations to be forged at these events.

MAKING THE DISPOSSESSED, OR THE AGENCY OF THE KNOWERS

It is worthwhile at this point to consider how the tribunal both represents (in the quasi-legal sense) and produces (in the epistemological sense) the social category of the "dispossessed." The tribunal process, generally, brings together and constitutes evidence and authority from multiple sources, yet it does not showcase any single particular subjectivity. Instead, it acts as a forum for the sharing, the revision, and, occasionally, the amendment of different experiences, epistemologies, and ontologies as voiced by the different persons airing their claims. My ethnographic research indicates that the tribunal process thus acts to articulate distinctly placed and entitled subjectivities (see also Aparicio and Blaser 2008: 81). As noted earlier, the PPT—which sees itself as a "people's courts for the dispossessed . . . for marginalized voices" (Klinghoffer and Klinghoffer 2002: 164)—not only epitomizes but also crafts categories of the dispossessed as the groups that (in the view of the organizers) need to be represented and perhaps to be subjoined to a larger conception of those people deprived of their rights. As Sökefeld (1999) suggests, in Foucauldian terms, what we witness here is that the subject is not simply a source of knowledge but is "itself a product or effect of networks of power and discourse" (417). By the linking of the individual to a group, a legal and/or political subject has been created and represented.

Stories and narratives can be used to take apart and reconfigure social relations. It is in this way that knowledge-making practices produce new subjects, subjects who may in turn have the power to speak and make new knowledge themselves, as seen through the case of the prehearings and hearings of the PPT process. By remolding subjectivities, the tribunal processes demonstrate activism's dynamic nature, as its hearings act to strengthen the legitimacy of those looking to bolster their own stories by conjoining them with others' experiences and with broader senses of human rights violation, or violation more generally. Individuals and groups push up against the narratives and authority of the tribunal, even as the tribunal derives its authority from their participation. In these interactions and exchanges, a new collective subjectivity is continually fashioned through the language of justice. Those people with the knowledge to contest corporate wrongdoing are not merely the agents of communities, but they also become dynamic actors with their own capital in the form of narrative, symbolic, and legal expertise, each drawing on the fund of pain and outrage that legitimates them. As experiences are negotiated and redirected in the interactions with others, prehearings and hearings work to open up spaces that allow for the expression of the agency of the participants, an agency that hinges on the knowledge they bring to meetings. The tribunal's appropriation of certain kinds of the knowledge so articulated is thus also an act of agency, as participants leverage their subjectivity into a form of hopeful social effectiveness: the hope of making multinational companies socially accountable. By recounting their experiences of the impact of multinational companies on their worlds, subjects share their knowledge through verbal disclosure, and by doing so seek justice.

"JUSTICIA AÚN NO LLEGA!"[11] (JUSTICE YET TO COME)

This chapter explains how the prehearings set out the terms of a political discourse that insists on the need to call to account multinationals' impunity in their dealings with specific communities. The prehearings serve as a forum in which specific communities can assert their views on both the impact of the coal mine Cerrejón in the Guajira Peninsula and of oil drilling installations in North Santander on their environment, livelihood, health, and broader well-being, especially given that surrounding areas have become militarized as a result of their presence.

The PPT aims to invoke the authority of the law to reassert the rights of peoples who have become dispossessed. Crucially, this authority is being underwritten by the articulation of subjective knowledge and collective experience through the mechanism of the tribunal process. The moral authority of the PPT verdict itself emerges from this leaning on the subjective knowledge and experience of those negatively impacted by the transnational companies.

Knowledge as a socially produced performance in these various hearings is itself an articulation of the different individuals' and groups' participations in the collection of their stories—the stories of the dispossessed. The category of the dispossessed becomes attached to particular persons as a new legal subjectivity is created through the formalized collection of their testimonies. A discursive construction of social justice, based on and illustrated by certain kinds of knowledge, renders the stories of the community legally meaningful. Taking part in the hearings can thus be seen as a means through which individuals and groups craft and claim legal subjectivity and obtain agency, an agency they hope will be manifested in the form of a justice about to come.

A reading of the prehearings as knowledge-producing activities is necessarily complex, as the hearings span multiple sites of the production and in turn circulate various forms of knowledge showcasing multiple sources of legitimacy. In collecting and exchanging many kinds of knowledge—in the form of stories, ideas, and kinds of expertise—the meetings are a source of legitimation for organizations affiliated with the PPT process. The tribunal as the nexus of multiple experiences and hopes illuminates the interests at stake for the organizations as they intersect with one another. It is a nexus where some of the complex stories and local debates converge and can thus be formed into a constellation of certain kinds of usefully edited—that is, objectifiable—knowledge. Once objectified as valid, this knowledge can then be endlessly circulated, exchanged, and appropriated according to any acting person's or group's agenda.

This process of objectification—of making certain kinds of knowledge visible as useful knowledge—requires the translation of abstract political visions into on-the-ground actions. The tribunal process enables such translations: in producing alliances, it constitutes a political space that may be generative of new social imaginaries or utopian visions. Any vision of a (just) society, as Gledhill (2004) explains, and with which I concur, "need[s] to translate utopias into some kind of viable politics" (343). The prehearings I have analyzed here try to do just this. They facilitate the production of narratives that not only value the present and project hope for the future, but once recalled, can be connected to a legal process that the participants hope will, in turn, produce social change. At the very least, testimony is fashioned to inform the final verdict in Bogotá, where a proclamation about social justice is crafted.

While leaders clearly are using the tribunal process to shape their own social visions, tribunal participants, in articulating their own versions of utopian discourse, are also empowered by the political space that is opened up, a space in which they attempt to drive through certain transformations (Postero 2007: 19). At the end of the process a verdict arises through which legitimacy, knowledge, and differing senses of justice are channeled. As such, we can see how the PPT and its preliminary hearings can work to carve out new sources of legitimacy, accountability, and sociality based on the articulation and display of knowledge identified as useful, even as they accept that justice is something still "yet to come."

NOTES

1. ONIC, or Organización Nacional Indígena de Colombia (National Indigenous Organization of Colombia), founded in 1982, is one of the two national organizations in Colombia. The other is AICO (Indigenous Authorities of Colombia).
2. These knowledges, as Casas-Cortés, Osterweil, and Powell (2008: 21) depict, can have the shape "of stories, ideas, narratives, and ideologies," while they may also draw on expertise and theoretical acumen in their political considerations and critical takes on certain contexts. Both the generation of knowledge and its adaptation or local enactment stand as forms of "knowledge-practice," as Casas-Cortés, Osterweil, and Powell suggest. All these practices have their own authors and rest on their own agencies, and all are lively in disseminating their own experiences and knowledge.
3. PPT rulings are based on international law and legal precedent, and take into account the jurisdiction of the International Criminal Court. The PPT further draws on the Universal Declaration for the Rights of Peoples (or the Algiers Declaration), adopted in 1976 by a group of non-governmental actors, including union representatives, NGO participants, scholars, and representatives of liberation movements (Cassese 1998: 277). Originating from a conference organized by the Lelio and Lisli Basso Foundation in Algiers in the 1970s, it is again not legally binding, although it could well be seen as the statute of the PPT. This declaration recognizes the rights of all peoples—that is, in terms of political and economic rights and political self-determination (Leary 1979: 207).
4. Henrard (2000) argues that although the Algiers Declaration does not have legal force as such, "its de facto authority cannot be dismissed" (204). Hence, according to Henrard,

the declaration has been seen as a "potential source of inspiration" (204) for rights group, which worked on minority rights. It was the use of the term "peoples" and the elaborated meaning of the right to self-determination of the peoples in the declaration that drew the attention of rights groups.

5. The accounts in this chapter are from the author's attendance at the prehearings in 2008 and interviews with members of the different organizations in 2008 and 2009.

6. The Guajira Peninsula in Colombia's northeast is a region shared with Venezuela, although the major portion of it is in Colombia.

7. The company is currently owned as a joint venture by the mining firms BHP Billiton (from Australia), Anglo American (from South Africa), and Xstrata (from Switzerland).

8. This has been recorded and transcribed by the PPT team of ONIC and published under the heading "El Cerrejón es un mal vecino" (2008).

9. The Cerrejón case also was included in the Madrid Judgment of the Permanent Peoples' Tribunal, a similar but independent investigation and analysis of the operations of European companies in Latin America (Transnational Institute 2010: 12).

10. ONIC is not the only national indigenous organization; there is also AICO although ONIC has more regional organizations affiliated with it. Most indigenous communities are represented by a major organization, with most regional groupings branching to ONIC.

11. This quote is from a PPT leader who spoke at the Guajira meeting.

WORKS CITED

Aparicio, Juan Ricardo, and Mario Blaser. 2008. "The 'Lettered City' and the Insurrection of Subjugated Knowledges in Latin America." *Anthropological Quarterly* 81 (1): 59–94.

Brysk, Alison. 2000. *From Tribal Village to Global Village: Indian Rights and International Relations in Latin America*. Stanford, CA: Stanford University Press.

Casas-Cortés, María Isabel, Michal Osterweil, and Dana E. Powell. 2008. "Blurring Boundaries: Recognizing Knowledge-Practices in the Study of Social Movements." *Anthropological Quarterly* 81 (1): 17–58.

Cassese, Antonio. 1998. *Self-Determination of Peoples: A Legal Reappraisal*. Cambridge: Cambridge University Press.

Colvin, Christopher. 2002. "Limiting Memory: The Roots and Routes of Storytelling in Post-Apartheid, Post-TRC South Africa." In *Telling Wounds: Narrative, Memory and Trauma: Working through the South African Armed Conflicts of the Twentieth Century*, edited by Chris van der Merwe and Rolf Wolfswinkel, 234–244. Stellenbosch, South Africa: Van Schaik Content Solutions.

Coombe, Rosemary J. 2005. "Protecting Traditional Environmental Knowledge and New Social Movements in the Americas: Intellectual Property, Human Right, or Claims to an Alternative Form of Sustainable Development." *Florida Journal of International Law* 17 (1): 115–135.

Coxshall, Wendy. 2005. "From the Peruvian Reconciliation Commission to Ethnography. Narrative, Relatedness, and Silence." *PoLAR: Political and Legal Anthropology Review* 28 (2): 203–222.

Dictámen Final Audiencia Tribunal Permanente de los Pueblos. 2008. http://www.colec tivodeabogados.org/DICTAMEN-FINAL-AUDIENCIA-TRIBUNAL.

"El cerrejón es un mal vecino." 2008. http://www.colectivodeabogados.org/EL-CERREJON -ES-UN-MAL-VECINO-AQUI.

Escobar, Arturo. 1992. "Culture, Practice and Politics: Anthropology and the Study of Social Movements." *Critique of Anthropology* 12 (4): 395–432.

———. 2004. "Development, Violence and the New Imperial Order." *Development* 47 (1): 15–21.

Falk, Richard A. 2011. "Kuala Lumpur War Crimes Tribunal: Bush and Blair Guilty." http:// richardfalk.wordpress.com/2011/11/29/kuala-lumpur-war-crimes-tribunal-bush-and -blair-guilty/.

Final Session of Permanent Peoples' Tribunal in Bogota. 2008. http://lascartasmarcadas .blogspot.co.uk/2008/07/final-session-of-permanent-peoples.html.

Fisher, Edward F. 2009. *Indigenous Peoples, Civil Society, and the Neo-Liberal State in Latin America.* New York: Berghahn.

Fondazione Lelio e Lisli Basso-Issoco. n.d. "Introduction." http://www.internazionalelelio basso.it/?page_id=207&lang=en.

Foucault, Michel. 1980. *Power/Knowledge—Selected Interviews and Other Writings: 1972– 1977.* New York: Harvester Wheatsheaf.

Gill, Lesley. 2007. "'Right There with You': Coca-Cola, Labor Restructuring and Political Violence in Colombia." *Critique of Anthropology* 27 (3): 235–260.

———. 2009. "The Parastate in Colombia: Political Violence and the Restructuring of Barrancabermeja." *Anthropologica* 51 (2): 313–325.

Gledhill, John. 1999. "Official Masks and Shadow Powers: Towards an Anthropology of the Dark Side of the State." *Urban Anthropology and Studies of Cultural Systems and World Economy* 28 (3–4): 199–251.

———. 2004. "Neoliberalism." In *A Companion to the Anthropology of Politics,* edited by David Nugent and Joan Vincent, 332–348. Malden, MA: Blackwell.

Grupo de Memoria Histórica. 2010. *La masacre de Bahía Portete: Mujeres Wayúu en la mira.* Bogotá: Taurus.

Henrard, Kristin. 2000. *Devising an Adequate System of Minority Protection: Individual Human Rights, Minority Rights and the Right to Self-Determination.* The Hague: Martinus Nijhoff.

Jackson, Jean E. 2002. "Contested Discourses of Authority in Colombian National Indigenous Politics: The 1996 Summer Takeovers." In *Indigenous Movements, Self-Representation and the State in Latin America,* edited by Karen B. Warren and Jean E. Jackson, 81–122. Austin: University of Texas Press.

Jackson, Michael. 2002. *The Politics of Storytelling: Violence, Transgression and Intersubjectivity.* Copenhagen: University of Copenhagen, Museum Tuscalanum Press.

Jessop, Bob. 2007. "Knowledge as a Fictitious Commodity: Insights and Limits of a Polanyian Perspective." In *Reading Karl Polanyi for the Twenty-First Century: Market Economy as Political Project,* edited by Ayse Buğra and Kaan Agartan, 115–134. Basingstoke, UK: Palgrave.

Johnson, Björn, and Bengt-Åke Lundvall. 2003. "Promoting Innovation Systems as a Response to the Globalizing Learning Economy." In *Systems of Innovation and Development: Evidence from Brazil,* edited by José E. Cassiolato, Helena M. M. Lastres, and Maria Lucia Maciel, 141–184. Cheltenham, UK: Edward Elgar.

Keen, Benjamin, and Keith A. Haynes. 2012. *A History of Latin America.* Vol. 2: *Independence to the Present.* Boston: Wadsworth, Cengage Learning.

Klinghoffer, Arthur J., and Judith A. Klinghoffer. 2002. *International Citizens' Tribunals: Mobilizing Public Opinion to Advance Human Rights.* New York: Palgrave.

Lambek, Michael. 1990. "Certain Knowledge, Contestable Authority: Power and Practice on the Islamic Periphery." *American Ethnologist* 17 (1): 23–40.

Leary, Virginia. 1979. "A New Role for Non-Governmental Organizations in Human Rights: A Case Study of Non-Governmental Participation in the Development of International Norms of Torture." In *UN Law Fundamental Rights: Two Topics in International Law*, edited by Antonio Cassese, 197–210. Alphen aan den Rijn, Netherlands: Sijthoff & Noordhoff.

Liu, Sida. 2006. "Beyond Global Convergence: Conflicts of Legitimacy in a Chinese Lower Court." *Law and Social Inquiry* 31(1): 75–106.

Marsh, Betsy. 2004. *Going to Extremes: The U.S.-Funded Aerial Eradication Program in Colombia*. Washington, DC: Latin America Working Group Education Fund.

ONIC. 2008. *Convocatoria al Tribunal Permanente de los Pueblos*. Brochure.

Paley, Dawn. 2008. "Justice in Colombia? The Permanent Peoples' Tribunal Reads Its Verdict." http://www.dominionpaper.ca/articles/2002.

Polanyi, Karl. 1944. *The Great Transformation*. New York: Rinehart.

Postero, Nancy. 2005. "Indigenous Responses to Neoliberalism." *PoLAR: Political and Legal Anthropology Review* 28 (1): 73–92.

———. 2007. "Andean Utopias in Evo Morales's Bolivia." *Latin American and Caribbean Ethnic Studies* 2 (1): 1–28.

Rodríguez-Garavito, César A., and Luis Carlos Arenas. 2005. "Indigenous Rights, Transnational Activism, and Legal Mobilization: The Struggle of the U'wa People in Colombia." In *Law and Globalization from Below: Towards a Cosmopolitan Legality*, edited by Boaventura de Sousa Santos and César A. Rodríguez-Garavito, 241–266. New York: Cambridge University Press.

Ross, Fiona. 2003. "On Having Voice and Being Heard: Some After-Effects of Testifying before the South African Truth and Reconciliation Commission." *Anthropological Theory* 3 (3): 325–341.

Santos, Boaventura de Sousa. 2005. "The Future of the World Social Forum: The Work of Translation." *Development* 48 (2): 15–22.

Sawyer, Suzana. 2004. *Crude Chronicles: Indigenous Politics, Multinational Oil, and Neoliberalism in Ecuador*. Durham, NC: Duke University Press.

Shivji, Issa G. 1996. "Constructing a New Rights Regime: Promises, Problems and Prospects." *UTAFITI: Journal of Arts and Social Sciences*, n.s., 3 (1): 1–46.

Sökefeld, Martin. 1999. "Debating Self, Identity, and Culture in Anthropology." *Current Anthropology* 40 (4): 417–448.

Strathern, Marilyn. 2000. *Audit Cultures: Anthropological Studies in Accountability, Ethics and the Academy*. New York: Routledge.

Theidon, Kimberly. 2012. *Intimate Enemies: Violence and Reconciliation in Peru*. Philadelphia: University of Pennsylvania Press.

Transnational Institute. 2010. "Permanent Peoples' Tribunal. The European Union and Transnational Corporations in Latin America: Policies, Instruments and Actors Complicit in Violations of the Peoples' Rights." http://www.enlazandoalternativas.org/IMG/pdf/TPP-verdict.pdf.

Tsing, Anna Lowenhaupt. 2005. *Friction: An Ethnography of Global Connection*. Princeton, NJ: Princeton University Press.

Warren, Kay. 1998. *Indigenous Movements and Their Critics: Pan-Maya Activism in Guatemala*. Princeton, NJ: Princeton University Press.

Whitt, Laurelyn. 2009. *Science, Colonialism, and Indigenous Peoples: The Cultural Politics of Law and Knowledge*. New York: Cambridge University Press.

Wilson, Richard. 2001. *The Politics of Truth and Reconciliation in South Africa: Legitimizing the Post-Apartheid State*. Cambridge: Cambridge University Press.

Winter, Franka. 2009. "Giving Voice to the Voiceless? Second Thoughts on Testimony in Transitional Justice." *A Contracorriente* 6 (3): 90–107.

6 ON JUSTICE, INSECURITY, AND THE RIGHT TO THE CITY IN BRAZIL'S OLDEST METROPOLIS

Marta Magalhães Wallace

"Look here," said Aparecida on a rainy evening in April 2010, "this place is just not safe. Maybe if you only move by car, stay in the noble areas, maybe then, . . . but that is not security—that is a different kind of prison." A long pause ensued, followed by a disclaimer: "Don't get me wrong—I move about as much as I *have* to. I just know, most of the time, I am *not* safe." Aparecida's words were a response to my questions about a news article on "the epidemic of violence" that had taken over the city in recent years. The article, which had appeared in one of Salvador's leading newspapers on the eve of Salvador's anniversary, revolved around crime statistics. Aparecida's words echoed what I had been told repeatedly in the preceding four weeks—namely, that Salvador had become violent, insecure, even unpredictable, and this transformation meant, in turn, that things were changing in the way people related to the city and to one another. That change should be as clear to me as it was to most of the people I had come to know over the previous eight years, she said.

The 2014 *Mapa da Violência*, a government-sponsored annual report containing statistical information on violent crime in Brazil, places Salvador third among state capitals in total number of homicides in 2012 (Waiselfisz 2014).[1] The city comes just after São Paulo and one place ahead of Rio de Janeiro, but the number of homicides for the two larger metropolises is small by comparison: 1,752 and 1,372, respectively. In the same period, Salvador, which is four times smaller than the former and half the size of Rio, counted 1,644 homicides. The report was greeted with disappointment by both state and municipal authorities. Since June 2011, special military police units have been deployed in some of the state's most violent areas, including Salvador and its periphery. The strategy, brought into effect by law number 2.357, is known as the Programa Pacto pela Vida (Pact for Life Program). Envisaged as a partnership between the state and its citizens, the pact has brought together a series of different institutional actors—including the Judiciary, the Legislative Assembly, the Public Prosecutor's Office, the Public

Defense Offices, and individual municipal administrations—in a joint effort to curb criminal violence across the state. The police units of Bahia's Pact for Life operate from Community Security Bases (Bases Comunitárias de Segurança) set up in several of Salvador's most violent neighborhoods. The police are expected to both conduct police work and manage public welfare. Their presence is meant to be preventive, aimed at helping the vulnerable population of the areas under tutelage feel safe so that citizens can publicly reaffirm their right to the city and gain access to crucial public services (http://www.pactopelavida.ba.gov.br). Nine such units, covering a total of 14 neighborhoods, were in place by 2013.

The Pact for Life was designed to address the general concern with (in)security and violent crime that has become a major issue in Salvador's public life. By 2010, the press had begun to describe the city as a place "sequestered by fear," where the population was so "terrorized by crime rates" that it no longer dared go out (Azevedo 2010). Bahia's Public Security Secretary publicly acknowledged that crime rates had increased 30 to 40 percent every year between 2002 and 2010 and showed no sign of abating (Azevedo 2010). That all this coincided with a period of significant economic growth[2] defied the logic of straightforward socioeconomic explanation. For many *soteropolitanos*[3] (residents of Salvador), it also defied the belief that the struggle for citizen rights and social justice, especially rights to the city, that many had engaged in since the late 1980s could succeed without a firmer approach to (in)security on the part of the state.

In contemporary Salvador, calls for greater security measures are increasingly framed in the idiom of rights. This has happened to the detriment of the kinds of demands for social justice that animated many of the citizen struggles of the past. In effect, the association between insecurity and violent crime, especially homicidal violence, seems to be stripping citizenship bare, as security is equated with survival, eliding ideas about the right to justice more broadly. The term *bare* does not sit easily next to citizenship. *Bare life* (Agamben 1998) is usually the life of those stripped of citizenship, who may be killed but not sacrificed, "a form of life that is beyond the reach of dignity and full humanity and thus not even a subject of benevolent power" (Blom Hansen and Steppuat 2005: 17). My intention is not to suggest that the expansion of security, understood as a technique of government, turns *all* citizens into bare life—human subjects reduced to a naked depoliticized state without official status and juridical rights (Lee 2010: 57). Formal citizenship is not in question here. Yet, while declarations of a state of emergency have seldom materialized, "the state of exception has gradually been replaced by an unprecedented generalization of the paradigm of security as the normal technique of government" (Agamben 2005: 14).

Initiatives like the Pact for Life evince this transformation, but they also pose challenges to arguments about the way security negates citizenship struggles. It may be tempting to view the transformation of Salvador's public space over the last two decades exclusively as an attack on the fundamental rights of its citizens, a refusal to expand substantive citizenship (Caldeira and Holston 1999) or a perversion of its social movements' calls for justice. Yet, careful consideration of what many of Salvador's residents say and do suggests otherwise. For many soteropolitanos, violence and insecurity have turned their city into a "foreign" place, a world fraught with danger that they no longer *know* or recognize. This is a context where a security framework increasingly determines the meaning of justice, where a desire for inclusion perversely takes on the form of a demand for intervention, discipline, and regulation on the part of institutions usually regarded with ambivalence, suspicion, or fear. In other words, it is a context where fear of violent crime, born of real events or not, has significantly reconfigured the way justice and rights to the city are conceived, demanded, and enacted.

The material I present here is based on a decade of engagement with Salvador, where I first carried out research as a graduate student between 2002 and 2003. That research did not start out to address security or justice. Rather, I was interested in studying the challenges posed by the conversion of Salvador's old colonial center into a UNESCO World Heritage Site, where once was situated a red-light district inhabited by a population that was often characterized as marginal. My aim was to examine the potential impact that the approval of the 2001 City Statute, which recognized the right to the city (Harvey 2008) as a collective right, might have on a project of urban renewal prompted by the desire to commodify heritage. In time, although I remained interested in what was happening in the old city center, I found myself venturing further afield—first to the neighborhoods adjacent to the center, which many of my middle- and upper-class acquaintances still regarded with suspicion, and eventually to parts of the periphery, where many of my interlocutors' family and friends lived. It was then that my conversations with mostly working-class soteropolitanos first became inflected by their profound disquiet about a perceived increase in violent crime. It was also then that I first began to think about security, or the lack thereof. Since that time, each return has foregrounded the concern with violence and security further. During a visit in 2010, talk of violence had become so pervasive that, on looking through my notes, I found every conversation eventually turned to it.

Doing justice to the register of my interlocutors' voices as they seek to make sense of the predicament that has befallen their city is not easy. The transformation of Salvador from a relatively safe urban milieu into a space fractured by insecurity and violence has not happened overnight. Neither can the process be traced to any single cause, although one can safely say that no small part has been played by its administration's neoliberal orientation (Collins 2008). My intention here is to capture the violence, insecurity, and sense of uncertainty that permeate Salvador's public life, seen first in terms of what they do to the city—or what people say they do to the city—and, second, in terms of how it changes its residents' mundane routines and intimate and ethical practices. The first section of this chapter looks more closely at how Salvador has been represented, both in crime statistics and by the media, as a landscape marked by violence and fear. As Jean and John Comaroff (2006) noted, contrary to common assertions on numbers' ability to abstract from visceral experience, in Salvador, "statistics [can] reduce a mass of faceless incidents, disturbing things that happened elsewhere, into the objects of first-person affect: fascination, revulsion, pain" (211). As they proliferate, crime statistics are treated as an integral part of the experience of violence, a source of anxiety and fear in themselves. This ties into the predominance of medical metaphors in describing the city's transformation. Violence becomes epidemic, evoking comparisons with dengue fever, which is spread by mosquitoes. The second section turns from the city's condition to the ethical lives of its citizens, whose right to lay a claim to human personhood was said to hinge on the cultivation of a concern for the common good. Human personhood, in this sense, became an unstable category that could be either consciously or unconsciously relinquished. This posed a series of moral dilemmas, including whether someone can regain human-ness once relinquished and, if so, whether someone who is not recognized as a full human person deserves "justice" or security. The third section moves away from violence, subjectivity, and everyday ethics to focus on the transformation of Salvador's old historic district into a heritage machine. It seeks to show that the strategies of security aimed at fencing off the center from undesirable soteropolitanos provided a blueprint for the kind of managerial approach to security that would later find expression in the Pacto pela Vida. The last section sets the Pacto pela Vida alongside calls for greater security on the part of Salvador's residents in an attempt to demonstrate that although their objectives may seem aligned, the relationship between the police and many soteropolitanos is still one of tension, mutual distrust, and vigilance. The chapter emphasizes how ideas about insecurity have come to modulate public discourse on justice and fundamental rights in Salvador, modulating the experiences and the values that underpin soteropolitanos' idea of a good life. In other words, how has the city's current predicament changed the ethical register of citizenship upon which the idea of a good life so often rests? Can we speak meaningfully about a right to security? Is the right to security compatible with a broader sense of justice, understood in terms not just of access to legal and juridical protection but of the right to social, political, and economic inclusion?

A DYSTOPIAN LANDSCAPE

In November 2013, the *New York Times* printed an article on Salvador with the title "Boom Town of 'Eternal Beauty' Faces Dark Side" (Romero 2013). In it, Salvador is introduced as a baroque gem perched over a stunning harbor, "where musicians enthrall audiences with high-octane performances." Its "industrial park, on the city's outskirts contains cutting-edge plants opened by Ford and other multinational corporations." It reports that the city is experiencing an economic boom, but the upturn has come with a boom of a different kind. Once known for its affable, peaceable nature, Salvador now induces "revolt" at the violence and impunity that seem to have taken over its streets.

This characterization takes a certain degree of poetic license, but in doing so, it captures the mood of many a resident of Salvador. "Revolt," "fear," even "terror" were all words my interlocutors used in describing the transformation *their* city had undergone over the last decade. And looking at the numbers, soteropolitanos are right in regarding the rise in homicidal violence in the city with unease. In 2011, Salvador had 62 homicides per 100,000 inhabitants, up from 21.3 just a decade earlier (Waiselfisz 2014). To most, this represented an incomprehensible increase. Despite government's protests that they had taken measures to address the problem, 2012 offered no respite. Instead, by the end of January, the military police had decreed a strike and withdrawn from the streets. During the strike, which lasted 11 days, there were 177 murders, mostly execution style—a 156 percent increase compared to the same period in 2011 (Frazão and Garcia 2012).

For many years now, Salvador's residents have described their beloved capital as a city in the throes of an epidemic of violence (Magalhães Wallace 2013). The revolt that the *Times* article speaks of is partly a result of complaints that nothing has been done to address the problem. Decrepit mansions turned drug dens surround the historic district, where crack cocaine is smoked in broad daylight, and in 2010, a young Brazilian tourist was killed by a stray bullet (Romero 2013). In 2013, the breakdown of security was such that beheaded bodies appeared by the side of the road to the airport (ibid.). And most of all, in the city's periphery, poor residents feel abandoned to their fate. Soteropolitanos often speak of feeling that their city is hanging dangerously close to the edge of the precipice. While many have retreated behind increasingly higher walls, an even greater number have had to "learn (to exist) in the city anew."

"Learning the city anew" offered no guarantees, but not doing so was not seen as an option. In one of my last visits, I had the opportunity to witness the remarkable paths travelled by several of my interlocutors in their attempts to "be smart" and "stay safe." I noticed several things at the time. First, the need to avoid certain areas at specific times often added a substantial amount of travel time to what would otherwise be a quick trip. Second, living in certain areas prevented all movement by foot or public transportation after a certain hour. This was especially clear in the upmarket districts. The informal curfew emptied much of the city, which felt haunted and fraught with hidden dangers. Third, privatized spaces like shopping malls and exclusive clubs were often full by comparison. Fourth, many of the spaces frequented by tourists, although public, are effectively enclosed under the watchful guard of military police. Fifth, poor popular districts and peripheral neighborhoods tend to be livelier than the empty streets in the noble quarters (*bairros nobres*), but even there, residents were adamant that public space felt "risky" and "unpredictable" in new ways.

What people called "being smart" required careful topographic work, an inexhaustible ability to map, on the spot, a series of alternate routes to any given point. Yet, the constant need to be mindful of one's every step was often so overwhelming as to paralyze. Although Aparecida, whose words I started with, insisted that she moved as much as she *had* to, in reality, she would simply not venture out after a certain hour at all unless someone picked her up from her small apartment just off Salvador's main bus station. This was not in keeping with her character. I have known Aparecida for over ten years, and she has always been a fiercely independent woman who must travel all over the city for her job. She was born in Liberdade, one of the city's largest districts, a densely populated low-income neighborhood where life was, in her words, "fun, but never easy." Yet, the fear and isolation she felt "taking over her life" at the time of my last visit was unbearable. Now in her forties, she was the youngest of several brothers and sisters. She had never been married and had almost always lived alone. Her family tended to treat her as an eccentric and leave her to her own devices. She had never minded. She worked very hard to maintain her independence, studying for more years than any of her siblings and working long hours for different institutions as a "cultural consultant." Because she worked freelance, her position was relatively precarious. She did not own a car, nor did she have much else to her name. Yet, she had always been resourceful. An extrovert by nature, her charm and wit had taken her far. When I first met Aparecida, she had been quick to warn me that she took great pride in knowing the city like no one else and on being known in turn. But things had changed so radically that she would not hear of my coming to her place by foot, on my own, after dark because, as she explained, her standing in the community would no longer protect me. After I left, Aparecida moved to a smaller apartment in another of Salvador's old neighborhoods on the edge of Salvador's historic district—a place that felt safer and less isolated than her former neighborhood.

Aparecida's story is not uncommon. At the time of my last visit, her fears had seemed out of character, but they were not unfounded. In just a few years, she had lost several friends to violence, some of it random, some related to drug use. There had been few arrests and even fewer prosecutions.[4] She thought things were out of control and unlikely to get better any time soon. And she was not alone in thinking that this was the case. Everyone I spoke with, from public sector employees, to informal workers and poor periphery residents, recognized the same symptoms. Everyone agreed that the problem was very serious, but there was less agreement as to what caused it or what could be done about it. Most noticeably, when speaking about violence, medical metaphors were dominant. The city was often said to be "gravely ill" or "fighting for its life." The lack of security was likened to a lack of doctors, or hospital beds, or even hospitals. Abandoned to its own devices, Salvador's residents took measures to avoid contagion, but there was only so much one could do. As Samuel, one of my closest acquaintances, who had recently bought his first car, put it, it was hard to accept that now even prosperity seemed fated to cause tragedy.[5] The increasingly common reports of road rage, when drivers "lost it" and simply ran over anyone "in their way," confirmed his view that no one was immune to the madness that had taken over the city.[6]

The association between violence, understood as a medical ailment, and the city's intractable road traffic came up repeatedly in conversations about security. I was often taken by surprise when people turned from complaints about corrupt city officials making a mockery of traffic management to discussions of the terror one might feel in a traffic jam. It was frightening to realize that only a windshield or window separated one's body and a stray bullet or that frustration with other drivers was enough to make "good people" turn their vehicles into deadly weapons. This kind of narrative pointed toward a peculiar configuration, where Salvador's residents seemed to say that their city's illness was making them ill as well, and not merely as victims of potential violence but as potential perpetrators. This, in turn, poses problems for thinking about citizenship and justice, as soteropolitanos struggled to cope with the dilemma of wanting a solution to a problem that many suspected they were already a part of.

This sense that the problem may be too disseminated for a quick fix was foreground in discussions over the increasing privatization of space. Many of my better-off acquaintances lacked the resources to move to a private condominium, which often resulted in public shaming of friends who did. Yet, in private, things were never as clear-cut. By contrast, my low-income acquaintances, many of whom scraped by with some difficulty, thought that private condominiums were a wonderful thing—if you were lucky enough to be able to afford to live in one. There was some irony in their tone, but the fortified enclaves that had cropped up all over the city did not seem to bother most people. Indeed, many shrugged off (my own) concerns about the pernicious effect of an increasing retreat behind walls on citizenship and public life. The "rich" had never cared about citizenship, I was told. A citizen, for the rich, was still primarily "a John Doe" (Holston 2008). Citizenship mattered for the poor, who struggled to open it up, to see their rights respected, to be able to say that they are "human persons" (*pessoa humana*), wholly deserving of empathy.

ON HUMAN PERSONS

I first heard people use the expression "human person" in 2002. Initially, it looked like a term of appreciation used mostly among friends. In time, the term begun to crop up in conversations about everyday stranger interactions marked by solidarity, generosity, and openness, as in "I didn't have enough for the fare, but the guy standing next to me paid it, because he was a *pessoa humana*." Applied to acquaintances or friends, the expression seemed first and foremost to index moral worth. They were not just a person but, emphatically, a "human person." By the same token, the term was used to interpellate and accuse others if someone felt unjustly treated, as in "Don't speak to me like that! I am a *pessoa humana*." Whenever the expression was used, there was a forcefulness about it. It became a compound—a human-person—and that lent the term a particular gravity. To say that one's status as a human person was not acknowledged was, in a certain sense, to complain about a specific form of ontological elision. The term *person* (*pessoa*), like the term *citizen* (*cidadão*), can also mean a "John Doe." And the word *human*, on its own, is a generic term for the species. Both can, in fact, be used to suggest "bare life." When brought together, however, they are qualitatively changed. A human person turns into a humane person, who one "knows" is capable of humane-ness. In other words, the human person is an ethical category, a person to whom one can extend kindness and treat with a culturally appropriate sense of justice. Here "justice" in terms of the treatment of human persons carries an embedded sense of social equality, of fair access to and distribution of public resources. Human personhood formulates the right to the city "in terms of the . . . ethical and performative registers of citizenship" (Holston 2011: 337).[7]

During my last visit, the term *pessoa humana* became an inevitable theme in conversations about violence. It was no longer simply a matter of people addressing one another as "human persons" or demanding the courtesy in return. Rather, people increasingly elaborated their replies to my questions about the problem of insecurity by splitting the terms. Violent criminals were not "human persons," I was told, and they most certainly did not treat their victims as such. In a sense, insecurity broke the expression in half, leaving bare life in its place. This was clearly articulated for me by Manu, a 50-year-old black man of humble origins, who had worked in the same popular canteen for his entire adult life and whom I had known for a number of years. I was sitting at a table overlooking a square close to the house I had stayed in a few years back. I was there with Aparecida, waiting for a mutual acquaintance to join us. It was early in the evening, but the canteen was relatively empty. Manu came over to greet us with a big smile. Turning to Aparecida, he asked if she had heard the news of his ex-wife's death. His tone was casual and matter-of-fact. Aparecida was not surprised. "Better," she replied. I asked Manu what had happened. "Crack," he replied. "It was terrible, it consumed her." I expressed my condolences. He looked puzzled. I should not, he said, because she had been gone long before she had died. He paused briefly before explaining that they had no longer been together because she had robbed him and tried to stab his mother. Her body had been found just up the road, but the important thing to remember was that, by the time of her death, he had become incapable of thinking of her as a *pessoa humana*. From where he stood, crack turned good *human persons* into "animals" (*que nem bicho*). They became violent and unpredictable, making it impossible for anyone to feel anything for them. They were destroying the city. In the end, justice had prevailed (*se fez justiça*), he concluded with a sigh.

As I would later find out, Manu's experience was not uncommon. Neither was his apparent detachment. Manu's words—she had become *que nem bicho* (like an animal) and thus met with justice—were reminiscent of the logic of sovereign violence that founds the political community (Agamben 1998). Yet, he did not "exclude" his former partner on the grounds that she had become less than a human person. That may very well have been so, but all that did was justify their estrangement. Instead, what led him to speak of her unfortunate demise as just was that "they were destroying the city," or, as he told me later, she had ceased to care for the good of the community. "Justice," in Portuguese, can simultaneously evoke the juridical order and a principle of fairness. Although she had broken the law, Manu's prevailing justice was about the latter. In other words, she had been meted out justice, which was individually tragic but collectively correct.

Implicit in Manu's reasoning is the idea that the right to the city requires careful ethical work on the part of all good people (*pessoas de bem*), and good people must act for the common good in making sure the city is safe for everyone, including themselves. This view would resurface several times over the course of my stay. For Arnaldo, who had been shot and seriously hurt during an armed robbery at his workplace, rights got in the way of security, and that had nearly killed him. For Irene, who lived just off one of the old city's main squares, the city needed police "willing to take control of justice," to make everyday life safe for people like her, who may not have much to their name but worked hard and fought for everyone's right to a better existence. It was not fair that she had to live in fear, she said. The most ambivalent of all my acquaintances was Samuel, whose view had always been that a just society breeds security, but he had recently had a reason to falter in his convictions. It had happened in a shop close to the city center, where he had stopped to buy groceries on his way home. He heard gunshots and quickly realized something was wrong. As quietly as possible, he made his way to an office at the back of the shop, where shop employees and a dozen other customers had also taken refuge. They stayed there until the police had found them, after exchanging fire with the robbers. He was shaken to the core, he said. He was not sure what had upset him the most—the panic he had felt creeping over as he realized what was happening or the sight of dead bodies, "just lying there." Unlike Manu, Samuel did not think justice had prevailed. Neither did he think that the robbers had relinquished their right to be treated as *human persons*. He was, nonetheless, of the opinion that more police officers were needed, a comprehensive security apparatus capable of acting to prevent the kind of critical event he had inadvertently walked into.

Samuel's ambivalence was partly an effect of his own life experience. On the one hand, he had worked as a teacher in one of the city's public schools, where he taught mostly "kids from the periphery" and saw their uphill struggle to avoid falling in with the wrong crowd. On the other, he had spent years involved in citizen initiatives to improve the lives of Salvador's residents. For most of his life, he had felt the police were abusive, that they were part of the problem, not a solution.[8] Yet, now things were out of control. However one viewed the problem of violence, in looking for solutions, the stakes were raised. Violent crime had become the most glaring symptom of an intractable problem. What its underlying cause may be was neither clear nor consensual. It was true that inequality had decreased, but that seemed to have had the effect of exacerbating the problem. For many, violence was caused by addiction to drugs, particularly crack cocaine, which had "spread like an epidemic" (Nóbrega 2011).

Wherever one turned, there were visible signs of crack's presence. Its users had become a prevalent sight in the center. All over the city, there were billboard posters put up by the government—a pair of feet with a tag in the foreground, the body to which they belong under a sheet, the word "Crack" above it in boldface letters, the caption "80% of homicides: main cause of violence in Bahia" in smaller print. For others, a lack of institutional cooperation across the different levels and scales of government meant that the prosperous years had been wasted in petty infighting instead of used to build infrastructure and boost security. Thus, Salvador found itself in the most precarious of states, a city beset by fear and suspicion, where no one was safe from becoming either a victim or a "perpetrator."

RIGHTS TO A CITY OUT OF CONTROL

Images of a city out of control are difficult to square with widespread representations of Salvador as a place experiencing unprecedented economic growth, whose rich heritage, multicultural vibrancy, and joyful population would allow it to look to the future with renewed hope in its prospects. And in fact, 15 years ago, few would have been able to predict the turn things have taken. In 2002, Salvador had been transformed into a heritage machine, attracting large numbers of foreign visitors, international investment, and World Bank and Inter-American Development Bank funds. The development of the tourist industry had reconfigured the city, but it had done so at the expense of significant numbers of people, especially in the old baroque downtown turned UNESCO world heritage (Collins 2008). With the approval of the City Statute in 2001, many of Bahia's urban social movements felt there was an opportunity to redirect the government's efforts toward a more inclusive, more equitable model of development.

Federal law 10.257—the City Statute—identifies the right to the city as a collective right and sets out to regulate the use of urban property, according to the need to attend to the collective best interest, security, and welfare of citizens, and to safeguard the environment (Art. 1). The City Statute was put in place primarily to confront the problem of informality in urban land use and housing, which governed the social production of Brazil's increasingly unmanageable urban space (Fernandes 2007). Inspired partly by French theorist Henri Lefebvre's writings on cities, a coalition of diverse actors—including academics, politicians, urban managers, and urban social movements—would spend years enmeshed in a technical and political battle for legal reform. Indeed, the City Statute "helped consolidate and promote an active sense of 'insurgent citizenship' (as James Holston calls it)" (Harvey 2012: xii) and furnished the basis for a "new field of public law, namely urban law" (Fernandes 2007: 204).

The statute defines a more central role for municipal governments in urban planning, development, and management than had hitherto been the case.

Municipal authorities are, of course, in a better position to assess needs, consult with urban social movements and citizens' associations, involve local actors, and reach reasonably consensual agreement on potential solutions to specific problems. Yet, local authorities are also embedded in local realities, which often means that they are prey to particular clients and set in their own ways. Likewise, local realities have problems of their own. Though the problems of informality dog most Brazilian urban milieus, informality can present in many guises and generate different forms of "insurgent citizenships."

Salvador has, in this regard, posed its own challenges. Salvador was founded over 450 years ago. The city lay at the center of the Atlantic trade in goods and people for the better part of 300 years. This had a significant impact in its urban form, as well as in the makeup of its population. Salvador is frequently compared to an illustrious matriarch who has been around for as long as the nation that it has nurtured. Soteropolitanos proudly proclaim that "they" are the "cradle of Brazil" (Collins 2012). The city's heritage is often mobilized to support assertions of intrinsic exceptional value and make demands for more resources (Collins 2011). Although representations of Salvador tend to revolve around its historical landmarks, the city has experienced intense growth over the course of the twentieth century, with its population increasing fourfold since 1950 (IBGE 2012). Like elsewhere, many of the newcomers moved into informal settlements in the periphery, which has continued to grow at an intense pace (Gordilho Souza 2008). Yet, this process of urbanization happened against the backdrop of a rather distinctive set of circumstances. Unlike the southern capitals of Rio de Janeiro and, especially, São Paulo, Salvador was not subject to the kind of reconfiguration that would have old colonial centers erased to make way for new, healthier, thoroughly modern cities. Instead, the old historical town was "abandoned" to the poor but remained upright, which largely determined the shape the city would take as it grew outwardly, both along the oceanfront and toward the Bahian hinterland.

Salvador today is a diverse and fragmented city, marked by a superimposition of differentiated patterns of land occupation (Gordilho Souza 2008: 77). Here, there is no clear-cut border between the favela and the asphalt in the manner of Rio de Janeiro (Goldstein 2003). Although there is a periphery, informal settlements can be found across the entire city—next to historic landmarks, between private condominiums, inside decrepit old mansions in those parts of the historic center that have not yet been reconstructed. The periphery is both a network of concrete places and an affective category—that is, it is a network of places capable of producing renewed forms of insurgent citizenship (Holston 2008) but also a generative device without clearly defined limits, which can be turned on its head to question the legitimacy of its residents' right to the city. This periphery becomes quite simply a place inhabited by poor, marginal, mostly black sotero-politanos, whose complaints and demands for recognition are always subject to a form of ethical scrutiny whereby they must show that they are not, in fact, the source of Salvador's current predicament.

This is especially clear around the historic center turned UNESCO heritage. The area, which once housed Bahia's elite, was left to its own devices for most of the twentieth century (Borges 1992). Between 1940 and 1991, the Pelourinho functioned as a red-light district, frequented by local artists, writers, and musicians but deplored by a large section of the city's bourgeoisie. Once branded by UNESCO, the Pelourinho quickly became an object of intervention. In 1992, the government set out to rebuild its ensemble of colonial buildings and reconfigure its residents as producers of a distinctly Afro-Bahian culture. Most of the local population did not possess the cultural capital to lay a claim to the new Pelourinho. In the end, the majority of Pelourinho's inhabitants were removed from the area, either pressured into doing so by police or after accepting cash indemnifications ranging from $200 for individuals with no ties to the area to several thousand dollars for large family groups (Collins 2008). Some pooled resources with other family members and bought plots in the periphery. Many simply moved next door to the unreconstructed districts around the center (Gordilho Souza 2008). A few were able to make a case that they were, in fact, producers of Afro-Bahian culture, which enabled them to remain in restored homes in the new Pelourinho.[9]

The Pelourinho's reconstruction, which was always supposed to be phased, has yet to be completed. Residents of the less central areas have been able to remain in the vicinity of the Pelourinho despite its core's slow transformation into a heritage showcase. At the same time, the renewed Pelourinho has become a magnet for tourists, whose presence requires careful management and constant protection. The Pelourinho may be Salvador's picture postcard, but keeping it that way depends on there being a security apparatus to regulate the movement of its (nearby) residents, who have gone about their business as usual, just around the corner. Initially, there was some resistance to the project. Social movements and opposition politicians protested the forceful removal of Pelourinho's residents, pointing to the violence and human misery present all around it to question the wisdom of attempting to fence off the center by means of constant policing. In time, the objections faded away. By 2010, groups of local activists concerned with safeguarding good people's rights to the city were often the first to call for both more policing and an extension of the police's activities to include the kind of social work that would become a defining feature of the Pact for Life.

The transformation in local attitudes toward security in and around the Pelourinho is instructive. The reconstruction of the Pelourinho was part of a broader project that sought to capitalize on Salvador's heritage, both material and immaterial—in the form of its population's Afro-Bahian cultural practices. The project turned Salvador's historic downtown into a spectacle (Debord 1998), a perfectly preserved colonial enclave surrounded by poor, marginal, black sotero-politanos, whose lives and livelihood continued to revolve around the opportunities afforded by proximity to the Pelourinho. Like other heritage enclaves around the world (Little 2014), the area became an object of intense policing. The area around it, like most of Salvador, has experienced an increase in violent crime. Drug traffickers linked to national criminal organizations moved in, getting rid of the competition along the way. The population of "crack" users living rough on its streets increased exponentially, as did petty crime (Rondon 2013). Police presence did not act as a deterrent but rather circumscribed the effects of crime to specific areas, organizing the circulation of tourists as well as locals, preventing unmediated encounters to the best of its abilities. In other words, insecurity has continued to permeate the lives of soteropolitanos all around the historic center, as police manage the unruly spaces that threaten Salvador's heritage machine not so much by intervening to curb violent crime where it happens but by "cordoning" off the undesirable population.

As might be expected, soteropolitanos did not react to the recent developments in the historic districts by demanding that the City Statute's approach to urban development be adapted to prevent future interventions in the center from displacing its residents, recreating the problems that currently beset it in adjacent areas. Nor did they question the effectiveness of setting up a permanent police presence around the Pelourinho. Rather, they called for its security apparatus to be replicated across the city. This was a recurring theme in my acquaintances' reflections on what should be done. Police work was deemed to have been essential to every stage of turning the Pelourinho into a heritage zone capable of generating wealth—from its cooperation with the administration at the time of the first residents' removal to their watchful management of the area since. In calling for an expansion of security, what seemed to be at stake was not simply an increase in the number of police deployed to keep the order. Rather, what people repeatedly seemed to suggest was that the security apparatus installed in the Pelourinho in the wake of reconstruction showed that violent crime could be kept within "acceptable limits and around an average that [may] be considered optimal for a given social functioning" (Foucault 2007: 5). Of course, this only applied to the space that had become fenced in, an enclave without walls. And no one suggested that violent crime had ceased to pose a challenge. But everyone pointed to the mitigating effects of careful management by police to suggest that perhaps something else could be done elsewhere, that a security framework could, in some small sense, make life better for those people who were inherently good but trapped by the disorder of a chaotic world, where the individual must struggle desperately just to survive (Moodie 2010: 170).

A PACT FOR LIFE

In 2011, the government appeared to heed calls for a large-scale program to combat insecurity by launching the Pact for Life. The Pact for Life has been hailed as a new paradigm in security provision. Often compared to Rio de Janeiro's pacification policy, which has seen several of the city's most dangerous favelas occupied by military police tasked with wresting control of territory controlled by traffickers, the Pact for Life has installed military police in Community Security Bases (Bases Comunitárias de Segurança, CSBs) in several of Salvador's most problematic peripheral neighborhoods. Yet, important differences exist between Rio's Pacifying Police Units (Unidades de Polícia Pacificadora, or UPPs) and Bahia's CSBs, not least of which is their designation. While Rio's UPPs explicitly point toward an armed conflict between police and drug traffickers, the emphasis in Bahia's CSB is not on "pacification," but on community and security. And in effect, unlike in Rio, the installation of CSB has dispensed with militarized intervention to "clear out entrenched drug gangs" (Barrionuevo 2011). Some might cynically claim this is partly to do with CSBs' priorities, which are less about rooting traffickers out than about keeping the population in check. In practice, the CSBs are supposed to operate first as managerial nodes in community police operations and, second, as "citizenship centers" (centros de cidadania). In CSBs, residents are meant to be able to access literacy courses, traineeships, and basic health care; request identity documents; and register for social security benefits like the Bolsa Família.[10] Most significantly, CSBs have become an invaluable tool in enabling police to gather intelligence about the periphery. This intelligence in itself is often presented as a means toward greater "justice." With adequate intelligence, the police can act swiftly to repress, prevent, and preempt the actions of violent perpetrators—both actual and potential. Immersion into the community would allow the police to map and manage insecurity with greater efficacy.

In light of recent demands that the program be expanded, one might be tempted to conclude that the "Pact for Life" has been successful in its stated aims. Yet, despite the authorities' statements to the contrary, many residents of peripheral neighborhoods under police tutelage remain skeptical of the view that "more security" equals greater social justice. In fact, in much of the periphery, there is a sense that the new program does little to curb the violence that has been inflicted upon the community by the state itself, both directly and indirectly. Assertions to the effect that the periphery has become "risky" and "unpredictable" in new ways reflect this skepticism. Since the program has been implemented, it appears that the number of violent homicides in areas with CSBs in place has decreased, although that has been offset by increases elsewhere. Such increases have been especially pronounced in the municipalities that comprise Salvador's greater metropolitan region, which had long been a *ponto de desova* (dumping ground) for murders committed in Salvador itself (Noronha 2003). Furthermore, residents point out that drug trafficking has not abated. Rather, as Penglase (2009) writes about Rio de Janeiro, the police and drug traffickers have found that they can maintain control of the periphery by producing paradoxically well-managed states of disorder. In other words, the Pact for Life may very well have been conceived to safeguard the "right to city," but it is not clear whose right that may be. Despite best intentions, what violence and security are for residents of the periphery are qualitatively different from what they may look like at the center. Or as protesters put it, back in 2013, "Rubber bullets in the center are real bullets in the periphery." And in spite of all the skepticism, support for the program remains strong.

In his article "Toward a Critical Anthropology of Security," Daniel Goldstein (2010) wrote that the present is marked by an increasing attention to "security," where the latter "calls on the power of fear to fill the ruptures that the crises and contradictions of neoliberalism have engendered and so functions as a principal tool of state formation and governmentality . . . , albeit one that is constantly challenged and negotiated by a range of local actors and state subjects" (487). This insight is particularly relevant here. In contemporary Salvador, the lived experience of insecurity, captured by Aparecida in her descriptions of how one must permanently try to "know" the city anew, has engendered a degree of uncertainty—what Ellen Moodie (2010) describes as "not-knowing"—such that people increasingly feel they do not know how to manage risk. Talk of the individuals deemed to have relinquished their right to be called "human persons" (*pessoas humanas*), like crack cocaine users, point to this sense that danger emanates from spectral sources that seem to transcend people's ability to call on what they know or think they know about the world. The increase in violence in Salvador is related to a reshaping of the geography of violence in Brazil. This has seen murder rates increase there, even as they dropped sharply in the southeast, "home to Rio de Janeiro and São Paulo and to many of the country's most enduring stereotypes of shootouts and kidnappings" (Barrionuevo 2011). That this has happened within a context of significant economic growth, coupled with administrative reforms aimed at reducing inequality and expanding citizens' rights, only serves to compound the feeling of fragmentation, confusion, and unpredictability reported by many of Salvador's residents.

In calling for an expansion of the kinds of security apparatuses first established in the historic district to keep out its poor, black, marginal population, what is paradoxically called for is a regime of order originally put in place to advance a neoliberal project of heritage-making, which has played no small part in reproducing insecurity in the areas around the Pelourinho. And this is not "unknown" as such, but insecurity has the effect of creating a different kind of disarray. Amidst the disorder of insecurity, people must assemble modes of living and making-do that often run counter to what they know from experience. Calls for an expansion of the security framework, in contemporary Salvador, are this making-do, firmly anchored on the conviction that one may be able to creatively navigate the spaces in between, to carve out a place for claiming one's right to justice in a city where the meaning of justice has become increasingly contested. In light of what is known about the Pelourinho, as well as of what is, for the time being, known of the Pact for Life, this appears counterintuitive. Yet, while a framework like the Pact for Life cannot truly eradicate insecurity, it has proved adept at managing expectations. It has done so by including people who have always felt excluded in selective regulatory regimes of its own making. Security here has become an integral part of justice, understood broadly to encompass the law as well as the idea of substantive rights to the city in its ability to engender a desire for inclusion. In other words, insecurity has reduced calls for justice, dignity, and citizenship "to a problem of ensuring the minimal conditions for survival" (Dagnino 2003: 217), where poverty and inequality are dealt with as issues of technical management best left to the security forces.

CONCLUSION

The constellation of events and interpretations of institutional responses to the problem of insecurity presented in this chapter suggest that there has been a fundamental transformation in the understanding of justice, of the right to the city and of the police's role in maintaining public order within contemporary Salvador. Over the last decade, Salvador has become a violent and unpredictable city, whose residents have come to feel increasingly paralyzed by a sense of profound insecurity toward the world around them. The case of Salvador is hardly unique as far as a surge in violent crime is concerned. Numerous scholars have written about the paradox and dangers posed by the skyrocketing of brutality that besieges many of the newly established democracies in Latin American (Arias and Goldstein 2010; Imbusch, Misse, and Carrión 2011; Rodgers, Beall, and Kanbur 2012). What is noteworthy, in Salvador, is that the surge in crime encountered an urban milieu unprepared for the form it took: an impersonal, seemingly arbitrary deadly violence that has transformed soteropólitanos' sense of space from something akin to the air one breathes without thinking into a threatening landscape that one must continuously monitor if one is to remain safe.

Violence has changed the way residents of Salvador sense both their city and one another. This has made public security a top priority for Bahia's administration. More significantly, it has made public security a priority for citizens' social movements, too. Without public security, there can be no justice, I heard over and over again. This made sense, insofar as insecurity had made the world so chaotic and fragmented that many felt they could no longer rely on their knowledge of cultural norms to navigate the urban landscape, let alone on state laws and government institutions. The sense of "not-knowing" how to inhabit an urban landscape fractured by the threat of violence has reshaped the way residents of Salvador conceive of rights to the city. In a space of vulnerability, the desire for security takes center stage. The idea of rights to the city was always understood in terms of a right to justice, to a fairer (urban) existence. In contemporary Salvador, as security and justice became interchangeable in public debate on what can be done to thwart violence, concerns with the right to the city receded.

Much of what has been written recently about the disjunction between the formal and substantive aspects of citizenship has looked specifically at the urban context (Appadurai and Holston 1999). Cities have furnished social scientists with rich insight into the exclusionary tactics that have stood in the way of more egalitarian forms of citizenship.[11] Social scientists working in Latin America have called attention to the ways in which walls, fences, and other apparatuses of security have been sought as a solution to the problems posed by a refusal to expand substantive citizenship. For Caldeira (2006), the expansion of security strategies has led to the implosion of modern public life—even if its ideal form had never quite fully materialized. No longer guided by the principles of openness, anonymity, and accessibility, which had for so long informed depictions of the ideal modern city (Young 1990), interactions in this hypervigilant public space have become marked by tension, separation, discrimination, and suspicion (Caldeira 2006: 297).

The case of Salvador poses a series of contradictory challenges to this view. While apparatuses of security have undoubtedly become ubiquitous across Salvador's public landscape, one would be hard pressed to argue that this process results exclusively from a refusal to expand substantive citizenship. Salvador has experienced significant economic growth and an improvement in the material conditions of existence of a substantial part of its population. This has been accompanied by legal and administrative reform aimed at expanding its residents' right to the city, as set out in the City Statute. It could be argued that legal reform, particularly if it stays on paper, merely expands formal citizenship. However, there are two problems with that argument. On the one hand, the application of the law is always a matter of interpretation. It could, in that sense, be argued that programs like the Pact for Life do precisely what the law sets out to do. That is, it could be said that the Pact for Life acts, in practice, to guarantee a right to the city for those that have found themselves trapped by the violence and insecurity that has engulfed Salvador's public life. And this is certainly one of the many arguments explicitly put forth by Bahian authorities to support the strategy. On the other hand, Salvador's residents, including those in its periphery, have on more than one occasion mobilized to demand that the state take an even more expansive approach to security than it has already done. And tempting as it may be to see this as a perverse effect of a dearth of citizenship, as the product of an insipid "democratic culture," that would be tantamount to denying Salvador's residents the vitality of their desire for inclusion in debates about their place in a world fraught with danger.

In his 1977 lectures at the Collège de France, Michel Foucault asked if it may be the case that "the general economy of power in our societies is becoming a domain of security" (Foucault 2007: 10–11). He was getting at a fundamental transformation in the way modern power operates, whereby it moved from a concern with discipline—which "structures space and addresses the essential problem of a hierarchical and functional distribution of elements" (20)—to a concern with planning "a milieu in terms of events or series of events or possible elements, of series that will have to be regulated within a multivalent and transformable framework" (20). Salvador's case seems to illustrate such transformation. Yet, what has happened in Salvador is not so much that there has been a movement away from discipline as it is that the logic of discipline and the logic of security have been joined together, quite literally, in the person of the police tasked with putting them both to work in practice. The Bases Comunitárias de Segurança may very well manage security and distribute welfare, but they also surveil and set up boundaries—both figuratively and, as with the case of Pelourinho's police function as borders of sorts, literally. And, at this point, the relationship between insecurity and citizenship is turned on its head. For while many of Salvador's residents would claim that insecurity makes life impossible, a security framework based on occupation, surveillance, and selective, qualified assistance goes a long way toward stripping citizenship bare. It is a testament to Salvador's residents' ingenuity that they have continued to find their way around the problems that beset them in a city fragmented by all manner of borders and thresholds. It is even more impressive that, stuck between a rock and a hard place, they have continued to hold on to the idea that justice, minimal as it may seem to the outsider, is worth all manner of creative adaptation.

NOTES

1. The *Mapa da Violência* is an annual report put together under the auspices of Brazil's branch of FLACSO, the highly respected Latin American Social Sciences Institute (http://www.mapadaviolencia.org.br/).

2. According to the World Bank, social policies accompanied by rapid economic growth lifted a great part of the poor into the middle class in the 2000s, causing the poverty rate in Bahia to fall from 60 percent of the population in 2003 to about 39 percent in 2009 (http://www-wds.worldbank.org).

3. *Soteropolitano* is the term for a resident of Salvador. Much like the city itself is often called simply Bahia, its inhabitants refer to themselves both as *Baianos* (Bahians) and as soteropolitanos. In keeping with the decision to refer to Salvador mostly by its official name, I refer to its inhabitants mostly as soteropolitanos or residents of Salvador.

4. According to an executive report, in 2008, there were 223,451 crimes reported to the police. Of these, 32,637 (14.6 percent) were further investigated, and 14,548 (3.2 percent) were pursued by the public prosecutor's office, resulting in 2,871 (1.3 percent) convictions (da Costa Gomes 2009).

5. My acquaintance's reference to prosperity is an allusion to the way credit's greater availability has contributed to the expansion of Salvador's stock of automobiles. He had recently bought his own car, on credit, but he was increasingly regretful about his decision.

6. In October 2013, for example, soteropolitanos were shocked by the news that a local doctor, driving a black SUV, had deliberately run down two siblings on a motorbike, "crushing them to death against the fence of a hotel" (Romero 2013).

7. The *human person* is also a legal term. Brazil's 1988 Constitution establishes the "dignity of the *human person*" as its third fundamental principle (http://www.planalto.gov.br/ccivil_03/Constituicao/Constituicao.htm). The dignity and inherent value of the human person are also explicitly addressed in the preamble to the Universal Declaration on Human Rights (http://www.ohchr.org/EN/UDHR/Documents/UDHR_Translations/por.pdf).

8. According to the Brazilian Forum for Public Security, a highly regarded think-tank whose mission is to gather and disseminate information on police and public security management across Brazil, in the last five years, military police have killed 11,197 individuals. Bahia's military police occupied the third place in this ranking (http://www.forumsegur anca.org.br/storage/download//anuario_2014_20150309.pdf).

9. In total, 103 families were initially allowed to stay, with another joining after appeal (Gordilho Souza 2008).

10. The Bolsa Família is a social welfare program of the Brazilian government aimed at reducing short-term poverty by direct cash transfers and diminishing long-term poverty by increasing human capital among the poor through conditional cash transfers. The Bolsa Família is part of the Fome Zero network of federal assistance programs. For families with children, access to the program is conditional on evidence of school attendance and vaccination. An estimated 13.9 million families are currently getting this assistance (http://bolsafamilia.datasus.gov.br/w3c/bfa.asp).

11. Although cities have become increasingly important in contemporary struggles for citizenship, rural social movements like the Movimento dos Sem-Terra, Brazil's large Landless Peasant Movement, should not be underestimated. Movements like the MST have undoubtedly made invaluable contributions to debates about citizens' rights and duties within a number of different, but no less peripheral, contexts (see Wittman 2009).

WORKS CITED

Agamben, Giorgio. 1998. *Homo Sacer: Sovereign Power and Bare Life.* Stanford, CA: Stanford University Press.

————. 2005. *State of Exception.* Chicago: University of Chicago Press.

Appadurai, Arjun, and James Holston. 1999. "Introduction: Cities and Citizenship." In *Cities and Citizenship*, edited by Arjun Appadurai and James Holston, 1–21. Durham, NC: Duke University Press.

Arias, Raymond, and Daniel Goldstein. 2010. "Violent Pluralism: Understanding the New Democracies of Latin America." In *Violent Democracies in Latin America*, edited by Raymond Arias and Daniel Goldstein, 1–34. Durham, NC: Duke University Press.

Azevedo, Solange. 2010. "Cidade amedrontada." *Istoé*, May 25. http://www.istoe.com.br/reportagens/paginar/74678_CIDADE+AMEDRONTADA/2.

Barrionuevo, Alexei. 2011. "As Prosperity Rises in Northeast Brazil, So Does Drug Violence." *New York Times*, August 29. http://www.nytimes.com/2011/08/30/world/americas/30brazil.html.

Blom Hansen, Thomas, and Finn Stepputat. 2005. "Introduction." In *Sovereign States: Citizens, Migrants, and States in the Postcolonial World.* Princeton, NJ: Princeton University Press.

Borges, Dain. 1992. *The Family in Bahia, Brazil, 1870–1945.* Stanford, CA: Stanford University Press.

Caldeira, Teresa. 1987. *City of Walls: Crime, Segregation, and Citizenship in São Paulo.* Berkeley: University of California Press.

————. 2006. "'I Came to Sabotage Your Reasoning!': Violence and Resignifications of Justice in Brazil." In *Law and Disorder in the Postcolony*, edited by Jean Comaroff and John L. Comaroff, 102–149. Chicago: University of Chicago Press.

Caldeira, Teresa, and James Holston. 1999. "Democracy and Violence in Brazil." *Comparative Studies in Society and History* 41 (4): 691–729.

Collins, John. 2008. "'But What If I Should Need to Defecate in Your Neighbourhood, Madame?': Empire, Redemption, and the 'Tradition of the Oppressed' in a Brazilian World Heritage Site." *Cultural Anthropology* 23 (2): 279–328.

————. 2011. "Culture, Content, and the Enclosure of Human Being: UNESCO's Intangible Heritage in the New Millennium." *Radical History Review* 109: 121–135.

————. 2012. "Reconstructing the 'Cradle of Brazil': The Detachability of Morality and the Nature of Cultural Labor in Salvador, Bahia's Pelourinho World Heritage Site." *International Journal of Cultural Property* 19: 423–452.

Comaroff, Jean, and John Comaroff. 2006. "Figuring Crime: Quantifacts and the Production of the Un/Real." *Public Culture* 18 (1): 209–246.

da Costa Gomes, Carlos Alberto. 2009. "O desafio da segurança pública para a Bahia." http://www.observatorioseguranca.org/pdf/O%20Desafio%20da%20Seguran%E7a%20P%FAblica%20para%20a%20Bahia.pdf.

Dagnino, Evelina. 2003. "Citizenship in Latin America." *Latin American Perspectives* 30 (2): 211–225.

Debord, Guy. 1998. *Comments on the Society of the Spectacle.* London: Verso Classics.

Fernandes, Edésio. 2007. "Constructing the 'Right to the City' in Brazil." *Social and Legal Studies* 16 (2): 201–219.

Fórum Brasileiro de Segurança Pública. 2014. *Anuário Brasileiro de Segurança Pública.* São Paulo: Fórum Brasileiro de Segurança Pública. http://www.forumseguranca.org.br/storage/download//anuario_2014_20150309.pdf.

Foucault, Michel. 2007. *Security, Territory, Population: Lectures at the Collège de France 1977–1978*. London: Palgrave Macmillan.

Frazão, Heliana, and Janaína Garcia. 2012. "Greve de policiais termina com aumento de 156% de mortes na região metropolitana de Salvador." *UOL*, February 12. http:// noticias.uol.com.br/cotidiano/ultimas-noticias/2012/02/12/greve-de-policiais-termina -com-aumento-de-156-de-mortes-na-regiao-metropolitana-de-salvador.htm.

Goldstein, Daniel. 2010. "Toward a Critical Anthropology of Security." *Current Anthropology* 51 (4): 487–499.

Goldstein, Donna. 2003. *Laughter Out of Place: Race, Class, Violence, and Sexuality in a Rio Shantytown*. Berkeley: University of California Press.

Gordilho Souza, Ângela Maria. 2008. *Limites do habitar: Segregação e exclusão na configuração urbana contemporânea de Salvador e perspectivas no final do século XX*. Salvador, Brazil: EDUFBA.

Harvey, David. 2008. "The Right to the City." *New Left Review*, September–October, 23–40.

———. 2012. *Rebel Cities: From the Right to the City to the Urban Revolution*. London: Verso.

Holston, James. 2008. *Insurgent Citizenship: Disjunctions of Democracy and Modernity in Brazil*. Princeton, NJ: Princeton University Press.

———. 2011. "Contesting Privilege with Right: The Transformation of Differentiated Citizenship in Brazil." *Citizenship Studies* 15 (3–4): 335–352.

Instituto Brasileiro de Geografia e Estatística. 2012. "Perfil dos munícipios brasileiros—2011." ftp://ftp.ibge.gov.br/Perfil_Municipios/2011/munic2011.pdf.

Lee, Charles. 2010. "Bare Life, Interstices, and the Third Space of Citizenship." *Women's Studies Quarterly* 38 (1–2): 57–81.

Little, Walter. 2014 "Police and Security in the World Heritage City of Antigua, Guatemala." *Journal of Latin American and Caribbean Anthropology* 19 (3): 396–417.

Magalhães Wallace, Marta. 2013. "Thinking through (In)security." *Anthropology News*, July– August, 6–7.

Moodie, Ellen. 2010. *El Salvador in the Aftermath of Peace: Crime, Uncertainty, and the Transition to Democracy*. Philadelphia: University of Pennsylvania Press.

Nóbrega, José Maria. 2011. "Os homicídios no nordeste brasileiro." In *O panorama dos homicídios no Brasil*, edited by Secretaria Nacional de Segurança Pública. Brasília: Secretaria Nacional de Segurança Pública. http://www.uff.br/ineac/sites/default/files/ os_homicidios_no_nordeste_brasileiro_jose_maria_nobrega_junior.pdf.

Noronha, Ceci Vilar. 2003. "Violência, crime e pobreza na região metropolitana de Salvador: Um velhotema revisitado." In *O clássico e o novo: Tendências, objetos e abordagens em ciências sociais e saúde*. Rio de Janeiro: Fiocruz.

Office of the United Nations High Commissioner for Human Rights. 2015. "Declaração universal dos direitos humanos." http://www.ohchr.org/EN/UDHR/Documents/ UDHR_Translations/por.pdf.

Penglase, Ben. 2009. "States of Insecurity: Everyday Emergencies, Public Secrets, and Drug Trafficker Power in a Brazilian Favela." *PoLAR: Political and Legal Anthropology Review* 32 (1): 47–63.

Portal do Bolsa Família. 2015. "Homepage." http://bolsafamilia.datasus.gov.br/w3c/bfa.asp.

Presidência da République do Brasil. 2015. "Constituição da République Federativa do Brasil de 1988." http://www.planalto.gov.br/ccivil_03/Constituicao/Constituicao.htm

Rodgers, Dennis, Jo Beall, and Ravi Kanbur. 2012. *Latin American Urban Development into the Twenty-First Century: Towards a Renewed Perspective on the City*. New York: Palgrave.

Romero, Simon. 2013. "A Brazilian Boom Town of 'Eternal Beauty' Faces Its Troubled Side." *New York Times*, November 10.

Rondon, José Eduardo. 2013. "Pelourinho: A rota do turista e a rota do crack." *Carta Capital*, June 1. http://www.cartacapital.com.br/sociedade/pelourinho-a-rota-do-turista-e-a-rota-do-crack-743.html.

Waiselfisz, Júlio Jacobo. 2014. *O mapa da violência 2014: Os jovens do Brasil*. São Paulo: Instituto Sanginari / FLACSO Brasil. http://www.mapadaviolencia.org.br/pdf2014/Mapa2014_JovensBrasil.pdf.

Wittman, Hannah. 2009. "Reframing Agrarian Citizenship: Land, Life and Power." *Journal of Rural Studies* 25: 120–130.

World Bank. 2013. "Bahia Socio-Economic Development for Inclusive Growth Development Policy Loan (P126351)." http://www-wds.worldbank.org/external/default/WDSContentServer/WDSP/IB/2013/12/26/000461832_20131226131502/Rendered/INDEX/836280BR0P1263020Box382089B00OUO090.txt.

Young, Iris Marion. 1990. *Justice and the Politics of Difference*. Princeton, NJ: Princeton University Press.

7 WATER JUSTICE, MINING, AND THE FETISH FORM OF LAW IN THE ATACAMA DESERT

Alonso Barros

A commodity appears at first sight, a very trivial thing, and easily understood. Its analysis shows that it is, in reality, a very queer thing, abounding in metaphysical subtleties and theological niceties.
　　Karl Marx, *Capital*

Not even in its beginnings was capital "territorial": its deterritorializing power consists in taking as an object, not even land itself, but the "materialized work" or merchandise. . . . Property is not over land or soil, nor even over the modes of production, but over abstract convertible rights.
　　Gilles Deleuze and Félix Guattari, *Mille plateaux*

Tout objet historique est fétiche.
　　Maurice Merleau-Ponty, in William Pietz, "Problem of the Fetish I"

TROUBLED WATERS: MINING COMPANIES AND ATACAMA DESERT PEOPLES

In his preface to the 1867 German edition of *Das Kapital*, Karl Marx famously warned that things like value, capital, profit, rent, and tax cannot be discovered with the aid of a microscope and chemical analysis, hinting to the distinct socio-natural logics that underpin the production of different kinds of knowledges and conceptual abstractions. This chapter's sociolegal ethnography of the collective ecopolitical imaginations born out of commoditized interrelations in the Atacama Desert in Chile aims to carve out the social forces behind the "cultural" abstractions and legal mechanisms that "make sense" of water justice within the narrow biopolitical limits set by the Atacama Desert's extreme "natural" conditions. This desert is an ideal social laboratory of sorts. Here, the macro and micro effects of mega-extractive operations collide visibly with indigenous peoples' lives in the messy legal claims to labor, land, and water required by the mining operations.

Water is the ideal prism through which to observe the (re)productive forces behind the nature/culture fetish in terms of justice. Indeed, whether as God and the Devil; age, gender, race, and class; space, place, and landscape perspectives;

knowledge and conservation; population, territory, and resource extraction, use, and exchange values; or as biopolitics, "water justice"—information, access, quality, sanitation, reuse, sustainability—refers to problems that lend relevance to recent political ecology debates on the place of law in society. These debates address the multiplicity of socio-natural worlds (relational vs. dualist ontologies, networked vs. structural forms of analysis, radical particularity vs. extended juris-prudence) and a posthuman renewal of the question of what constitutes "life"— whether as pure immanence in Deleuzian terms or as the—Foucauldian—object/ function of "law" as a transcendent kind of "governmentality" (Foucault 2003a; Walby 2007). While rather intractable theoretically, such questions seem to stem from both the social and lived experience more clearly than ever before, due in great part to the decolonial practice and political ecology of some social move-ments (see Escobar 2010).[1] Like competing territorialities, then, water justice is incommensurable with the socio-natural worlds it gives life to.[2] Still, the senses of territorial justice involved have found their way into global and local human rights discourses and projects, becoming part of mainstream corporate respon-sibilities and socio-environmental due diligence issues and debates. But none of this is news: the extractive industry has shaped Chile culturally, politically, and economically across the centuries (Barros 1997: 2008a).

The political ecology of mining operations that extract water from Atacameño mountains, oases, and salt flats provides the context within which to observe the structural coupling of natural resources extraction for the global market with the ways in which local peoples come to (re)cast themselves and their water us-age practices in the fetishistic media "flow" of marketable identities and financial return. This chapter takes an ethnographic focus through two case studies, one of indigenous self-portrayal around a water dispute and the other the mediatiza-tion of 33 trapped Chilean miners in 2010. These examples of mediatized and commoditized indigenous knowledge practices aim to show the extent to which cultural commodity fetishism may directly result from the legal separation of land use and water rights (as traded separately in Chile)—and provide a background to understand the drying out and cultural evisceration of agropastoralist communi-ties.[3] Resulting "identity flows" also feed "water justice," as identities and water, simultaneously, are both commodified and culturally alienated.

So how have the soft law of mining social responsibility and global human rights standards enmeshed with indigenous territorial knowledge practices? Are they contributing to protect desert "ethnic identity" and "hydraulic culture" or merely substituting it with a future of marketable "water justice" with cultural con-sequences that both parties can afford to live with (or not)? Paraphrasing Escobar, this chapter analyzes how modern law does not describe ethnic subjectivities and territorialities so much as it actively constitutes them as culturally commodifiable objects of knowledge to be managed and policed through various techniques and modes of positive intervention—especially spectacular media (Escobar 1998: 56) but also by means of religious and legal schooling and disciplines (Supiot 2012). The Atacama Desert evidences those otherwise invisible tracks linking large-scale extractions to ethnocultural commoditization.

The conclusion addresses "law the fetish"—or the fetish form of modern law—directly as it succeeds to create a neoliberal sense of water justice that transmutes "stakeholder" cultural values into individualized commodity "shareholder" value in terms of corporate image. The point is that nature/culture binarism thrives in the form of law and indigenous rights or "hegemony and resistance" discourses (Bolados 2014), which tends thus to actively prefigure, naturalize, reify and "racialize" poverty, at best, in the law and media terms of deterritorialized cultural resistance and political violence, rather than to stand for indigenous territorial immanence and autonomy (Barros 2008c). More important, it is this very same fetish legal form that enables the Atacameño people to, inversely, reterritorialize their collective capabilities through a sense of ancestral ownership, by virtue of their own preexisting right and freedoms—the resulting flow of "water justice" being always "in the making."

The racialized background effect of mining water and metal extractions helps to consider and analyze mutually unintelligible or incommensurable values as hierarchically cast around water property, of course, but also as based on quasi-religious structures of distributional authority and inequality—as currently organized in the desert's demanding biopolitical arena, neoliberal Chile, and the world at large.

GEOPOLITICAL AND ETHNOGRAPHIC CONTEXT:
MINING PEOPLE, WATER ENERGY

The Atacama Desert is the hyper-arid middle depression between the cliffs of the northern Pacific coast and the so-called Puna de Atacama (an immense and unique highland habitat now divided between Argentina, Bolivia, and Chile), which in Chile is roughly 250 kilometers across and between the Loa River down south to Taltal (21° to 27° south); it has been historically and commonly known as the Despoblado de Atacama, or Atacama Desert—and roughly covers today's Antofagasta Region (former Bolivian territory).[4] Flowing from east to west over 400 kilometers, the U-shaped Loa River marks the northern limit of the region and hosts the (now) state-owned Chuquicamata copper mine and its mining camp city of Calama. A hundred kilometers east of Calama are the geothermal fields of El Tatio that give birth to both the Loa and Atacama basins. The Atacama River runs to the south, irrigating another rosary of oases that straddles the line of Capricorn and pours endlessly into the Atacama salt pan—site of the world's largest lithium extraction district and the favorite nesting place of three flamingo species.[5] The Atacama salt pan is considered a global conservation priority because plants and animals adapted to its forbidding geography are found nowhere else on earth (RIDES 2005).

Combined, the effects of mega-mining, drought, and accelerated privatization since Pinochet's rule (1973–1990) have resulted in the Loa River drying up well before it reaches the ocean. There are now over 650 mining operations in the Antofagasta Region (see SERNAGEOMIN 2011: 8). The Atacama River, which carried 1,000 liters per second (L/s) ten years ago, now carries only 400 L/s. More than ten Atacameño villages and ranches have depopulated over the past 50 years; entire villages are now Calama slums. My own work among surviving oases started in 1993, when I was fresh out of law school. At that time, surface water flows were recorded and protected as indigenous property in the public registry (at over 3,000 L/s). Groundwater has since become the focus of territorial disputes between the Atacameños and miners, especially over the lithium-rich brine that makes up 40 percent of the world's production.

Thirty-three of Atacama's miners were rocketed to fame after being trapped 700 meters underground for over two months during 2010. Over a billion people watched the live-coverage rescue effort, which showcased some of the biopolitical techniques and drew the world's attention to the region and transformed the Atacameño pueblo and miners into hyper-individualized icons. The global media's spectacular coverage of the rescue, however, also had the effect of diverting public attention inside Chile away from the badly handled mining royalty law that had been passed. Indeed, this occurred on the very same day that the miners were rescued (additionally covering up Mapuche territorial claims and cries for justice).

The global story of copper is firmly enmeshed with the history of Chile. Nationalized by the unanimous decision of the Chilean Congress in 1971 under socialist president Salvador Allende, copper was re-reprivatized following a U.S.-supported military coup in 1973—and later with the help of José Piñera, brother of ex-Chilean president Sebastián Piñera (2010–2014). This privatization policy has never been revised since: at the time of this writing, Pinochet's ex-son-in-law still controls Chile's world-leading brine, lithium, potash, and iodine extraction business, SOQUIMICH, or SQM.[6] Although Pinochet's 1980 Constitution incorporated the declaration that mineral resources belong to the nation, José Piñera, who served as his secretary of mining and of labor and social security, convinced mining concessionaires that he could guarantee them full ownership of the minerals they extracted, along with special rights to labor, land, and water.

Despite this wealth in natural resources, income inequality in Chile is striking and acute. Chile has now a per capita GDP of roughly US$20,000, but the richest 5 percent of the country has an income 830 times greater than the poorest 5 percent: the average household debt is equivalent to 7.5 monthly incomes.[7] While mining bonanzas are known to redefine hinterland cluster properties and territorial borders (national, regional, and local) (Barros 2008a), less is known about the impact such booms have on the traditional knowledge practices of local indigenous populations and the workforce of the precariously floating population of subcontractors that arrive, attracted by the bounty. We will see in this chapter how extractive booms and busts latch onto disputes over other resources, with the result of deepening inequalities and thus water injustice in the country and the region at large.

Resulting socioeconomic differences are constantly being naturalized and spun by the media in terms of racialized caste-type social hierarchies. This is nothing new: at least since the time of the Spanish Conquest, wealth and poverty rates in all of Latin America have been historically indexed along racialized lines—the darker one's skin, the lower one's income and property; the whiter, the richer. Chile is no exception to this rule nor to the endurance of modern endogamous neocolonial practices and related rather insular, society-wide class-reinforcing mechanisms and segregations (Barros 2008b; Bello and Rangel 2000; Busso, Cicowies, and Gasparini 2005; Hall and Patrinos 2005; Psacharopoulos and Patrinos 1994).

Why is it, then, that darker-skinned Chileans do not benefit commensurately from the riches of the country's "white" mining manifest destiny? One major reason, aside from mining companies paying the state one of the lowest royalty rates in the world, is that legal loopholes allowed miners to declare huge losses or no profit at all and avoid taxation—and thus redistribution of the wealth they generate.[8]

By far the largest single energy consumer—using up to 90 percent of the power generated by the country's northern energy grid and close to 40 percent of the national total—mining has other, more pervasive effects on Chileans' quality of life. Privatized water utility companies are likewise vertically controlled by large economic groups, some of which also happen to be large mining groups. More to the point, in order to supply 40 percent of the world's copper, the mining industries require massive amounts of energy and fresh water (it is estimated that three-quarters of copper's value is owed to water, but there is not enough reliable information on this). Indeed, water is also needed to produce the copper-rich granulate and transport it down the mountain to the privatized ports and then off to the world at large. Coincidentally, water was also privatized by José Piñera under Pinochet's rule and completely separated from land ownership. This means that ownership of land does not include ownership of the water that flows through or under it. The transnationalization and proprietorial concentration of potable water has Chilean households footing the most expensive water bill in Latin America.[9]

It is from within this context that this chapter examines the Atacameños' defense of local water sources. Until 1997, I collaborated to protect and register the Atacameños' 1,000 rivulets in conformity with Pinochet's water privatization law. Afterward, the extractive industry began to concentrate on, explore, and tap groundwater aquifers. Despite the fact that highland *vegas* and *bofedales* wetlands also became officially protected by a 1992 law, specialized "water-pinching" companies soon were pumping water alongside the protected zones inside Atacameño territory. Freshwater depletion has since generated severe ecological havoc in indigenous wetlands, salt pan lagoons, and torrential water collection areas (see Sánchez, Marchant, and Borsdorf 2012). Some water tables have plunged hundreds of meters deeper than they were a few years ago, resulting in irreversible damage to the subsistence base of traditional agropastoralists. Pastures are now found ever higher and farther away from the foothill oases, making seasonal transhumance impossible.

Chile's National Water Directorate estimated that it would cost between US\$300 and US\$2,500 per square kilometer to determine how much groundwater there is in order to manage it more sustainably—a sum they claim not to have at their disposal, although it is relatively small considering the commercial value of water for mining. Clearly, TNCs know how much they are effectively finding, pumping out, and/or exporting free of charge. But the general public's knowledge about water remains artificially "small"—that is, made irrelevant to resource decision makers who do not have (or press to have) reliable facts in the face of public scrutiny.[10] Mining companies claim groundwater belongs to those who can find and extract it, essentially getting away with trumped sustainability models used first to obtain environmental license and then to explain away rapid depletion levels by "correcting" the models' mistakes and finally, in the best of cases, by compensating indigenous communities for the complete destruction of their habitat.[11]

Once registered as mine property, water is effectively used and exported out of Chile free of charge (neither royalties nor taxes apply to water; again, it is originally acquired as a "free" commodity that can be bought, sold, externalized, or discounted from tax bases at comparatively high market value). Nor does this water return to the regional hydrogeological cycle: because the water tables that feed the wetlands and salt pans go deeper into the ground every day, local cloud formation has become increasingly rare. According to my informants, the drought has lasted for 50 years (see Bonilla and Norero 1999).

LOS ATACAMEñOS

> And as I here have painted them and made them of stone so they will come out of the sources and rivers and caves and mountains in the provinces that I likewise have told you and named and you will go, all of you, by that place, signaling to them where the sun comes out, dividing them, each one in his own and signaling the right that he would henceforth carry.
>
> Juan Diez de Betanzos, *Suma y narración de los Incas*

Ten thousand or so Lickanantay or Atacameños live on the territory. They are the largest indigenous people in the region of Antofagasta. Although a majority inhabits in the fringes of major mining cities like Calama (in the Middle Loa basin) or in the port of Antofagasta, Atacameños keep strong links with their over 4,000 homeland relatives living in the foothill pueblos, oases and mineral hinterland, more than 100 kilometers away. Central to ethnic reunion rituals among Atacameño professionals, businesspeople, miners, and agropastoralists, water, in any sign or whatever form, is laden with the deepest importance (Barros 1997, 2008a; see also Pourrut 1995).

A conception widely held among the indigenous Andean, as among most indigenous peoples in Latin America, is that the earth and mountains produce humans, animals, plants, minerals, and all material things. Each mountain is said to have a distinct mythos that describes its age, sex, and rank, along with its productive, reproductive, and technical capabilities. The Atacameños likewise endow their mountain suppliers with autonomous distributional authority over water. This embedded sense of interrelation can be further seen in shared values and everyday knowledge practices of reciprocity and exchange (Strathern 2005). Ritual specialists known as *cantales* regularly address and petition each mountain owner (*Mayllku* in Quechua, *Achache* in Aymara, or "ancestor") in sight by its toponym in Kunza (a now extinct language). Before the work of collective irrigation channel cleaning takes place, and especially during harsh drought periods, the *cantal* and his helpers will have driven to the sea, which is four hours away, to fill and bring back bottles of seawater. I observed this ceremony on many occasions in different villages. Seawater is given as an offering to their particular tutelary patron by being poured on a ritual *mesa* (stone table). In addition to the patron mountain owner, the timeless and spaceless feminine receiver and giver of life, Pachamama, is also ritually paid and literally begged to further accept the Mayllku's water. Ice, snow, clouds, mist, rain—water in all its recognizable forms is sung from a print-out written in the extinct Kunza language (Barros 1997). Together, Mayllku and Pachamama have biopolitically generated and regenerated the communities that they water but failed to perpetuate their common—now fossilized—language.

The insides of these mountains and caves, so filled with coveted riches, are watched over by the Mayllkus' jealous guard of devils (*supay*) that, whether in the guise of a whirlwind or a mestizo rider, also form part of the desert's supernatural equation. Such anthropomorphized mountains and their keepers punish and strike with lightning and flash floods. They can, and do, bless, maim, or kill. They decide whether to impart drought or rain, holding real power over life and death. Mayllkus become infuriated when not adequately revered, cajoled, and paid; when that happens, they will viciously take the lives of Indians and miners alike (see Barros 1997; Bouysse-Cassagne 2005, 2008, 2012).

It is in this context that Atacameños, like the Andean miners depicted by Michael Taussig (1980) and June Nash (1979), perform their material and spiritual hopes for the better in highly choreographed processions and dance. By all accounts, ritual dance troupes and *cofradía* (brotherhood) memberships have grown at a steady rate during the mining bonanza, with more money having been invested in new gear and accessories in the last decade than in the past 70 years.

The Atacama Desert's main salt pan town, San Pedro de Atacama, is now a tourist and scientific hot spot that is experiencing rapid urbanization and uneven economic development. The monetary value of individually owned property in the better-preserved oases has risen 50-fold in the last decade alone. Most indigenous landowners have sold their plots for admirable sums and moved to the shabby houses and flats they have in Calama or Antofagasta. Oases populations dwindle as authorities sign away their habitats' groundwater, drying out the rivers and making traditional irrigation impossible because there are more canals to clean than the number of people required to do so. The remaining indigenous villages are being quickly abandoned when the mestizo owner-of-the-mountain bursts on the scene. Most of the mineral and water extraction in the Antofagasta region takes place within 5 million hectares of "community" and "patrimonial" Atacameño territory that was officially measured and mapped by the state over 15 years ago. If, in the abstract, Atacameño communities legally own their territory, in practice, they lack the written and formally registered title deeds normally required to prove rightful possession in court. Thus unrecorded, Atacameño territory is in practice considered to be terra nullius and thus remains registered as "fiscal territory." It is the Chilean state, then, through its Ministry of National Goods (previously titled the Ministry of Lands and Colonization) and the National Water Directorate, that grants groundwater exploration licenses. It does so without consulting local populations and invariably against the will of the Indigenous communities whose territories are directly impacted.

TNCs naturally have every reason to follow suit and likewise deny indigenous territory in practice as if it didn't exist, despite industry standards saying otherwise (Barros and Schönsteiner 2014). Since land and water were legally separated by Pinochet's water privatization code and policies, groundwater exploration and exploitation constitute a gray economy. Although surface water can be freely traded, groundwater exploration licenses require the prior authorization of the owner of the land in which water is found.

TNCs will, however, still insistently seek to sign Corporate Social Responsibility (hereafter CSR) agreements with Atacameños, contracts with which they can easily obtain the coveted "social license" from the state that allows them to operate and access the minerals and water in indigenous territory (territory labeled as a mere expectation or "ancestral land claim"). Over 30 Atacameño communities, which combined inhabit millions of hectares, thus end up negotiating legally binding contracts with the global extractive industry's biggest players, practically on their own. Under pressure for cash and better livelihoods, such isolated communities often end up both letting strongly state-backed mining companies get away with their carefully monitored drainage operations, and trade their unprotected territory in exchange for secure urban jobs and facilities (sewage systems, schools, roofed multisport fields, community houses, nursing homes, etc.).[12] Many villagers build shacks and make a living by renting them out to a large floating population of miners and contractors, putting further pressure on available drinking water and normal village life. In fact, most Atacameños aspire to work in mines near their villages and therefore form a substantive part of the precariously unskilled workforce of subcontractors, 70 percent of which have no union rights or health, pension, or education benefits. Ninety percent of Peine's male population works in the potash and lithium extraction facilities in the salt pan nearby.

Disguising practical legally based territorial asymmetries and negotiations, CSR company officials will recommend their Corporate Affairs managers to avoid mentioning transactions over property and natural resources in their compacts with "host" communities, lest this be used against them. Contracts should instead provide the positive impression of agreed, neighborly, and sustainable development and capacity-building programs, where large amounts of cash are mentioned but water is not. This entire dispossession process occurs despite Chile being a signatory to ILO Convention 169, a binding human rights treaty that recognizes indigenous peoples' ownership of the total habitat of the region they occupy.

The social life of water among and between Atacameños and Chile's mining, media, and political elites takes us even further into the unevenly plural field of cosmopolitan politics we have seen take shape. This field is one where state-recognized indigenous groups struggle against large-scale plunder and commoditization in the fixed managerial terms of the state's and Atacameños' competing claims to territorial ownership of property. The following cases show how the law does not describe subjectivities so much as it actively constitutes them as culturally commodifiable objects of knowledge to be managed and policed through various modes of positive intervention, especially through spectacular media (Escobar 1998: 56; see also Supiot 2012). As we will see, racialized "cultural" commoditization is the direct consequence of "natural" extractions by the mining industry.

Case 1: Pampa Colorada

In the summer of 2007, Minera Escondida—the largest open-pit copper mine in the world—announced its US$300 million Pampa Colorada water supply project.[13] Based on a 20-year extraction model, it expected to pump 648 million cubic meters of water (1,027 L/s) south across 100 kilometers of environmentally fragile, indigenous highland habitat and protected wetlands to the mine's main pit, and from there another 100 kilometers to its private port in Antofagasta, where the copper concentrate is shipped abroad. The people of Peine brought their concerns to both company and state officials directly on many occasions. After a few meetings with company officials and shifting crews of professionals, it became clear that the company refused to acknowledge the community's territorial rights, and Peine's assembly decided to take legal steps to stop the project from materializing.[14] Once again, the Andes collective distributional reputation was called into ecopolitical action.

Despite the many land surveys it made in the 1990s, the Chilean state (heavily influenced by the mining lobby) had thus far demarcated and handed over title deeds for only 5 percent of the Atacameño territory that was identified. The official land survey still allowed the Atacameños to claim, at least rhetorically, that the disputed territory belonged to them, despite not having registered paper titles to prove it. In any case, Peine's first major legal step was to make sure its voice was heard in the national media, thereby exposing the mine to public scrutiny. The Pampa Colorada project was covered on national television that Saturday evening of the Easter weekend (Foncea 2007).[15]

Afterward, to everyone's surprise, the Regional Environmental Commission (COREMA) reached the landmark unanimous decision to reject the Pampa Colorada project (a particularly brave choice considering all members were government-appointed). COREMA took explicit heed of human rights and "observations of the Indigenous Communities of Peine, Socaire, Río Grande, Catarpe, Coyo, and Solor, the Pueblo Atacameño Council, the Asociación Atacameña de

Regantes y Agricultores of San Pedro de Atacama."[16] No matter how invisible and deep underground, water had been finally recognized as belonging to the people who depended on it to survive.

Although such COREMA rulings have little weight outside the case they directly apply to, the fetish of ethnic incorporation had temporarily paid off in Peine's David and Goliath "lawfare" over water and inequality (see Comaroff and Comaroff 2009). Yet even if law the fetish is always evoking, calling up, addressing, and even disguising problems of racial discrimination and profound material inequality, it can never bury them. My ethnographic fieldwork was undertaken in the context of deeply racialized divides that forced the Atacameños (a heretofore rather unobtrusive ethnicity) to become a more prominent player in the uneven field of natural resource dispute, protest, law, and media. This time the fetish form of law had helped us to win—technically. Pampa Colorada highland wetlands, lagoons, and groundwater were henceforth left alone and allowed to flow according to the Andes's generous injunctions. Although there was no prior or intrinsic need to communicate local opposition in the corporative terms of ethnic concreteness (i.e., Ethnicity Inc.[17]), Atacameño authorities knew that in order to be effective, opposition had to be necessarily argued on the basis of the notion that the desert water was native water.

One of the functions of law is to reify relationships by making them commensurable in terms of life, value, property, and revenue. Law thus commoditizes people and things—like culture and nature—as kernels of mutually constitutive opposites, further commoditized schizogenically by financial flows. If it is to avoid becoming colonized by the process of individualistic commoditization, indigenous socio-nature has no choice but to reterritorialize as a collective form of ontonomy that can be perceived as a properly racialized biopolitical subject. Although forecasted on the back of liberal equality, such territorial "reappropriation" invariably ends up enacting, combining, and reifying economic relations in the naturalized terms of caste and class inequalities, the "poor" Indian becoming a spectacular token to cover up and normalize poverty in the country at large (Barros 2008b). Modern law is seen again as the transformative fetish that enacts this split temporality as split materiality, thus reinforcing the tenets and deep grammar of neoliberal value, identity, and resource politics but especially the judicialization of natural resource property relations and its racialized enforcements.[18]

A RACE FOR WATER

Out of concern for and in explicit consideration of the human rights of the Atacameño community of Peine, the COREMA of Antofagasta decided to back the

Atacameños because the mine had refused—and ultimately failed—to provide any sound assessment of the impacts that highland water extraction might have on the continuity of Atacameño culture. Had the Pampa Colorada project materialized, it would have destroyed what Chile's environmental protection law calls "local customs and systems of life," as are indeed the beliefs that the Mayllkus and Pachamama are the supernatural providers of life in their isolated oases and immense highland pastures. After this scathing, unprecedented defeat by the Atacameño's Mayllkus and Pachamama, the corporation decided to both dismiss its environmental manager and put an end to its water exploration and extraction policy in the indigenous highlands. It has since invested more than US$3 billion instead in a seawater desalination facility and pumping complex on the Antofagasta coast.[19]

A brief interview with two village elders as they returned to the—now ravaged—Punta Negra salt flat of their infancy where they used to collect flamingo eggs to eat (from which Minera Escondida already extracts over 1.000 L/s on a continuous basis), shows that practically none of the water mirrors and lagoons of old are left: "What will we leave to our kids? We will only have this story to tell them" (quoted in Foncea 2007).

Investigative journalist Valeria Foncea introduces the next section in "off," saying that the Atacameño people are willing to give their life for the water they consider to be sacred. The news clip then shows the village's weavers' club at the background, in which elderly ladies are seen spinning and weaving woolen clothes, socks, and the like, to sell to tourists. María Barreda, then president of the community, had set up the scene deliberately in order to render her brilliant summary:

It goes like this, if I sell the water, the water will finish, it's a cultural issue. . . . It is a cultural issue that gives us strength to continue living in this great desert. That is why we are affected, because we are sure that the water that comes down from the high Cordillera is the same that reaches the salt pan and feeds us as a community, so to say.

Aliro Plaza, an elder from the nearby village of Socaire, said, "They say they will replace the water, but where from? All the same, they will have to take out water, and waters are the same" (quoted in Foncea 2007).

So, legal notions contribute to substitute indigenous direct ownership over water and its uses, with marketable cultural property (itself forecast as a commoditized future in the tourism industry). If law enables this operation technically, it's because its fetish form is a two-timer that creates split temporalities managed as historical debt and/or judicialized wait (the Salar of infancy vs. the Salar today).

Atacameños are then left to their own devices and lack the money they need to force a proper judicial dénouement. Again, law is the fetish that enacts this split temporality, especially through the judicialization and mediatization of territorial politics.

The lawfare over water considered in this case, has brought together the names, creeds, and deeds of global elites and Andean agropastoralists, all within the easily observable legal framework of things (assemblages) and persons (groups, dead or alive) in the Atacama Desert, as bared legally and naturally from any unessential attribute, leaving only water. Media coverage of diversely territorialized capabilities faring in concrete natural resource negotiations has since become increasingly and matter-of-factly coded, cast, observed, and couched in terms of nation, race, territory, ethnicity, culture, working class, and neoliberal property definitions. Yet, neither money nor culture nor race are at stake but entire basins, water becoming the ultimate commodity cum biopolitical fetish that secretly animates CSR compacts with supernatural powers (Barros and Schönsteiner 2014). The point is that this struggle and conflicts over water were always already commoditized along with the water.

This is how mainstream media tells the story of Peine, the village that had most actively fought and won, in Pampa Colorada:

> Peine was a forgotten village, lost among the desert mountains, until 1984, when lithium changed it forever. That year, Foote Minerals, a Montana-based company, bought a national brand name, Sociedad Chilena del Litio, SCL, and started to extract a mineral substance which was hardly known to the local inhabitants. With the arrival of company workers and contractors, Peine had to adapt to the new customs and the new people who went to live there. Today, close to 30 years later, Peine *is* lithium. (Mandiola 2012, emphasis in the original)

> "In Peine there is unconformity with these projects that have been authorized by the State, because all the resources that should reach our pueblo due to the effects operations of lithium plants have on our life are not coming. Everything is basic here: education is rural, we have a dispensary with a doctor that comes once every month. We are abandoned," Ramón Torres, Peine's strongman says. (Mandiola 2012)

> It is night-time and 12 workers are playing a football match in the encampment's synthetic field. Four spotlights brighten the scene. Three [Atacameño] men walk by in the dark street alongside the camp-site and look at the [non-Atacameño] workers play.
> —See how unfair it is? We have nothing they have.
> —Well, so it is. Beers anyone? (Mandiola 2012)

Case 1 suggested how although the Atacameño communities and authorities are fully recognized in all kinds of public and private property deals, their salares and oases are still losing out on the competition for diminishing freshwater supplies and are being further urbanized and commoditized in fetishistic terms, deterritorialized as "dead" archaeological phenomena readied for consumption— only to be reborn in the powerfully schizoid neoliberal terms of media celebrity cultural politics, as Case 2 will show, next.

Case 2: From Collective Native Devil to Individualized Media God

We are alive and well in the shelter.
    The 33

Variously translated from the Spanish, these words on a scrap of paper launched hundreds of headlines and encapsulated the eventual happy ending to the ordeal of the Chilean miners who, in late 2010, survived more than two months deep underground in the hot, dark tunnel of the Atacama Desert's San José mine. Not only were the miners rescued and then celebrated, but the image of Chile and its president, Sebastian Piñera, got a boost in the eyes of the world. President Piñera even came to the London School of Economics and Political Science to show his video trailer of Chile's most recent brush with fame.[20]

The miners were trapped in the San José mine on August, 5, 2010, a month when the Mayllkus, the fabled Andean devil-owners of the mountain, are petitioned with special devotion to surrender the riches they jealously guard. Indeed, if inadequately tended to, mountains produce bodily injury and death, and the 33 were no doubt paying the price for a lack of proper devotion. Agricultural plots are more the field of ancestors, who are asked permission to sow. But somebody else paid the miners' ransom: the rescue of the 33 by Operation San Lorenzo cost about US$23 million (Lawrence being the Catholic patron saint of miners). CODELCO, the state-owned mining company, contributed US$15 million, while mining TNCs BHP Billiton (Escondida, Spence, Cerro Colorado) and Anglo American (Collahuasi, Soldado) covered the remaining sum (including US$2 million for the renowned T-130 Schraam drilling machine).[21] Sixty-nine days later, the miners were freed from the "devil's bowel"—to use President Piñera's inspired term. The now world-famous Phoenix capsule extracted them individually in an explicitly hierarchized manner. Every aspect of the broadcast was carefully monitored by the private production company hired to film and broadcast the saga live to over a billion viewers.

Lawrence Golborne, Chile's Minister for Mining and Energy, later declared that the rescue operation he oversaw well might have not been undertaken because it was "completely irrational in economic terms." Indeed, considering how many miners have died since that time from different accidents, even with the benefit of hindsight, a deeper rationale for this spectacularly "irrational"—and highly emotional—rescue can be regarded as a corporate publicity stunt, of course, but also as a ritual or symbolically "waterless" rebirthing of the trapped miners as free, God-fearing individuals.

The first of the 33 was extracted from this hell on October 12, when Latin American countries—still—officially commemorate Columbus's landing, also known as Día de la Raza (Day of the Race). That very same day, two substantial new legal packages were railroaded through the Chilean Congress. One was passed guaranteeing that mining TNCs continue to pay less than 20 percent taxes on profit until 2023 in spite of skyrocketing global copper prices (the state-owned CODELCO alone contributes 50 percent of what the private sector does in total, while only accounting for a third of total copper production). That Day of the Race, President Piñera also formally submitted a constitutional reform to Congress for "urgent discussion," a reform ostensibly to recognize indigenous peoples.[22] Yet, this was done without duly consulting its supposed beneficiaries, as is required by national and international laws (Convention 169 of the ILO, among others). Unsurprisingly, the reform project's fine print only recognized "communities," not indigenous peoples, as such international rights-bearers. At the same time, it indirectly sought to erase previous legal recognitions of collective land and water ownership rights. What is important to note here is the juxtaposition of the media frenzy of hyper-individualization (rescuing one miner at a time) and the legal assault on indigenous land rights and collectivity to the media-corporate benefit of TNCs in terms of low taxation.

More is now known regarding the measures taken by the (government-hired) private production company to avoid communication glitches and filter messages and images as the miners were pulled out of the pit. Unlike other messages, "Fuerza al pueblo Mapuche"—a cheer of support for the plight of the Mapuche people in southern Chile—was not conveyed by the media, with the government's production team going so far as to suppress the message, "causing unease amongst the miners' families."[23] Moreover, throughout the media-frenzied ordeal of the miners' accidental captivity (and for over 80 days in total), a group of 34 Mapuche prisoners were engaged in a hunger strike for ancestral land rights and to protest the application of Pinochet's long-lived antiterrorist law (for which the Chilean state has been recently summoned by the Inter-American Court of Human Rights). In contrast to the minute-by-minute coverage of the miners' plight, the Mapuche prisoners received no attention from the mainstream media.[24]

Media "undercommunication" (Goffman 1959: 319) of the life and trials of the Mapuche and others like them makes the indigenous come through as if they were nonexistent, dead, or invisible with an abstract and waterless cultural history. The Atacama 33 rescue effort reveals a few connections between state law, extractive companies, and media celebrity culture, enough to enable a brief exploration of the biopolitical techniques that were combined to transform both the miners and Atacameños into equally disposable, devilishly exposed, flesh-and-blood icons of racialization (see Collier, Maurer, and Suárez-Navaz 1995). In effect, poor miners and natives are likewise culturally and politically exploited and programmed as exclusive "relic" or dead identities that, rather than being the product of collective territorial knowledge practices, are reduced to the individual indigene—the "barest life" of Chile's national casting machine.

Different religious denominations likewise fought over the rescue's hidden purposes: the day that the final miner emerged, October 13, is also the day on which the Virgin of Fatima appeared before Portugal's lucky shepherds, and many others saw similar signs through a variety of coded lenses. "God and the Devil were fighting over me. God won," said Mario Sepúlveda, the second miner rescued and the first to speak with the media. Indeed, it seems very natural to thank God for the success of the technical efforts that extracted these living bodies from the clasp of death, so much so that the t-shirts the miners were asked to put on after their rescue read "Thank you Lord" (conveniently written in both Spanish and English; see Figure 7.1). On the back, the t-shirts read "In his hand are the depths of the earth, and the mountain peaks belong to him" (Psalms 95:4).[25]

LAW AND TERRITORY UNBOUND: ETHNO-TECHNICAL DETERRITORIALIZATIONS

The assertion of individual rights is related directly to the "western idiom of ownership (that) construes agency in terms of what persons do to or with [other people or] things by means of their [actions,] labour, and knowledge" (Mundy and Pottage 2004: 34). The "health, sanitation, birth rate, longevity," and, most important, race, and even the religion of a population, on the other hand, all come to be regulated by the gaze and mechanisms similarly displayed by state in its enterprise to make life (Foucault 2003b: 73; Sanderson 2006).

Foucault thought racialization was indelibly carved into the workings of the state, which necessitates racism as "the break between what must live and what must die" (Foucault 2003c: 254). By imposing distinctions along racial differences in a population, the death of the racially categorized other is posited as allowing

FIGURE 7.1   "¡Gracias Señor! Thank you, Lord!" T-shirt worn by one of the rescued Atacama 33 as they emerged from "the devil's bowels." Photo by Hugo Infante / www .hugoinfante.cl. Reprinted with permission.

"bio-politically correct" life to proliferate. Foucault states, "In a normalizing society, race or racism is the precondition that makes killing acceptable," since only racism can serve as "the precondition for exercising the right to kill" of the state (Foucault 2003c: 256).

This understanding of the fetishistic power of law to "let live" was first highlighted by Foucault and later realigned with the sovereign "power to kill" by Achille Mbembe's theorization of necropolitics. Foucault locates the transformation from sovereign power "to take life or let live" to the current power to "make" life and "let" die in the nineteenth-century definition that "does not erase the old right but which does penetrate it, permeate it" (241). In Mbembe's words, such politics do indeed appear to be "the work of death," where sovereignty is expressed as "the right to kill" (16).[26] In simpler terms, Albert Camus wrote that "property is murder" (1989: 64), and indeed, in the neoliberal era, without property, one might as well be dead (Barros 2008c). By reversing the life of water, neoliberal property has become one of Chile's most powerful fetishes, allowing the extractive industry to thus "cannibalize" oasis life, draining and substituting it with "lighter," prepackaged transcendent culture to be displayed just like the t-shirts on the miners' fragile bodies.[27]

The rescue boosted the country brand along with Piñera's public image, while simultaneously downplaying the extractive industry's abusive market position in the energy and water sectors to the greater sorrow of Chile's citizens and their pockets. Global media coverage of the 33's rescue also had the indirect effect of diverting attention from the responsibilities behind the accident along with Mapuche territorial claims and sense of injustice tied to their relative lack of (legal and media) power, so much so that the naturally shared values and emotions brought on by the miners' drama were transformed into company share value in terms of corporate image.

Because two former CEOs of BHP Billiton were heading CODELCO and TVN (Televisión Nacional de Chile), Chile Inc. (copper and media) was at one point firmly in the hands of Anglo-Australian and Chilean financial capital and their partners worldwide. Commodity fetishism sources nature/culture divides at the highest of capitalist logic. What did the common citizen do? How did the 33 fare? In 2011, after a year touring the globe in a road show that took them to Greece, New York, Disneyland in California, Israel, and Jordan (among other places), the rescued miners found themselves without jobs or pensions. Some sued the Chilean state that had rescued them because "now they are like stray dogs," jobless. Corporate media immediately began reporting on the "public outrage" at such an ungrateful judicial action.[28] A film sponsored by Chile's wealthy miners, starring Antonio Banderas, was released in 2015.

But the story of mining in Chile doesn't begin or end with los 33. My field work exposes a much more complex, and darker, view of life in and around Chile's mining industry and racism.[29] Piñera's right-wing government openly embraced Pinochet's economic legacy of commodity oligopsony and oligopoly, putting Chile right back at the colonial stage. One would not necessarily know this from the Chilean news media, nor are many aware that 45 miners died in mine "accidents" the same year that the 33 were rescued.

THE FETISH FORM OF LAW

Let us accept, then, Michael Taussig's argument that traditionally Andean peoples seek to cajole capitalism in native terms through the fetishistic imagery and worship of the Devil, who would have hence taken over the previously reciprocal and redistributive relations with the kindred spirits of nature. Inversely, we also may presume that the Atacama 33 were "extracted" from the mountain-devil's abode by virtue of the media god's "extractive" pull of iconic "bare life" fetish forms.[30] Fetishized in the image of the mountain-devil, social evils are mediated between precapitalist and capitalist modes of objectifying the human condition. The metaphoric "deal with the Devil" would itself be an indictment of political forces that make people barter their souls and senses of belonging to a broader population for the attractive yet no less destructive power of commodities.

Modern law parallels fetishism in the understanding that they are both self-alienating acts, the consequence of which is such that they are seen to be supernatural and thus unaccountable (like mountain owners and water sources). Modern law commoditizes mutually incommensurable values and rights like fetishes enthral their creators—people who thus become the passive recipients of the very power they have created, a power that is deified and animated to the degree that humans deny their collective authorships.

Chile is a world-class example of how humans' natural and cultural essences and their products can be dislocated into properly marketable things when "life" engages in a supernatural debt of sorts (bought and sold). Of necessity, commodity-based biopolitical societies like Chile, abiding by such colonizing legal forms produce things and persons by "extracting" them as property from the shrinking pools of shared territorial values and political ecologies (dead or alive). The mining TNCs schizogenic denial/recognition of Atacameño collectivity and territoriality (a particular form of socio-natural relationality) comes out reborn as a mystical appraisal of the phantom legal subjects and objects thus extracted from social life, as propertied. This magical passing from the collective "nature" of Atacameño hydraulic societies to the deterritorialized individual's "culture" brings forth the financial predation or "undermining" of indigenous peoples' socionatural base, its fractal "collective nature" proper, which is less and less expressed in terms of kinship (Barros 1997). Some internationalists have called this ecocide (Willemsen-Díaz 2010) and cultural genocide (Nersessian 2005).

According to Pietz, when Gilles Deleuze asserts that the fetish is the natural object of social consciousness as common sense or recognition of value, he uses the word *fetish* as an affirmative term of fundamental theoretical significance congenial to his project of radically revaluing and "reversing" the tradition of Western philosophical thought (Deleuze 1972: 269, in Pietz 1985). The fetish, Pietz adds, "not only originated from, but remains specific to, the problematic of the social value of material objects in situations formed by the encounter of radically heterogeneous social systems" (6). In this light, it is fair to add that in the era of digital reproduction and celebrity culture, media fetishes represent complex social realities "as if" they were radically heterogeneous societies, in which Indians and extractive companies have "productive misunderstandings" about water and are seen to talk "right" past each other. This is what happens in most CSR contracts where mining company "operation managers" meet indigenous stakeholders and related grieving parties in the leveled language of development money (not water or living bodies). In the context of such contracts, law the fetish informs the language of rights and obligations through which mutual—yet no less fictional—responsibilities are set so that a decade ago every care was put into drafting that which referred only to "sport, education, and capacity building," "health and hygiene," or at the most, "care for the environment." No mention is made of the hundreds of thousands of hectares that the Atacameño community of Peine owns according to the law, with full knowledge of the mining companies, to no avail. Everyone around the negotiation table has a transparent commodity in mind that nobody wants to talk about. Indeed, water's silence can magically make people, things, and TNCs commensurate in a contract.

Even if it is to oppose them, we tend to accept hegemonic discourses at face value, and in so doing, we often adopt and adapt their conceptual tools and narrative tropes (Narotzky 2006).[31] But we also tend to discard nonhegemonic discourses that do not necessarily counter anything but pertain to totally different or incommensurable emotional and intellectual leagues seeking their own desires in common. A nonhegemonic human rights–based water culture might help counter the many evils of mining extractivism, one that does not reactualize the false dichotomy opposing the Devil's naturally darker "community" of indigenous poor to the modern gods' celebrity heaven of the rich, whiter chosen few. The fetish form spins the fractal wheel of all such hierarchic imaginations.

CONCLUSIONS: LEGAL FORECASTS AND TERRITORIAL IDENTITIES

> And the Lord said unto Satan, "From whence comest thou?" And Satan answered the Lord, "From going to and fro in the earth, and from walking up and down in it."
> Job 2:2

> It is not at all the same sense of Land: following the legal model, one never ceases to reterritorialize on a point of view, in a domain that takes after a set of constant rapports; but, following the ambulatory model, it is the process of deterritorialization itself that constitutes and extends the territory.
> Gilles Deleuze and Félix Guattari, *Mille plateaux*

Technical action over water's extreme "nature" in the desert reminds one of the ways that background "culture" feeds the collective imaginations that corporate finance wishes to grow and manage separately from nature. Considering that the notions of land and people have mutually constitutive intellectual properties in modern law, then territoriality and culture can be fractally conceived as mutually reinforcing intellectual projections of each other (Barros 1997, Grinlinton and Taylor 2011; Strathern 2004).

Recent inquiries into the modern workings of law in society acknowledge the weight of religious underpinnings that anchor this legal common sense (Agamben 1998; Tierney 1997). In his book *Homo Juridicus*, for instance, Supiot considers the ongoing influence of Judeo-Christian dogma in law and classic scientific reasoning, where contract and research projects function much the same as contracts between parties that invoke a monotheistic deity as guarantor. The state (and the international community by extension) is pictured to be the guarantor of human dignity and freedom to engage in such conventions. While this analysis hints at the history of a sociocultural mentality that might account for the pervasiveness of contract law today, this particularistic—and indeed quite positivistic—model has yet to provide an overarching analytical framework that may account for the existent plural intercourse of the religious and the legal on how related normative ideas flourish by moving from one dogmatic sphere to another. (In response to Supiot's remarks, I have argued it is because of the fetish form of both.) Supiot's understanding of the anthropological functionality of law provides ample means, moreover, with which to historicize the fundamentals of transnational legal pluralism (Sawyer and Gómez 2008; Szablowski 2007; Walby 2007; Zumbansen 2010), a task that has been partially undertaken in his book *The Spirit of Philadelphia* (2012).

Indeed, in all cases, law is plural and works out relationships among the notional groups, persons, and things that it creates from its own rhetorical environment, and such notions usually rely on religious assumptions and related "secularized" declinations or dogma (ideas like community, property, dignity, and freedom). Yet, this should not blind the observer from seeing how law at the same time successfully categorizes, mediates, mixes, and often confuses repertoires of notional persons and things that are by definition incommensurable. This happens not only because of modern law's common language with the transcendentals of religion but rather owing to one of law's properly metalinguistic cross-cultural (and cross-religious) functions: as biopolitical fetish.

In the hands of the mining company, law the fetish naturalizes Atacameño culture as a given, both immutable and real, a substantial commodity that emerges like a ghost from specific ways of organizing persons relative to one another and to both material and intellectual resources. But this living fetish law is even itself further commoditized as today's so-called zombie rights. Like other commodities (dead and alive), subjective rights and laws come thus to be cherished as real objects akin to inert things that on the other hand are conceived as supernatural animate entities with a life force of their own—akin to spirits of God (money just like water). Mountain owner, God or Devil, fetish authority is likewise abstracted from Atacameño relations of production as supernatural injunctions that represent relationships over water as ritual reciprocity, in an ideal world of words and deeds where all is "right," albeit impossibly so.

While Taussig's depiction of commodity fetishism in the Andes has often been criticized for caricaturizing the religious phenomenon and reducing its complexity—hence reducing its sociality and materiality—Pietz's more cross-cultural analysis of "the problem of the fetish" explores the material circumstances from which religious phenomena are extracted and abstracted in the first place, later recast in the fetish form of "law." So instead of looking at traditional Andean devil worship and religious masks, dances, and traditions as wily fetish forms of accommodative resistance/insistence in the masterful line of Bouysse-Cassagne, Taussig, or Gruzinski, I have here attempted, inversely, to show how the fetish form of modern law enables mining companies to actively conceal the plights of collective nature/culture differentiation—"multi-nature" in Latour's sense—by deifying the technical means by which, say, the Atacama's 33 were extracted from tragedy and made into spectacular icons of hard-working poverty. Mass media publicly extract miner bodies from hell, while mining companies surreptitiously drain the land of its tantalizing wealth.

Mainstream media's parallel silencing or strategic "undercommunication" of hydraulic cultures and indigenous peoples has had a similar effect and on a different scale of organization when the Atacameño people are represented archaeologically, as dead and inert things of the tradable past (Barros 2010).[32] Modern Atacameño culture thus relies on the subvention and fabrication of other racialized commodities, like country brands, ethno-chic designs, world class heritage, and archaeological sites or the promotion of "special" capacity building schemes, all of which are further abstracted through mainstream media's light-cultured, fit-for-tourism packages as commonly "sold" to the Atacameños and their avid public by mining and government agencies and clientele alike. Yet, such token devolution of archaeological sites and free light-cultural shows obscure deeper-running problems and rampant inequality.

The Comaroffs' assertion that global Ethnicity Inc. is the upshot of cultural commoditization (aka ethnic branding—just as nation branding and Divinity Inc.) overlooks how this itself is the direct product of resource extraction and environmental degradation. A further by-product of cultural commoditization, individualization can in effect be seen as being the immediate effect of the extraction of water and minerals as a dead or technically racialized "nature" of sorts. Indeed, privatized water is the "transparent commodity" or vital substance informing the racialized backdrop of extractivism, and working through this idea in a Foucauldian vein has helped us to understand how legally and racially encoded properties and inequalities are legitimized and governed spectacularly by means of the fetish form of law.

So if Atacama Desert peoples do sometimes successfully defend their mountains' water and manage to reenact their hydraulic sociality by insisting on their own territorial sense of water justice, on the longer "necropolitical" run (Mbembe 2003), they cannot prevent the overall diminishing returns of sui iuris revenue streams-cum-zombie (living dead) rights, draught, ethnic dislocation, and crushing deterritorialized suburban poverty. More precisely, hydraulic communities are deterritorialized by the same force that groundwater and community life are extracted as commodities, against their will, by the power of Chile's mine-controlled media and state (Bonilla and Norero 1999). This is why Atacameño territorial identity has today become the token (silent) answer for unequal relations to water.[33]

Atacameño lawfare grafts new corporate skins as so many knowledge-skills or masks on their Andean semblance of collective action, always-growing paper fences as so many "incorporated" fetishes "inside" the law. Informed and recast thus, partial restitutions and substitutions in terms of "neighborly social responsibility" in turn feed Indian "stakeholder grievances" against extractive TNCs that put traditional livelihoods in peril. The paper-chase environment generated by this possessive nominalism is inherent to justice in the fetish form of law, relentlessly stripping the Mayllkus of their riches.

The neoliberal paradox here is that, reified, mediatized, and readied for individual consumption, Atacameño culture becomes the "other" of water and copper as "extracted nature," precisely as the embodiment of capitalism's paradigmatic contradictions, a biopolitical "object" too often accounted for in terms of racialized premature death. Indeed, it is this very fetish ambivalence that lends law its universalistic claim to power over life and death.

The global extractive industry uses Transnational-Ethnicity Inc. as a legal trope that operates as a human rights clearinghouse for the state, the biopolitical task then being to account for the people in and out of the loop, dead or alive, and certainly not to act as guarantor of human dignity, as any human rights practitioner would hope. This reality is today exemplarily reframed in the terms of the complex legal subjectivities that have crystallized around the 2007 United Nations Declaration on the Rights of Indigenous Peoples (UNDRIP), an order of things also partially achieved by the UN's intricate human rights accountability program, as deployed through the High Commissioner's Office for Human Rights. A sense of inevitability arises from the DRIP's legal chronicle of an announced ethnic group, "sense of inevitability" that heralds unfettered genocide in resource-rich indigenous territories across the world, often under the guise of what one might call called "low intensity" lawfare.

The much-awaited irruption of the DRIP leaves no semantic room for cheating with indigenous peoples' rights, however: uncloaked from their previous "domestic" postcolonial condition, indigenous peoples are now more fully recognized as international legal subjects than ever, and they have no choice but to claim their territorial self-determination as a basic human right related to legal notions of sovereignty, autonomy, and property; life and death; water, and all, by still using the scripts of colonization (Narotzky 2006). Inscribed in the international legal sphere as "soft law" with pretensions to redress and repair historical injustices committed against indigenous peoples, the legal historicity of governments' disciplines and punishments dominate so unbearably so that past and present injustices become ever more pressing, despairing, and violent, to paroxysm.

In sum, while commodity fetishism obscures the relations of production, it also commodifies reproduction (of bodies), labor (as wage), and distribution (as exchange). Mountains, like law, refer to distributional authority. The first have slowly been eroded and drained of their immanent power by state and TNC extractions, where law operates the competing relationships at virtual stake. This fetishism is intrinsic to the living law, or law from below (power-subjective rights). The higher, institutional order of fetishism (or super fetish) regulates lower order simulacra, this is to say, regulates the relationships between relationships (as limit to power or objective rights) in terms of their VALUE (dead or alive)—hopefully, not left into the sole hands of the market.

Like law, anthropology concerns itself with social variability: difference and change, people and resources—writ large: power, techniques, skills, desires, beliefs, attitudes, values or to retake Sen's phrasing, "capabilities" (Sen 2009). In such instances of changing political ecology and "flat" ontologies engaging multifarious socio-natural worlds, it becomes necessary to reterritorialize the notion of capabilities.[34] In the Atacameño case, this means having to defend sustainable hydraulic cultures, while avoiding the pitfalls of cultural commoditization around water disputes where "light culture" supplants "natural" water justice at the price of ecocide. Modern market water divides produce socio-natural differentiations that become legally (de- and re-)fetishized to reinforce the rationalist nature/culture dichotomy at the root of all inequalities, including unequal access to water-justice in the desert.[35] The idea of water justice, in this context, has become the fetish possibility of territorial commensurability.

For it remains the case that Chile's rampant social inequalities can be largely explained in terms of copper, energy, and water; while all Chileans are getting slowly crushed by the corrupt political and economic forces that prey and feed on Chile's resource curse boom, none more so than the country's indigenous peoples who are chipped off the landscape with each blow (along with birds and plants and things). This is not necessarily the picture the world took away from the rescue of los 33, but it is a picture worth bearing in mind. In Chile's Atacama Desert, law in society still pits God with the Devil in more supernatural terms than ever.

NOTES

1. Escobar (2010) notes the existence of "non-hegemonic" place-based cultural groups with profoundly different political and knowledge systems that are guided by a wish to live creatively in and with certain places (in "constant peaks of territorialization"). Such communities relinquish ways of thinking based on binaries, assumed unities, rigid laws, and political structures to embrace multiplicities, autonomously evolving place-based responses, networks, and micropolitics based on radical particularities and extended differences (see Grinlinton and Taylor 2011).

2. "Not even in its beginnings was capital 'territorial': its de-territorializing power consists in taking as an object, not even land itself, but the 'materialized work' or merchandise. . . . Property is not over land or soil, nor even over the modes of production, but over abstract convertible rights" (Deleuze and Guattari 1980: 567).

3. Cultural commodity fetishism transforms a cultural commodity (picture, icon, sound, frame) into a product with a "life of its own" that is independent of the volition and initiative of the artist or the culture that produced it. In his book *The Society of the Spectacle*, Guy Debord goes so far as to elaborate on how intimacies of intersubjectivity and personal self-relation are commodified into and presented as discrete "experiences" that can be bought and sold. The Society of the Spectacle is the ultimate form of social alienation that occurs when a person views his or her being (self) as a commodity that can be bought and sold, because he or she regards every human relation as a (potential) business transaction. Cultural commodity fetishism is the misperception that the social relationships involved in the production of cultural commodities do not take place among living, breathing people and cultures but as objective ties between "money" and "commodities" exchanged in market trade. As such, cultural commodity fetishism transforms the *subjective* and abstract collective value of socio-nature into *objective*, real things and people that have (only) individual, deterritorialized economic value.

4. Copper has a long pre-Columbian history, the Atacama Desert being considered the cradle of metallurgy in the Southern Cone. For an in-depth discussion of Atacama Desert law, anthropology, and mining geopolitics, see Zapata (1992) and Vergara (2008).

5. For a state-of-the-art analysis of the legal situation of lithium exploitation in Chile (41 percent of world production), see http://www.quepasa.cl/articulo/negocios/2012/03/16-7940-9-la-ilusion-del-litio.shtml.

6. See *The Economist*'s characterization of Pinochet's mining corruption legacy at http://www.economist.com/news/business-and-finance/21617153-chiles-stock-exchange-regulator-dishes-out-huge-fines-over-series-illegal-share.

7. http://fundacionsol.wordpress.com/2011/11/15/chile%E2%80%99s-4000-families-that-live-in-a-dream-world/.

8. Until 2005, only Escondida effectively paid income tax. That year, under social democratic president Ricardo Lagos, mining tax laws were rewritten to be more effective. The industry won deep concessions, however, that were guaranteed to last until 2017, allowing it to pay advantageously little in Chile compared to countries like Australia. Escondida made close to US$6 billion in profit in 2007 (it being but one of three copper mines controlled by BHP Billiton in Chile). Overall, private copper companies made nearly US$25 billion in 2010, while paying less than US$1 billion in taxes.

9. Interview with Máximo Pacheco, Chile's Ministry of Energy, who reported that Chile's household average electricity bill is Latin America's highest and whose gas bill is the highest in the world. http://www.eldinamo.cl/2014/08/05/ministro-pacheco-el-mayor-desafio-de -chile-es-bajar-los-precios-de-la-electricidad/.

10. COCHILCO (2007: 5–6).

11. Wetland water extraction models have been known to fall apart after only three or four years.

12. For an interesting analysis of "impression management" in the Atacama basin, see Carrasco (2010).

13. It is controlled by the Anglo-Australian poly-mining giant BHP Billiton.

14. This can be seen as an example of the kind of "judicialization" of political activism and claims-making described in Sieder, Angell, and Schjolden (2005) and Couso, Huneeus, and Sieder (2010).

15. I unintentionally had a prominent role at the meetings, acting both as representative lawyer and researcher. As the official environmental evaluation process of the Pampa Colorada project unfolded, I was told that one of the mine's CEOs had asked my university employer to terminate me. Instead, they asked me "for my own good" to "stop talking about indigenous peoples' rights, their territories and human rights in general," forbidding me explicitly from speaking to the press. They went on to explain that the situation was delicate because the university had been given a multimillion-dollar donation from the miner to build a scientific park, two new archaeology museums, a new geology department, a meteorite exhibit, and more. My "activism," they told me, seriously jeopardized the university's otherwise excellent relationship with the miner, who had conditioned the receipt of any further funding on my leaving the university. Unfortunately, it was too late. My interviews had already been published. By doing the exact opposite (and being "outspoken" and "honest"), the magic of public support eventually helped me to break the mining group's spell (although, ironically, my employer later complained that I had not mentioned the university by name in a glossy magazine interview). In the end, my own "bare body" had become immune to mediatized exposition and "light" political discrimination, blacklisting, censorship and persecution— while Atacameno voices rose to successfully denounce their collective plight over water.

16. See page 1 and starting on page 86 for the final decision of the COREMA of Antofagasta rejecting Escondida's Pampa Colorada Project on behalf of atacameño communities. https://www.e-seia.cl/externos/admin_seia_web/archivos/6502_2007_11_19_RE.pdf.

17. See Comaroff and Comaroff (2009) for an in-depth treatment of this concept.

18. There is no better example of this trend than Anglo American's corporative image stunt at http://www.appfly.com/work/anglo-american-get-the-full-story. It explains how the company obtained "share value from shared values: real mining, real people, real difference." The article is accompanied by studio portraits of carefully made-up hard-working miners and employees from operations the world over.

19. There was also another, slightly more negative, outcome (that lasted at least until the left-wing New Majority block took power in early 2014, with Bachelet replacing Piñera). Wary of the media's role in the environmental evaluation process, transnational mining companies have since bought themselves more direct influence in the public media than ever before. Until 2014, the main public television channel was under the direct influence of the mining lobby. Chile's most recent corruption scandals have since pushed the country further into the trail of Spain, Argentina, and Brazil, taking it to an institutional standstill—as evidence of serious wrongdoings is mounting to unprecedented heights. See the May 28, 2015, interview with Chile's President Bachelet in *El País* at http://elpais.com/elpais/2015/05/28/inenglish/1432817255_353853.html; and "Corruption in Politics: Chile's Gordian Knot: Successive Scandals Jeopardize Prized Institutional Stability" at http://panampost.com/malgorzata-lange/2015/04/20/corruption-in-politics-chiles-gordian-knot/.

20. See http://www2.lse.ac.uk/publicEvents/events/2010/20101018t1830vLSE1.aspx.

21. The global private sector has received due praise for its spontaneous technical reaction: Kansas-based Layne Christensen, for instance, operated the drills that located the miners initially and drilled the shaft that was ultimately used to rescue them. The South African firm Murray & Roberts supplied a 40-ton drilling machine called the Strata 950. And the Canadian Precision Drilling Corp. created a backup rescue shaft in case the primary one collapsed. Center Rock Inc., headquartered in Berlin, Pennsylvania, designed the specialized drill bits and automated hammers that made the hole. The Chilean government commissioned Schramm Inc. of West Chester, Pennsylvania, for the drill rig. Milwaukee's Atlas Copco Construction Mining Co. helped rescuers integrate the drilling equipment from these different sources, and NASA worked closely with Chilean authorities to design the custom-made Phoenix capsule used for extraction. Soon after the miners were found, the Chilean Embassy reached out to UPS to ship drilling tools from America. In less than two days, UPS transported seven shipments of equipment—totaling more than 50,000 pounds—from Pennsylvania to Chile. The Aramark Corporation was responsible for keeping the miners fed. Working with the Chilean Health Ministry, NASA, and other experts, a chef and a staff of 12 created a menu that could meet the miners' nutritional needs. They also developed a means to transport, at final count, approximately 6,000 vacuum-packed meals down the 2,300-foot-deep shaft. Zephyr Technologies of Annapolis, Maryland, provided the digital tools used to monitor the miners' health while they were underground. Its BioHarness employs digital sensors to read the wearer's vital signs and wireless technology to send that data aboveground. Physicians and psychologists, using that data and advanced video camera technology furnished by Aries Central California Video, were able to conduct one-on-one health assessments with each miner multiple times a week.

22. The Atacameño, Aymara, Coya, Diaguita, Kaweskar, Quechua, Mapuche, Rapa Nui, and Yagan peoples—about 1.5 million, or 8 percent of Chile's population.

23. See http://diario.latercera.com/2010/10/19/01/contenido/pais/31-42024-9-las-diferencias-que-supero-el-equipo-de-rescatistas-para-cumplir-la-mision.shtml.

24. Another heated dialogue took place via Twitter while the miners were trapped. President Piñera's brother confronted activist and *Shock Doctrine* author Naomi Klein, who had blamed capitalism for the accident and said, "It was President Piñera's brother José who wrote the law privatizing the mines under Pinochet, helping create the disaster." José Piñera replied, "What are you smoking, Naomi?" See http://www.josepinera.com/articles/articles_debate_naomiklein.htm.

25. See also http://religion.blogs.cnn.com/2010/10/14/the-story-behind-the-chilean -miners-jesus-t-shirts/.

26. See also Walter Benjamin's "Critique of Violence" (1999).

27. For a detailed analysis of the media's coverage of the rescue, see http://www.funda cionimagendechile.cl/Recursos/Documento/D2610172520-documento-an%C3%A1lisis -mineros-fundaci%C3%B3n-imagen-de-chile.pdf.

28. See http://globedia.com/afectan-atacama-problemas-psiquiatricos-desempleo; and http://www.elmundo.es/america/2011/05/09/noticias/1304903639.html.

29. On Chilean castes, poverty, and indigenous peoples, see Barros (2008b).

30. See Agamben (1998) on the notion of "bare life."

31. See Sanhueza and Gundermann (2007), Boccara and Ayala (2011), and Gundermann, González, and Durston (2014) for racialized, mainstream, neocolonial, state-centered social critiques of modern indigenous collective agency (and rights discourse) in the Atacama Desert—as deterritorialized or "non pre-existent" to Chilean national sovereignty or as "essentialist," "un-historical," "inauthentic," and boldly subservient to neoliberal capitalism.

32. Goffman (1959) defines such "impression management" as a world stage in which actors are framed with reference to normality. Impression management is a response to the perception that one or more people sense something to be abnormal or wrong. These impressions need to be managed to reestablish an impression of normalcy. In the process, some information is "overcommunicated," whereas other information is "undercommunicated," and law is a perfect medium for both.

33. See Sanhueza and Gundermann (2007) and especially Gundermann, González, and Durston (2014) for the sociohistorical justification of the Chilean state's neocolonial implementation of the universally condemned *terra nullius* doctrine that deprives Atacama Desert indigenous peoples of their preexisting land rights—to this day (Barros 2008c).

34. See Escobar (2010).

35. See Sahlins (2008).

WORKS CITED

Agamben, Giorgio. 1998. *Homo Sacer: Sovereign Power and Bare Life*. Stanford, CA: Stanford University Press.

Barros, Alonso. 1997. "Desarrollo y pachamama: Paisajes conflictivos en el Desierto de Atacama." *Estudios Atacameños* 13: 75–94.

———. 2008a. "Agua subterránea: Autonomía, discriminación y justicia ambiental en el Salar de Atacama." In *Globalización, derechos humanos y pueblos indígenas*, edited by Álvaro Bello and José Aylwin, 347–372. Santiago: Fundación FORD, Observatorio Ciudadano e IWGIA.

———. 2008b. "De las castas y la pobreza indígena en Chile." In *Anales del Instituto de Chile. N° 27, La pobreza en Chile II*, 213–262. http://www.institutodechile.cl/home/ images/stories/anales_2008_web.pdf.

_____. 2008c. "Identidades y propiedades: Transiciones territoriales en el siglo XIX atacameño." *Estudios Atacameños* 35: 119–139.

_____. 2010. "Charqui por carne: Arqueología, propiedad y desigualdad en el Desierto de Atacama." In *El regreso de los muertos y las promesas del oro: Significados y usos del patrimonio arqueológico en los conflictos sociales frente al estado y a los capitales transnacionales*, 83–105. Córdoba, Argentina: Editorial Brujas.

Barros, Alonso, and Judith Schönsteiner. 2014. "Due Diligence: Investment Projects, Property over Natural Resources and the Free Prior Informed Consultation of Indigenous Peoples and Communities Concerned." In *Informe anual sobre derechos humanos en Chile 2014*, edited by Tomás Vial, 203–244. Santiago: Universidad Diego Portales.

Benjamin, Walter. 1999. "Critique of Violence." In *Selected Writings*, edited by Marcus Bullock and Michael Jennings, 1:237–252. Translated by Edmund Jephcott. Cambridge, MA: Harvard University Press.

Bello, Alvaro, and Marta Rangel. 2000. *Etnicidad, "raza" y equidad en América Latina y el Caribe*. Santiago: CEPAL, División de Desarrollo Social.

Bernand, Carmen, and Serge Gruzinski. 1988. *De l'idolâtrie: Une archéologie des sciences religieuses*. Paris: Seuil.

Betanzos, Juan Diez de. 1987. *Suma y narración de los Incas*. Transcribed by María Carmen Martín Rubio. Madrid: Atlas.

Boccara, Guillaume, and Patricia Ayala. 2011. "Patrimonializar al indígena: Imaginación del multiculturalismo neoliberal en Chile." *Cahiers des Amériques Latines* 67: 207–230.

Bolados, Paola. 2014. "Los conflictos etnoambientales de Pampa Colorada y el Tatio en el Salar de Atacama, Norte de Chile: Procesos étnicos en un contexto minero y turístico transnacional." *Estudios Atacameños* 48: 228–248.

Bonilla, Carlos, and Aldo Norero, eds. 1999. *Las sequías en Chile: Causas, consecuencias y mitigación*. Santiago: Universidad Católica de Chile, Facultad de Agronomía e Ingeniería Forestal.

Bouysse-Cassagne, Thérèse. 2005. "Las minas del centro-sur andino, los cultos prehispánicos y los cultos cristianos." *Bulletin de l'Institut Français d'Études Andines* 34 (3): 443–462.

———. 2008. "Minas del sol, del Inka, y de la gente: Potosí en el contexto de la minería prehispana." In *Minas y metalurgias en los Andes del Sur, entre la época prehispánica y el siglo XVII*, edited by Pablo José Cruz and Jean-Joinville Vacher, 278–301. Sucre, Bolivia: Instituto Francés de Estudios Andinos et Institut de Recherche pour le Développement (IRD).

———. 2012. "Partición colonial del territorio, cultos funerarios y memoria ancestral en Carangas y precordillera de Arica (siglos xvi–xvii)." *Chungara, Revista de Antropología Chilena* 44 (4): 669–689.

Busso, Matías, Martín Cicowies, and Leonardo Gasparini. 2005. *Etnicidad y los objetivos del milenio en América Latina y el Caribe*. Buenos Aires: CEPAL, PNUD, BID, Banco Mundial.

Camus, Albert. 1989. *Carnets III: Mars 1951–Décembre 1959*. Paris: Gallimard.

Carrasco, Anita. 2010. "A Sacred Mountain and the Art of 'Impression Management': Analyzing a Mining Company's Encounter with Indigenous Communities in Atacama, Chile." *Mountain Research and Development* 30 (4): 391–397.

COCHILCO. 2007. *Gestión del recurso hídrico y la minería en Chile: Diagnóstico para Mesa Público-Privada Nacional*. http://www.cochilco.cl/productos/pdf/estudios2007/mesa_agua.pdf.

Collier, Jane F., Bill Maurer, and Liliana Suárez-Navaz. 1995. "Sanctioned Identities: Legal Constructions of Modern Personhood." *Identities* 2 (1): 1–27.

Comaroff, John L., and Jean Comaroff. 2009. *Ethnicity Inc*. Chicago: University of Chicago Press.

Comisión Nacional de Riego. 2008. *Diagnóstico y propuestas de fomento al riego y drenaje para la pequeña agricultura y etnias originales.* Santiago: MOP.

Coombe, Rosemary, and Nicole Aylwin. 2011. "Bordering Diversity and Desire: Using Intellectual Property to Mark Place-Based Products." *Environment and Planning* 43 (9): 2027–2042.

Couso, Javier, Alexandra Huneeus, and Rachel Sieder, eds. 2010. *Cultures of Legality: Judicialization and Political Activism in Latin America.* Cambridge: Cambridge University Press.

Deleuze, Gilles. 1972. *Différence et répétition.* Paris: PUF.

Deleuze, Gilles, and Félix Guattari. 1980. *Mille plateaux: Capitalisme et schizophrénie II.* Paris: Minuit.

Escobar, Arturo. 1998. "Whose Knowledge, Whose Nature? Biodiversity, Conservation, and the Political Ecology of Social Movements." *Journal of Political Ecology* 5: 53–82.

———. 2010. "Postconstructivist Political Ecologies." In *International Handbook of Environmental Sociology,* edited by Michael Redclift and Graham Woodgate, 91–105. 2nd ed. Cheltenham, UK: Elgar.

Foncea, Valeria. 2007 "H2O." News report in Spanish broadcast by Chile's National Television. https://www.youtube.com/watch?v=9AM9UlhJPD4 (translations by the author).

Foucault, Michel. 2003a. "Governmentality." In *Ethics: The Essential Foucault 1954–1984,* edited by Paul Rabinow and Nikolas Rose, 229–246. New York: New Press.

———. 2003b. "The Birth of Biopolitics." In *Ethics: The Essential Foucault 1954–1984,* edited by Paul Rabinow and Nikolas Rose, 202–208. New York: New Press.

———. 2003c. "17 March 1976." In *Society Must Be Defended: Lectures at the Collège de France, 1975–1976,* edited by Mauro Bertani, 239–264. New York: Picador.

Gell, Alfred. 1998. *Art and Agency: An Anthropological Theory.* Oxford: Clarendon.

Goffman, Erving. 1959. *The Presentation of Self in Everyday Life.* Garden City, NY: Doubleday.

Grinlinton, David, and Prue Taylor, eds. 2011. *Property Rights and Sustainability: The Evolution of Property Rights to Meet Ecological Challenges.* Vol. 11 of *Legal Aspects of Sustainable Development.* Boston: Martinus Nijhoff.

Gruzinski, Serge. 1985. *Les hommes-dieux du Mexique: Pouvoir indien et société coloniale 17e et 18e siècles.* Paris: Archives Contemporaines.

———. 1988. *La colonisation de l'imaginaire: Sociétés indigènes et occidentalisation dans le Mexique espagnol: XVIe–XVIIIe siècle.* Paris: Gallimard.

———. 1999. *La pensée métisse.* Paris: Fayard.

Gundermann, Hans, Héctor González, and John Durston. 2014. "Relaciones sociales y etnicidad en el espacio aymara chileno." *Chungará (Arica)* 46 (3): 397–421.

Hall, Gillette, and Harry Anthony Patrinos. 2005. *Indigenous People, Poverty and Human Development in Latin America: 1994–2004.* Washington, DC: World Bank.

INDH—Instituto Nacional de Derechos Humanos. 2014. "Derechos de los pueblos indígenas: Territorios y consulta previa." In *Informe Anual del Instituto Nacional de Derechos Humanos de Chile 2014,* 231–250. Santiago: INDH.

Mandiola, Carla. 2012. "El pueblo del litio." *La Tercera,* October 21. http://diario.latercera.com/2012/10/21/01/contenido/la-tercera-el-semanal/34-121061-9-el-pueblo-del-litio.shtml.

Marx, Karl. 1887. *Capital: A Critique of Political Economy.* Vol. 1. Chicago: Charles H. Kerr.

Mbembe, Achille. 2003. "Necropolitics." *Public Culture* 15 (1): 11 40.

MBN. 2011. *Chile: Superficie de Territorio Fiscal. Ministerio de Bienes Nacionales Junio 2011.* http://www.bienesnacionales.cl/wp-content/uploads/2011/12/ChileSuperficie -Territorio-Fiscal-Jun-2011.pdf.

Mundy, Martha, and Alain Pottage. 2004. *Law, Anthropology, and the Constitution of the Social: Making Persons and Things.* Cambridge: Cambridge University Press.

Narotzky, Susana. 2006. "The Production of Knowledge and the Production of Hegemony: Anthropological Theory and Political Struggles in Spain." In *World Anthropologies: Disciplinary Transformations within Systems of Power,* edited by Gustavo Lins-Ribeiro and Arturo Escobar, 133–154. Oxford: Berg.

Nash, June. 1979. *We Eat the Mines and the Mines Eat Us: Dependency and Exploitation in Bolivian Tin Mines.* New York: Columbia University Press.

Nersessian, David. 2005. "Rethinking Cultural Genocide under International Law." *Human Rights Dialogue Series* 2 (12). http://www.carnegiecouncil.org/resources/publications/ dialogue/2_12/section_1/5139.html.

OECD—Organization for Economic Cooperation and Development. 2015. *Why Less Inequality Benefits All (Chile).* http://www.oecd.org/chile/OECD2015-In-It-Together -Highlights-Chile.pdf.

Pietz, William. 1985. "Problem of the Fetish I." *Res: Anthropology and Aesthetics* 9: 5–17.

Pourrut, Pierre, ed. 1995. *El desierto, el hombre y el agua: Agua, ocupación del espacio y economia campesina en la región atacameña: Aspectos dinámicos.* Antofagasta, Chile: UCN.

Psacharopoulos, George, and Harry Patrinos. 1994. *Indigenous People and Poverty in Latin America: An Empirical Analysis.* Washington, DC: World Bank.

RIDES. 2005. *Bienestar humano y manejo sustentable en San Pedro de Atacama, Chile Resumen Ejecutivo.* Santiago: RIDES.

Sahlins, Marshall. 2008. *The Western Illusion of Human Nature.* Chicago: Prickly Paradigm.

Sánchez, Rafael, Carla Marchant, and Axel Borsdorf. 2012. "The Role of Chilean Mountain Areas in Time of Drought and Energy Crisis: New Pressures and Challenges for Vulnerable Ecosystems." *Journal of Mountain Science* 9 (4): 451–462.

Sanderson, Jorge. 2006. "La población indígena en Chile, censos y encuestas territoriales." In *Pueblos indígenas y afrodescendientes de América Latina y el Caribe: Información sociodemográfica para políticas y programas,* edited by Fabiana del Popolo and M. Ávila, 109–134. Santiago: CEPAL-ECLAC. http://www.eclac.cl/publicaciones/xml/0/25730/ pueblosindigenas_final-web.pdf.

Sanhueza, María, and Hans Gundermann. 2007. "Estado, expansión capitalista y sujetos sociales en Atacama (1879–1928)." *Estudios Atacameños* 34: 113–136.

Sawyer, Suzana, and Edmund Gómez. 2008. "Transnational Governmentality and Resource Extraction: Indigenous Peoples, Multinational Corporations, Multilateral Institutions and the State." UNRISD Identities, Conflict and Cohesion Programme Paper 13.

Sieder, Rachel, Alan Angell, and Line Schjolden. 2005. *The Judicialization of Politics in Latin America.* New York: Palgrave Macmillan.

Sen, Amartya. 2009. *The Idea of Justice.* Cambridge, MA: Harvard University Press.

SERNAGEOMIN. 2008. *Atlas de Faenas Mineras (Antofagasta y Atacama): Servicio Nacional de Geografía y Minería.* http://www.sernageomin.cl/pdf/mineria/estadisticas/atlas/ atlas_faenas%20Anfo_Atacama.pdf.

SINIA. 2008. "Análisis de vulnerabilidad del sector silvoagropecuario, recurso hídricos y edáficos frente a escenarios de cambio climático." http://www.sinia.cl/1292/ articles-46115_capituloIV_informefinal.pdf, chap. 4.

Strathern, Marilyn. 2004. "Land as Intellectual Property." In *Oxford Amnesty Lectures, 13: Land Rights*, edited by Timothy Chesters, 39–46. Oxford: Oxford University Press.

Supiot, Alain. 2007. *Homo Juridicus*. London: Verso.

———. 2012. *The Spirit of Philadelphia*. London: Verso.

Szablowski, David. 2007. *Transnational Law and Local Struggles: Mining Communities and the World Bank*. Portland, OR: Hart.

Tierney, Brian. 1997. *The Idea of Natural Rights*. Cambridge: Eerdmans.

Taussig, Michael. 1980. *The Devil and Commodity Fetishism in South America*. Chapel Hill: University of North Carolina Press.

Vergara, Angela. 2008. *Copper Workers, International Business and Domestic Politics in Cold War Chile*. University Park: Pennsylvania State University Press.

Walby, Kevin. 2007. "Contributions to a Post-Sovereigntist Understanding of Law: Foucault, Law as Governance, and Legal Pluralism." *Social and Legal Studies* 16: 551.

Willemsen-Díaz, Augusto. 2010. "Cómo llegaron los derechos de los pueblos indígenas a la ONU?" In *El desafío de la Declaración: Historia y futuro de la declaración de la ONU sobre pueblos indígenas*, edited by Claire Charters and Rodolfo Stavenhagen, 16–33. Copenhagen: IWGIA.

World Bank. 2006. *World Development Report 2006: Equity and Development*. Washington, DC: World Bank.

Zapata, Francisco. 1992. *Atacama: Desierto de la discordia: Minería y política internacional en Bolivia, Chile y Perú*. Mexico City: Colegio de México.

Zumbansen, Peer. 2010. "Transnational Legal Pluralism." CLPE Research Paper 01/2010. http://papers.ssrn.com/sol3/papers.cfm?abstract_id=1542907.

CONCLUSION

Justice at the Limits of Law

Mark Goodale

SERÁ JUSTICIA

My first encounter with the complicated imaginaries of justice in Latin America was deceptively understated. The year was 1998, and I had just begun ethnographic research far from the centers of ongoing civil war, ethnic atrocities, and indigenous mobilization. The sleepy capital of Sacaca in the province Alonso de Ibañez in Bolivia's norte de Potosí was notable beyond its borders both within Bolivia and abroad primarily for its *tinkus*, rituals that brought hundreds of *campesinos* from their hamlets to town to fight one another on important days in the yearly agro-religious calendar. But outside of these periods of relative chaos, the region was marked mainly by its quiet poverty and simmering land disputes, low-grade local political power struggles, and both geographic and symbolic isolation from the national consciousness.

Sacaca was (and still is) a classic colonial *reducción*, one of the hundreds of Spanish-style towns that were the result of Viceroy Toledo's reforms of the sixteenth century through which the empire's indigenous population was forcibly "reduced" from their dispersed pre-Columbian settlements into civic spaces that reflected the colonial Spanish ideal of civilization. The *reducción* typically featured a central plaza surrounded geometrically by the symbols of sacred and secular power: the mayor's administrative building, a police station, a legal court, perhaps an office of a notary public, and, most important, the church. In most of Bolivia's rural provincial towns like Sacaca during the ancien régime,[1] the legal court was a court of first instance with a single judge and two other functionaries: a *secretario*, whose primary task was to record court sessions on a typewriter, and a right-hand man (always a man) called an *actuario*, who kept the records, opened and closed the court sessions, received visitors to the small waiting room, and maintained the court's calendar. As in Sacaca's court—technically a *juzgado de instrucción*—the docket in Bolivia's rural courts of first instance was light—perhaps one or two hearings a week and weeks would often pass without any cases at all on the court's calendar. Even given this relatively light workload, the official court vacations—around Todos Santos, Christmas, Carnival—were disproportionately lengthy. During Carnival, for example, the court was shuttered for an entire month.

But when the court was in session, it always began with the same ritualistic process. The parties gathered in the courtroom, which also doubled as the judge's chambers, a small room that contained an office desk and chairs arranged along three of the walls for witnesses, victims, the accused, and different kinds of legal counsel. The *actuario* would place himself next to the judge's side at a small table with his manual typewriter positioned in front of him. Some minutes after everyone was in place, the *actuario* would announce, "The court of Dr. [X] is now in session. Please rise." At that moment, everyone would stand, the door would open, and the judge would enter. Immediately, everyone in the room would make the ancient "sign of the cross" with their thumb and crossed forefinger, which they held in front of their faces. After collectively taking the oath, each person in the room was obligated to kiss a large crucifix that was placed upright on a stand at the front of the judge's desk. After each person in the room kissed the cross, he or she would intone solemnly, "será justicia"—"there will be justice."

This terse phrase, which can be heard in legal processes and courts throughout Latin America, always intrigued me, in part because of the use of the simple future tense, which carries with it a sense of certainty that has important implications for how formal legal procedures are conceptualized in Latin America. But more than anything, the phrase lingered in the analytical imagination because, at least in Sacaca, it was the only time one heard the word *justice* spoken, even by those who worked at the court. Justice was just a word to be intoned, mechanically, unthinkingly, even somewhat begrudgingly, rather than something concrete to be achieved, whether in the form of a specific legal resolution or, more generally, in the form of righting past wrongs, fighting against impunity, or acting to change unequal social or economic conditions. At a certain point, I asked the judge directly what he thought justice meant? A man not given to deep analysis, he considered for a moment and then replied, "Work." He did not mean work in the sense that justice is an abstract ideal that one must constantly work toward—a sort of clichéd understanding that hovers over our preoccupation with justice as a foundational keyword (Williams 1976)—but work as in his job as an obscure *juez instructor* assigned to the remote margins of Bolivian judicial and social life, as far from the clubby Ilustre Colegio de Abogados as a Bolivian lawyer could get. As least for this particular rural Bolivian judge, "será justicia" meant "my dreary life here in Sacaca will go on, and on, and on."

During later research on law and culture in Bolivia, I would confront a similar problem with the multiple possible meanings and practices of human rights. However, it was soon clear as a question of both ethnographic research and ideological history that human rights, as an admittedly "protean" (Baxi 2002) referent, nevertheless functioned in qualitatively different ways than did justice. Justice remained vague as a social signifier and remote in practice. Human rights, by contrast, evoked the flood of non-governmental organizations (NGOs) to rural Bolivia throughout the 1990s and early 2000s; the debates at the national level over the ratification of late-generation rights documents like ILO 169; and the rearticulation of long-standing social and economic grievances (particularly by the indigenous movements) in the language of rights, self-determination, and dignity. As a legal-anthropological problem worthy of close ethnographic attention, human rights was thick, while justice seemed to be either frustratingly thin or too closely intertwined with the kinds of formal, particularly state, legal domains that (at that time, at least) had less appeal as sites of anthropological scrutiny.

But as Sandra Brunnegger and Karen Faulk argue in their introduction to this book, the elasticity and apparent remoteness of justice in Latin America—which must be understood at multiple scales and within multiple registers of social practice and experience—have had important consequences. Even if the trajectories of justice have intersected with those of human rights, particularly over the last 20 years, it is the key differences revealed by an archaeology of justice that require the kind of renewed empirical and analytical focus that the chapters here reflect. In many ways, the idea of a "sense of justice" captures these differences with precision. It also foregrounds the anthropological encounter, in particular, with what might be described as the "paradox of justice." Despite its deep, even essential, heterogeneity (and heterodoxy), within the kinds of phenomenologies of conflict, resistance, and suffering that are revealed so powerfully across this book's seven substantive chapters, one trans-theoretical conclusion emerges more starkly than others: the fact that justice is associated with various kinds of disembeddedness but that it is this very character of dis-articulation that infuses the practice of justice with power, with promise, and with social force within lived experiences. That is, far from standing apart as an empty referent with little resonance within some of the most critical moments in contemporary Latin America, the concept and social category of "justice" has hovered just in the background or, perhaps more accurately, just in the distance, even as its meanings have resisted easy parsing.

In her wide-ranging ethnography and critique of the first wave of prosecutions undertaken by the International Criminal Court in Sub-Saharan Africa, Kamari Maxine Clarke (2009) suggestively adapts the Derridean concept of "spectrality"

to explain this diffuse ontology of justice, this hovering just out of reach. A spectral sense of justice allows us to disrupt, on the one hand, its clichéd, often official,
often legal, invocation that can appear as solid and impenetrable as the almost
absurdly elaborate neoclassical edifice that houses Argentina's Supreme Court,
the "imagined court" whose own specters Leticia Barrera confronts in her contribution here. But on the other hand, a spectral reading of justice in contemporary Latin America establishes a critical analytical distance between aspiration
and teleology. As Clarke argues, official accounts of justice processes that suggest
inevitability or consequence must be rejected. However, the desire for particular
consequences, the hope for alternative futures, the willingness to embody new social categories (like "victim" or "perpetrator"[2]) should be made part of a centrifugal theory of justice, one in which the spectral and the ideological ("será justicia")
remain in constant and productive tension. And as Clarke reminds us, this tension
is one that must always be negotiated. Indeed, as the chapters in this book demonstrate, the many facets of negotiation between the spectral and the ideological
provide rich material for a newly conceptualized anthropology of justice in which
the "terms of aspiration must be negotiated, amended, compromised; through that
process, new fictions [of justice] will be derived to meet the memories of our past
and the needs of our pluralist social worlds" (Clarke 2009: 22).

It is in this spirit, therefore, that I make my own contribution to this book
with reference to ongoing research on the relationship between law and social
change in Bolivia; through a selective engagement with the book's other chapters and case studies; and, finally, through more general reflections on the relative
poverty of alternatives—beyond what is becoming a routinized package of neoliberal or late-liberal reforms and models for good governance and postconflict
reconciliation—for challenging enduring inequality and vectors of marginalization in Latin America. If Marta Magalhães Wallace can write in her chapter about
perceptions of a "deficit of justice" in the dystopian city of Salvador, Brazil, one
can also think of this lack in another way. Within the steady march in Latin America toward what James Ferguson (2006) called the "neoliberal world order," one
can hear the ever so faint tune of alternatives (see, e.g., Escobar 2010; Goodale and
Postero 2013). Yet, as a relative question, the sheer marginality of these "alternative
modernizations," as Escobar describes them, only reinforces the sense that we have
all become, in Harri Englund's (2006) chilling phrase, "prisoners of freedom." In
this way, the manifold invocations of and negotiations around "justice" that we
find in this book can be understood as a *response* to deficit, rather than the reflection of one, that is to say, an engagement with a paradoxically opaque moral,
cultural, and legal category as a way to create space within which at least the possibility of alternative futures can be envisioned.

LAW'S LABOR'S LOST

The Preamble to revolutionary Bolivia's 2009 constitution is a masterpiece of post-modern political literature. If the lines from the iconic 1967 Velvet Underground song promise to show us our true selves—"I'll be your mirror / Reflect what you are, in case you don't know"—then the sweeping claims and hybrid images that begin Bolivia's new social contract likewise reflect both the creative possibilities and normative ambiguity of post–Cold War social change and legal experimentation. After acknowledging the foundational importance of an indigenous universe in grounding the Bolivian revolution—an ontology that the Andeanist anthropologist and ethnohistorian Frank Salomon (2001) has described inimitably as a "unified biological-technological productivity unfolding seamlessly from human-telluric bonds through matrimonial alliance outward to very wide regional alignments and toward cosmological forces" (654)—the Preamble lists the catalogue of moral values, political objectives, and social principles that will define a "re-founded" Bolivia. It is an exhaustive list: respect and equality among all; commitment to sovereignty, dignity, complementarity, solidarity, harmony, and equity in the distribution and redistribution of social goods; living well (the now paradigmatic "vivir bien," which is contrasted elsewhere in revolutionary rhetoric with "vivir mejor," or living better); respect for pluralism in economics, society, law, politics, and culture; and collective coexistence with equal access to water, work, education, health, and housing for all.

But nowhere in the Preamble—which also declares that the Bolivian people have "left in the past" the "colonial, republican, and neoliberal" forms of government—is "justice" invoked. This despite the fact that the lead-in to Bolivia's "new history" is deeply anchored in moments in Bolivia's contested past that have been traditionally infused with the ideology of injustice and its consequences. As the Preamble puts it, the revolution was "inspired by the struggles of the past, the anticolonial indigenous uprising, independence, the popular struggles of liberation, the indigenous, social, and trade union marches, the Water War and the October War, and the struggles for land and territory."[3]

Despite the fact that "social justice" is included briefly in another long list of official revolutionary values and essential state functions and ends (in Articles 8[II] and 9[I]), "justice" does not makes its appearance with any significance until the new social contract begins outlining the legal dimensions of the new bureaucratic structure of the Estado Plurinacional—that is, in Article 179 and later. Here, within the radical establishment of three separate and ambiguously interrelated legal systems (the "ordinary," or state, the "agro-environmental," and the "indigenous originary peasant"), justice is clearly associated to, even synonymous with, law—that is, the third bureaucratic pillar of the state, along with the legislative and the executive.[4] In other words, within the structure of revolutionary Bolivia, "justice" has become delimited and circumscribed; it is no longer a general value or organizing principle for social action. It is, within the flow of experimental policies and objectives, simply another way to refer to the mechanisms of state and society that are intended to resolve disputes within particular forms of governmental organization and social control.

So it is an important fact that Bolivia's postmodern revolution does not make the broad framing of justice the anchor of its contested collective imaginary— whether as an absence, or a vague teleology, or an individual value that characterizes the ideal revolutionary subject. In this way, contemporary Bolivia couldn't be further from the Islamic Morocco that is the basis for Lawrence Rosen's seminal *The Anthropology of Justice* (1989). As Rosen writes:

> Everywhere one encounters in Islamic life the idea of justice: Respected figures are acknowledged for being just; relationships are valued when they partake of just arrangements; particular historical periods are admired because they were days when men acted justly. The Muslim concept of justice is thus one of those domains in which a host of social, political, and ethical ideas come into uneasy coalescence. (74)

In this conceptualization of justice as the pervasive, even elemental, force in Islamic Moroccan life, Rosen explains that rights—whether human, collective, or divine—are not the central normativity. As he puts it:

> It is not rights that are at the center of Islamic justice, for no one expects rights to be recognized that are not granted by God or forcefully ensured by networks of obligation. Rather what is central is the process by which one's claims may be validated before the community in accord with local practice and the attestation of people who with their own eyes know what is so and will not risk their credibility as allies by refusing to say it. (74)

This is a multivalent and entirely anthropological account of justice, but I dwell on it at some length for two reasons that are relevant here. First, even though the essence of Rosen's anthropological theory of (Islamic) justice has its basis in the social performance of legitimacy, through which people make claims and have these claims publicly acknowledged as valid, it is nevertheless true that justice in this sense is circumscribed by the boundaries of legal disputes within formal institutions. Second, and more bedeviling, is the fact that although Rosen embeds his anthropology of justice in the conceptual and comparative analysis of a wide array of Arabic legal, social, and religious terminology, he does not do the same with the first principle—justice.[5] Rather, the sense of justice emerges from Rosen's descriptions of the cultural performance of Islamic law. In this way, Rosen seems to be saying, it is neither possible as a matter of anthropological theory nor as a matter of ethnographic analysis to offer an interpretively generalizable account of "justice." Instead, it ranges as an "implicit idea" that suffuses the entirety of contemporary Moroccan life (38). Elsewhere, he explains that this implicit idea should not be understood monolithically, but in the plural: "Moroccan *concepts* of justice" (45; emphasis mine).[6]

Nevertheless, we should not take Rosen's anthropological framing to mean that the Latin-derived English word *justice* is necessarily incommensurable with the Arabic word *adl* (assuming that *adl* was the word that Rosen encountered repeatedly in his study of Moroccan *qadis*, or judges). Rather, it is that the concepts that these words connote emerge from cultural, political, and legal histories that make strict linguistic comparison a fruitless exercise and the attempt to arrive at a trans-historical conception of justice an arid exercise in theoretical sleight-of-hand.[7]

It is no wonder, then, to return to the Bolivian revolution, that "justice" is marginalized within the vernaculars of "refoundation." On the one hand, as we have seen, justice is tightly bundled with a particular face of state power, and as with any vestige of the ancien régime, justice-as-law plays an ambiguous role in the revolution's ideology. But on the other hand, because Bolivia's revolution, as we will see later, is being instantiated *through* the mechanisms of law and legal regulation, the broad and necessarily ambiguous conception of justice was supplanted in the Constitution and within follow-on legislation by a long list of moral-juridical hybrids whose radicalness was meant to be commensurate with the far-reaching, even utopian, *cosmovisión* of Bolivia's new history. To make this point another way, Bolivia's revolutionaries were compelled, for both historical and ideological reasons, to follow the post–Cold War script, one written in many ways through the experience of South Africa's collective reimagination after apartheid (see Klug 2000; Wilson 2001).[8] This script insists on certain forms of governance and thereby excludes others. It is open to far-reaching expressions of postmodern revolutionary ideology, while restrictive of the means by which revolutionaries can do "what is to be done." Finally, this post–Cold War script demands, above all else, that social change, even radical social change, take place in terms of the ordering logics of law—in its creative, legislative, and interpretive modes.

In this way, the meaning and sequence of revolution themselves have undergone a profound shift. Rather than putting the pieces of society back together after a period of disruption, fracture, and violence, law is now the means through which revolutionary change itself must be funneled. But is law adequate to the task of revolution? In the next section, I take up this question more generally. But using the ongoing ethnography of Bolivia's revolution as a starting point, the empirical answer is quite mixed. From 2006 to 2009, Bolivia went through alternating periods of social turmoil and the reestablishment of order, often through the use of state power to discredit the opposition movements. As Vera Lugo writes in his chapter on the relationship between law and conflict in Colombia, so too in Bolivia was the apparatus of legal governance used to both "mobilize emotions" toward a particular understanding of contemporary history and constrain those emotions that came into conflict with the state-sanctioned version of revolutionary ideology. After the twin political and moral catastrophes for the antigovernment right in Bolivia—the atrocities committed against indigenous pro-government activists in Sucre on the day known as the "Plaza de Rodillas" (May 24, 2008), and the massacre of unknown numbers of pro-government peasants in and around the town of Porvenir in the Department of Pando in September 2008—the constraining power of law-as-revolution became even more pronounced as the MAS government consolidated political control through the mundaneness of legal-bureaucratic implementation.

Much of this revolutionary bureaucracy has developed far below the radar of both the international media and academic critical scrutiny. For the first, attention has been occupied with a range of narratives, particularly from hegemonic neoliberal vantages points like the United States, in which Bolivia was intermeshed with Chávez's Venezuela (itself constructed to fit certain dystopian imaginaries; see Contreras Natera 2013) as the joint exemplar par excellence of something described as the "new left" (see, e.g., Kozloff 2009). Interestingly, this discursive move was also a key tactic of the antigovernment movement based in Santa Cruz, which often featured cartoon images in its pamphlets and posters of a menacing figure of Hugo Chávez in his red beret with a tiny Evo Morales growing from one of Chávez's shoulders.

But from the academic perspective, the bureaucratization of Bolivia's revolution has often been obscured by obsessions with several spectacular social conflicts after the passage of the constitution in 2009 (e.g., McNeish 2013), or with Bolivia's apparently self-contradictory reliance on what is described as an economy of "extractivism" (see, e.g., Crabtree and Crabtree-Condor 2012: 52–53). In the meantime, the regulatory interaction between the executive and Bolivia's new legislative body, the Plurinational Legislative Assembly, has continued to produce a steady flow of *reglamentaciones*, which function even after the *refundación* to specify, articulate, parse, and implement the normative and ideological principles of the constitution.[9]

It is not a coincidence that Bolivia's revolution has become encapsulated within the pages of governmental regulations and that civil servant functionaries have taken over from the political visionaries and social leaders who often risked their lives so that a new epoch could take root. As early as 2007, before the passage of the constitution, close advisors to President Morales made the case that the revolutionary government was an embodiment of the social movements that brought it to power; that it was not a representative government, comprised of politicians who spoke *for* the people but, rather, that it *was* the people (Goodale n.d.). In this sense, legislative acts are seen as the direct expression of power and will by the social movements whose perspectives are privileged in the new Bolivia, rather than second-order agreements between political representatives that reflect compromise, individual idiosyncrasy, and the culture of legislative governance. So law is being conceptualized and deployed here in several novel ways that provoke a number of reflections, the most immediate of which is "Is law adequate to the task of revolutionary embodiment?" That is, is law—in its acknowledged multiplicities and social expressions—a form that is capable of both signifying and instantiating radical social change at the same time? If law absorbs the currents of revolution and is thereafter reconceptualized in its name, what is gained and what is lost? And if, on balance, the ethnography of revolutionary Bolivia suggests a balance sheet on which more is lost than is gained in this experimental—if inevitable—rearticulation of law's ways and means, what alternatives exist for better advancing what is known locally as simply "el proceso de cambio," the process of change?

AN ODE TO THE GHOST OF E. P. THOMPSON

In his 1975 study of the infamous Black Act of 1723, the British Marxist historian E. P. Thompson (1977) revealed—with a fine sense of the ethnographic infusions of history—the ways in which the rising landed class in early eighteenth century England had turned to the law as a primary mechanism for consolidating class power. The Act mandated death by hanging for an unprecedented list of offenses to property, such as appearing on private land armed with the intention to poach deer, or maliciously killing or maiming cattle, or even "cutting down trees 'planted in any avenue, or growing in any garden, orchard, or plantation'" (22). The "black" in the Black Act referred to the fact that peasant deer poachers and tree barkers at the time had taken to blackening their faces before entering the boundaries of the massive estates of people like Lord Craven and the Earl of Cadogan. And as Thompson himself acknowledges, it didn't take five years of painstaking and frustrating historical research with a spotty archival record to come to the conclusion that could "in its essential structures, have been known without any investigation at all" (260)—namely, that judges, the landed gentry, and members of Parliament worked together to use the law to legitimate their interests and suppress or eradicate the traditions of communal land tenure that were seen as an obstacle during the emergence of modern Britain.

Nevertheless, the use of law as an instrument of class power was not all Thompson could say about the Black Act. Writing against his own Marxist inclinations, he was forced to admit that something more was needed, because of the simple fact was that not all defendants were found guilty and executed; some managed to be exonerated and set free by the very process that was meant to destroy them. Thompson attributes this slippage in the exercise of class power to what he calls the "forms of law," which emerge through a historical process that is not merely the evolution of "relations [of power] translated into others terms, which mask[ ] or mystif[y] . . . reality" (262). Rather, even the blatant manipulation of law by elites is subject to shaping and constraint beyond the intention to use law to legitimate the expression of power. As Thompson argues:

> Most men have a strong sense of justice, at least with regard to their own interests. If the law is evidently partial and unjust, then it will mask nothing, legitimize nothing, contribute nothing to any class's hegemony. The essential precondition for the effectiveness of law . . . is that it shall display an independence from gross manipulation and shall seem to be just. It cannot seem to be so without upholding *its own logic and criteria of equity*; indeed, on occasion, by actually *being* just. (263; first emphasis mine; second emphasis in original)

Now what most interests me here is not the use of law as an instrument of class domination per se. Instead, I want to argue that if the "forms of law"—with all accommodation made for cultural and historical variation—are structured and structure (see Giddens 1984) in part through logics that are separate from the working of law as a particular form of governance, then this applies as much to the progressive, emancipatory, socially expansive uses of law as it does to uses (as with the Black Act) that are regressive and exploitative. And if what is being tempered by the logics of law in cases of "gross manipulation" is precisely the capacity to deploy law as a weapon of class power, then what must be tempered in times of revolution is the potential to use law as a mechanism of progressive social transformation. The problem here is not only that the logics of law, if Thompson is right, prevent its effective use to shepherd social change or even ground massive projects of "re-foundation," as in contemporary Bolivia.

The problem is also that if the "judicialization of politics" (Couso, Huneeus, and Sieder 2010; Sieder, Angell, and Schjolden 2005), or what might be called the "legalization of revolution," creates a large enough gap between general expectations of social, political, and economic change and the mundaneness of bureaucratic governance, then disenchantment can take root and threaten to rot the process away from within. As Jessica Greenberg (2014) has recently shown, disenchantment is fatal to processes of revolutionary transformation in an era in which expectations for radical social change have been paradoxically both dramatically raised and narrowed at the same time. (Raised, because the transnational culture of revolution, fueled by social media, has made everyone a potential revolutionary, even if the revolution is directed from a computer keyboard; and narrowed, because the ideological resources for shaping revolution have tightened after the end of the Cold War, leaving few alternatives that are not, in one way or another, dependent on the hegemonies of the Fergusonian "neoliberal world order.")

This is not an either/or claim—that is, that the necessarily expansive, even utopian, promises of revolution are either met across the board or they are not. If there is many a slip 'twixt the cup and the lip, as the adage has it, then, in conditions of social transformation, there will likewise always be space between the ideological vision toward which structural changes are put in motion and the uncertain practices of structural change themselves. Rather, it is merely to heighten awareness to the fact that the consequences of the legalization of revolution are only partly dependent on the range of contingencies, unintended alignments, and hidden intentions that have taken up so much of the critical scrutiny of Bolivia's radical experiments with postneoliberal state- and society-making; the very fact of legalization itself acts to contain the revolutionary *cosmovisión* and thereby change its meaning.

The ultimate consequences of this dual movement—the first, the Bourdieuian slippage that is a normal part of social practice, the second, the specific historical emergence of what Ran Hirschl (2004) would call the "juridification" of revolutionary social relations—are uncertain. At the very least, the evolution from utopian revolutionary politics to bureaucratic revolutionary practice in Bolivia is changing the constitution into a different kind of symbol, one that is paradoxically more remote from people's lives even as its articles are steadily converted into policies that affect thousands of citizens. And some Bolivians, including those in the powerful indigenous movements, have begun to act on their growing disenchantment by creating the conditions for radical social change outside the boundaries of Bolivia's juridified revolution—for example, during the crisis over the proposed interdepartmental highway through the Territorio Indígena y Parque Nacional Isiboro Sécure, or TIPNIS (McNeish 2013; Svampa 2013; Villanueva 2012). What is clear, however, as Denyer Willis shows in his study of policing in Brazil in this book, or as Vera Lugo demonstrates in his chapter on Colombia, is that alternatives to constitutional revolution, especially those that involve the direct exercise of extra-legal violence, have a difficult time finding ideological traction even in periods of extended transition.

CONCLUSION: "RUBBER BULLETS IN THE CENTER ARE REAL BULLETS IN THE PERIPHERY" (OR THE EMPTY BUT NECESSARY SIGNIFIER)

If the Bolivian revolution has been structured by a hybridity that does not give "justice" a central role in its ideology of radical social change, the same is not true in other regions of Latin America. As we see throughout the chapters in this book, claims for or against or in terms of justice have become key markers of the perpetuation of various forms of inequality and violence even in the face of political reform and economic experimentation. These studies reveal a central tension for the reconstituted anthropology of justice that this book proposes.

On the one hand, the chapters demonstrate in rich ethnographic detail the ways in which the capaciousness of justice as a social, moral, and legal category functions to frame various kinds of contentious politics and the pursuit of interests. As Faulk shows in her study of the aftermath of a bombing in Buenos Aires, different constituencies first constructed, and then acted upon, a quite different conception of what justice meant for the same historical atrocity. Each group understood itself to be pursuing justice as a fundamental mode of social practice, but the meanings of justice—and therefore their structuring effects on social action—spanned a wide range. Likewise, in her ethnography of the Argentine Supreme Court, Barrera uses Haraway's concept of "partial knowledge" to account for the fact that even among elite legal actors in Argentina, conceptions of justice emerged from situated and idiosyncratic positions—social, gendered, even physical, as the architecture of the court building itself shaped what she calls the "imagined court and the real court." And in her study of the obscure, but analytically fascinating, Permanent Peoples' Tribunal, Brunnegger examines the way conceptions of justice can emerge in an entirely symbolic way; disputes, in this sense, over the meaning of justice are thus disputes over the content of public performance of grievances.

But on the other hand, the chapters in this book force us to look past the epistemological, symbolic, and pluralistic content of "justice" to confront the immediacy of structural violence, historical vulnerability, and what Barros, in his chapter, describes as the "commodification" of justice subjects. Here, claims for justice get subsumed within the quotidian struggles of everyday life from urban Brazil to the barren region of the Atacama Desert, where transnational extractive industries corner the market for the precious water that is needed to keep the mines open and the profits flowing. In these case studies, an overly academic concern with the discursive dimensions of justice claims would be naive at best. A sense of justice rebels against what is revealed by the ethnography of systemic racism and the ways in which transnational capital accommodates so-called soft law claims only in order to further consolidate control over labor and resources. But the starkness of *injustice* in these cases is the dominant variable, and the role of justice institutions—whether national or international—is ambiguous. Meanwhile, broader structures of inequality, which often span the centuries, continue to curtail life-chances in ways that are visceral and undeniable. As Magalhães explains, through an unforgettable ethnographic extract, "rubber bullets in the center are real bullets in the periphery."

So we are left with this dual formation in the anthropology of justice: the move to unpack and understand the multiplicity of justice as an ethnographic and social category, and the move to penetrate the level of interpretive analysis—which often becomes a part of claims-making itself—in order to unmask the relations of production that often lie at the heart of social conflict and chronic immiseration. But even when we turn to a hard-edged political economy of justice, even when we are willing, as anthropologists, to confront forms of violence that cannot be encapsulated within the kinds of symbolic categories in which we readily traffic, a "sense of justice" nevertheless remains in all of its essential ambiguity. In his chapter, Barros attributes this lingering uncertainty to what he calls the "unreason at the core of law." Better yet is Brunnegger's more elusive, and thus paradoxically more accurate explanation, that the endless search for justice, even in the face of a dark reality, is the necessary search for the forever "yet to come."

NOTES

1. Despite the fact that Bolivia's revolutionary constitution of 2009 radically restructures the country's legal architecture (specifically in Articles 179–205), the effects of these changes—like the establishment of independent indigenous tribunals and the closing of "state" courts in regions that have been reorganized into autonomous indigenous zones—have yet to be felt throughout much of the country as of 2015.

2. For a provacative analysis of how the category of "perpetrator" gets constructed within and after mass atrocity, see Hinton (2013).

3. "Anticolonial indigenous uprising," phrased in the singular, almost certainly is a reference to the failed uprising led by Túpac Katari and his wife Bartolina Sisa against the Spanish royalist forces in La Paz in 1781. After being defeated in battle, Katari was brutally tortured and then drawn and quartered (see Thomson 2003). The "Water War" refers to a series of protests in Cochabamba over the privatization of the valley's water concession, a disastrous arrangement that was later annulled (see Olivera 2004; Shultz and Draper 2009). The October War, also known as Black October, was a series of large-scale protests against transnational natural gas contracts in 2003 that were violently suppressed by the administration of Gonzalo Sánchez de Lozada, leading to dozens of deaths and the eventual resignation of Sánchez de Lozada and his exile to the United States.

4. On "community justice" and the Bolivian Constitution, see Goldstein (2012).

5. Among the many keywords from Moroccan Islamic jurisprudence that are translated and analyzed are *'aqel* (reason), *fatwa* (scholarly opinion), *haqq* (truth, reality, obligation),

Ijma' (consensus), *m'ulem* (expert), *nafs* (passions), *niya* (intention), *qiyas* (analogic reasoning), and *shari'a* (Islamic law).

6. The usual Arabic word that is translated in the singular as "justice" is *adl*. For a comprehensive discussion of the historical evolution of *adl* within Islamic jurisprudence, see Khadduri (2001). His analysis supports Rosen's emphasis on the Moroccan concept(s) of justice as inhering in people as a kind of moral-juridical quality. As Khadduri explains, this sense of justice was never fully lost, even with the rise of legal and political institutions, so that "justice" can still be understood in part as a personal quality that combines truthfulness and good behavior (145).

7. For an idea of how fruitless such an approach to the problem of justice would be, one need only take a peek into a source like the magisterial *Black's Law Dictionary* (1979), which functions as a comprehensive linguistic and conceptual archaeology of Anglo-American (and thus, at some remove, French-Norman, and thus, at an even further remove, Roman) law and jurisprudence. In the entry for "justice," after giving meanings that refer to legal officials ("title given to judges") and the act of exercising jurisdiction—that is, state power—over a conflict, we arrive at the following: Justice means "proper administration of laws. In Jurisprudence, the constant and perpetual disposition of legal matters or disputes to render every man his due" (776). Even though "to render every man his due" begins to gesture toward something of interest, what precedes it is of little value.

8. Indeed, as my research has uncovered, this trans-historical linkage between the South Africa of 1994 and the Bolivia of 2009 is more than just analytical speculation. Close advisors to President Evo Morales have described in interviews how and why the first presidential trip taken after the historic election of 2005 was to South Africa. *Movimiento al Socialismo* (MAS) lawyers and political activists wanted to know from their African National Congress (ANC) counterparts what lessons could be taken from the South African experience to be applied to the Bolivian. For what these lessons were and how they were put into practice through the 2009 constitutions, see Goodale (n.d.).

9. See, for example, the new law on child labor, which controversially lowers the age of work to 10 (under parental supervision) and allows children between the ages of 10 and 12 to enter into work contracts independent of their parents. The new mining law, which passed in 2014, restructured national mining relations to bring them in line—problematically—with the terms of the 2009 constitution.

WORKS CITED

Baxi, Upendra. 2002. *The Future of Human Rights*. New Delhi: Oxford University Press.

Black's Law Dictionary, 5th ed. 1979. St. Paul, MN: West Publishing.

Clarke, Kamari Maxine. 2009. *Fictions of Justice: The International Criminal Court and the Challenge of Legal Pluralism in Sub-Saharan Africa*. Cambridge: Cambridge University Press.

Contreras Natera, Miguel Ángel. 2013. "Insurgent Imaginaries and Postneoliberalism in Latin America." In *Neoliberalism, Interrupted: Social Change and Contested Governance in Contemporary Latin America*, edited by Mark Goodale and Nancy Postero, 249–269. Stanford, CA: Stanford University Press.

Couso, Javier, Alexandra Huneeus, and Rachel Sieder, eds. 2010. *Cultures of Legality: Judicialization and Political Activism in Latin America*. Cambridge: Cambridge University Press.

Crabtree, John, and Isabel Crabtree-Condor. 2012. "The Politics of Extractive Industries in the Central Andes." In *Social Conflict, Economic Development, and Extractive Industry: Evidence from South America*, edited by Anthony Bebbington, 46–64. New York: Routledge.

Englund, Harri. 2006. *Prisoners of Freedom: Human Rights and the African Poor*. Berkeley: University of California Press.

Escobar, Arturo. 2010. "Latin America at a Crossroads." *Cultural Studies* 24 (1): 1–65.

Ferguson, James. 2006. *Global Shadows: Africa in the Neoliberal World Order*. Durham, NC: Duke University Press.

Giddens, Anthony. 1984. *The Constitution of Society: Outline of the Theory of Structuration*. Berkeley: University of California Press.

Goldstein, Daniel. 2012. *Outlawed: Between Security and Rights in a Bolivian City*. Durham, NC: Duke University Press.

Goodale, Mark. N.d. "Revolution in the Brackets: Law, Ideology, and Social Change in Bolivia." Unpublished manuscript.

Goodale, Mark, and Nancy Postero, eds. 2013. *Neoliberalism, Interrupted: Social Change and Contested Governance in Contemporary Latin America*. Stanford, CA: Stanford University Press.

Greenburg, Jessica. 2014. *After the Revolution: Youth, Democracy and the Politics of Disappointment in Serbia*. Stanford, CA: Stanford University Press.

Hinton, Alex. 2013. "The Paradox of Perpetration: A View from the Cambodian Genocide." In *Human Rights at the Crossroads*, edited by Mark Goodale, 153–162. New York: Oxford University Press.

Hirschl, Ran. 2004. *Towards Juristocracy: The Origins and Consequences of the New Constitutionalism*. Cambridge, MA: Harvard University Press.

Khadduri, Majid. 2001. *The Islamic Conception of Justice*. Baltimore: Johns Hopkins University Press.

Klug, Heinz. 2000. "Co-operative Government in South Africa's Post-Apartheid Constitutions: Embracing the German Model?" *Verfassung und Recht in Ubersee* 33: 432–453.

Kozloff, Nikolas. 2009. *Revolution! South America and the Rise of the New Left*. London: Palgrave.

McNeish, John-Andrew. 2013. "Extraction, Protest and Indigeneity in Bolivia: The TIPNIS Effect." *Latin American and Caribbean Ethnic Studies* 8 (2): 221–242.

Olivera, Oscar. 2004. *¡Cochabamba! Water War in Bolivia*. Boston: South End.

Rosen, Lawrence. 1989. *The Anthropology of Justice: Law as Culture in Islamic Society*. Cambridge: Cambridge University Press.

Salomon, Frank. 2001. "Review of *To Make the Earth Bear Fruit: Ethnographic Essays on Fertility, Work and Gender in Highland Bolivia*, by Olivia Harris." *Journal of Latin American Studies* 33 (3): 654–656.

Shultz, James, and Melissa Draper, eds. 2009. *Dignity and Defiance: Stories from Bolivia's Challenge to Globalization*. Berkeley: University of California Press.

Sieder, Rachel, Alan Angell, and Line Schjolden, eds. 2005. *The Judicialization of Politics in Latin America*. New York: Palgrave Macmillan.

Svampa, Maristella. 2013. *Bolivia, modelo 2013, en perspectiva*. http://www.sinpermiso.info/articulos/ficheros/6boliviams.pdf.

Thompson, E. P. 1977. *Whigs and Hunters: The Origin of the Black Act*. London: Penguin.

Thomson, Sinclair. 2003. "Revolutionary Memory in Bolivia: Anticolonial and National Projects from 1781 to 1952." In *Proclaiming the Revolution: Bolivia in Comparative Perspective*, edited by Merilee Grindle and Pilar Domingo, 117–134. Cambridge, MA: Harvard University Press.

Villanueva, Arturo. 2012. "Bolivia: Balance y perspectivas de la gestión gubernamental y el proceso de cambio." *ALAI, América Latina en Movimiento*, July 25.

Williams, Raymond. 1976. *Keywords: A Vocabulary of Culture and Society*. London: Fontana.

Wilson, Richard. 2001. *The Politics of Truth and Reconciliation in South Africa: Legitimizing the Post-Apartheid State*. Cambridge: Cambridge University Press.

INDEX

INDEX

Page numbers in italics refer to figures.

abject subjectivities, 27
acerto de conta (payback) killings, 90–91
aerial fumigation, 135
Agamben, Giorgio, 148, 155
Alfonsin, Raúl, 111
Algiers Declaration, 127, 142–143nn3–4
alternative justice, 129
AMIA/DAIA movement, *55*, *56*; and APEMIA, 57–58, 65, 67–69; appealing TOF3 verdict, 65; arguments over meaning of justice, 53–54, 68–70; bombing of building, 52, 60; direct family members of victims, 59–60, 62; Ginsberg's accusations, Bereja's disavowal, 54; Iranian connection with bombing, 70–71n4; Kirchner's acceptance of responsibility, 66–67; weekly memorial assemblies, 53, 58. *See also* Memoria Activa
Angell, Alan, 5
Anglo American, 183
Antequera, José Darío, 47n25
anthropology of human rights, 3
Anthropology of Justice, The (Rosen), 208
Antze, Paul, 62
Anzorreguy, Hugo, 65
APEMIA, 57–58, 65, 67–69. *See also* AMIA/DAIA movement
Appadurai, Arjun, 164
Aretxaga, Begoña, 36–37
Argentina: amnesty laws in, 111; constitutional amendments and judicial reform, 111–112, 115–116n7; IACHR case against, 63–68; judiciary a "double-faced" body, 113–114; knowledges of the Court, 114; legal protocol and etiquette in, 116n9; military selecting judges, 111; role of judicial power and

practice in, 104–108. *See also* AMIA/DAIA movement
Arias, Enrique Desmond, 83, 84
Arias, Luis Fernando Arias, 123, 134, 138
ASFAMIPAZ, 28
Atacama Desert, 172–173; Atacama 33, 183–185, *186*, 187, 196n21; land and water rights in, 176–178; as social laboratory, 170
Atacameños (Lickanantay), 176–179, 190–191
authoritative legal knowledge, 7, 10–12
Azevedo, Solange, 148

Bahia, Brazil, 148, 159–161, 164–165, 166n3. *See also* Salvador, Brazil
Bahía Portete massacre, 133, 137
Baixada Fluminense incident, 80
Banderas, Antonio, 187
bare life, 148, 154–155
Barí communities, 134–135
Barreda, María, 181
Barrionuevo, Alexei, 161, 162
Bases Comunitárias de Segurança (Community Security Bases), 148, 161, 165
Basso, Lelio, 126–127
Battaglia, Debbora, 109
Baxi, Uprendra, 205
Beckett, Greg, 45n7
Beraja, Rubén, 54, 65, 71n8
Betanzos, Juan Diez de, 176
Bhopal, 126
BHP Billiton, 183, 187, 195n8
Black Act (1723), 211
Black's Law Dictionary, 216n7
Blom Hansen, Thomas, 148
Blomley, Nicholas K., 18n5

Bogotá, PPT hearing in, 128, 134
Bolados, Paola, 172
Bolivia, 3; aftermath of revolution, 210–211; "justice" and revolutionary constitution, 207–208, 209–210, 213; "new left" in, 210; Sacaca, 203
Bonilla, Carlos, 192
Bourdieu, Pierre, 12, 41
Brazil: Bahia, 148, 159–161, 164–165, 166n3; Pact for Life Program, 147–150, 159, 161–163, 165; policing in, 86–95; prisons in, 89, 91; Rio de Janeiro, 147, 161; São Paulo, 91–94, 147; state capitals, violence in, 147. *See also* Salvador, Brazil
Briceño, Ignacio, 46–47n25
Buenos Aires. *See* AMIA/DAIA movement
bureaucracies, study of, 113
Butler, Judith, 46n24

Cabo de Vela, Colombia, 131–132, 135–136, 138–139
Caldeira, Teresa, 80, 90, 149, 164
Camacho, Marcos Willians Herbas (Marcola), 79, 86–89
Camus, Albert, 186
Candelária incident, 80
Capps, Lisa, 46n23
Carandiru incident, 80
care ethic versus rights ethic, 57
Casas-Cortés, María Isabel, 142n2
categories of justice, 4
centrifugal theory of justice, 206
Cerrejon, PPT hearing on, 131–134, 137
Chávez, Hugo, 210
Chile: antiterrorist law, 184; Atacama 33, 183–185, *186*, 187; and Inter-American Court of Human Rights, 184. *See also* Atacama Desert
Chuquicamata copper mine, 172
citizenship: and legal reform, 164–165; and memory, 63
Ciudadanos de la Plaza (Citizens of the Plaza), 60–63, *61*, 68–69
Civil Police (Brazil), 90–94
Clarke, Kamari Maxine, 4, 53, 205–206
Cochabamba, Bolivia, 3
CODELCO, 183–184, 187
cofradía (brotherhood) memberships, 177
collectivity: in Atacameño communities, 179, 183–185, 188, 191–192; meaning of, 71n5; and territorial "reappropriation," 180
Collins, John, 150, 157–158

Colombia: concept of victimhood in, 27–28; guerrilla groups in, 25, 28–30, 128, 135; historical truth reconstruction, 32; internal displacement in, 27–28; Justice and Peace Law, 25–26; multiple factions within, 128–129; paramilitary groups in, 25–26, 30–32, 36, 44, 132–135; polarization of society in, 30; political violence in, 29–30, 43–44, 45n6; state possessing power for good and bad, 28–29; state violence by proxy in, 26; victims becoming political actors, 31, 43. *See also* MOVICE; PPT (Permanent Peoples' Tribunal)
coloniality/modernity inextricably coupled, 6
Comaroff, Jean, 150, 191
Comaroff, John, 150, 191
"commodification" of justice subject, 214
commodity fetish, 171–172, 187, 191, 193, 194n3
"commodity fiction," 136
communitarianism, 56–57
"community justice," 3
Community Security Bases (CSBs), 148, 161, 165
Coombe, Rosemary J., 128
copper. *See* mining in Chile
Corach, Carlos, 54, 65
COREMA (Regional Environmental Commission), 179–181
Couso, Javier, 5, 112–113
crack cocaine in Salvador, 156–157
CSBs (Community Security Bases), 148, 161, 165
CSR (Corporate Social Responsibility) agreements, 178
Cúcuta, PPT prehearing in, 129, 134–135, 138
cultural commodity fetishism, 171
Cultures of Legality (Couso, Huneeus, and Sieder), 5
cynicism within judiciary, 107

Dagnino, Evelina, 163
Da Matta, Roberto, 113
Das Kapital (Marx), 170
Debord, Guy, 160, 194n3
de la Rúa, Fernando, 64, 99
Deleuze, Gilles, 44, 170, 188, 189, 194n2
Derrida, Jacques, 51
devils and fetishes, 176–177, 181, 183, 185–191, *186*, 194
dignity, struggle for, 29
discourse as law, 41
dispossessed, making of, 139–141
drugs and "right to the city," 156–157
"due obedience" law (Argentina), 116n14
Duhalde, Eduardo, 54, 99

Ecopetrol, 131
Eilbaum, Lucía, 116n9
emotions, mobilization of, 36
Englund, Harri, 206
Escobar, Arturo, 128–129, 171, 179, 194n1, 206
Escondida, 179, 181, 183, 195n8
escraches, 51
Ethnicity Inc., 191
ethnocultural commoditization, 172
ethnography of law, 3
ethno-technical deterritorializations, 185–187
European Union corporations, 127
extractivist economics, 6, 210

Falk, Richard, 126–127
Familiares y Amigos de las Víctimas del Atentado a la AMIA, 55–57, 65, 68
"family member of victim" position, 53
FARC guerrillas, 28, 29
Fayt, Carlos, 117n15
fear of violence, 147–151
Ferguson, James, 206
Fernandes, Edésio, 157
Fernández, Cristina, 71n4
"final stop" law (Argentina), 116n14
fingerprinting, 92
first- and second-generation human rights, 26
flagrante crime arrests, 93–94
Foncea, Valeria, 181
Fondazione Lelio e Lisli Basso-Issoco (Lelio Basso Foundation), 126
"forms of law," 212
Foucault, Michel, 160, 165, 171, 185–186
"Fuerza al pueblo Mapuche" censored, 184–185

Gal, Susan, 42
Galeano, Juan José, 54, 64–65, 73n30, 73n33
Gammeltoft, Tine, 11
García Márquez, Gabriel, 45n6
Gasper, Des, 3
Giddens, Anthony, 17–18n5
Ginsberg, Laura, 54, 57–58
Giovanola, Benedetta, 3
Gledhill, John, 128, 142
global and local normativities of justice, 5–6
GMH (Grupo de Memoria Histórica), 27; advocating reconciliation, 33; compared to MOVICE, 33–34; distinguishing historical and judicial truth, 32–33, 40; importance of testimonies, 38; mandate of, 31–32; power of memory, testimony, 39; reports on Colombian violence, 31–32, 47n29

Goffman, Erving, 185, 197n32
Golborne, Lawrence, 183–184
Goldman, Michael, 17n4
Goldstein, Daniel, 3, 162
good name (buen nombre), restitution of, 29
Gordilho Souza, Ângela Maria, 158
Gramsci, Antonio, 44
Greenberg, Jessica, 213
Grossman, Claudio, 64–66
groundwater ownership/rights, 175, 177
Guattari, Félix, 44, 170, 188, 189, 194n2
guerrilla groups in Colombia, 25, 28–30, 128, 135
Gurevich, Beatriz, 53–54, 56–57
Gutierrez, Francisco, 45n13

Haraway, Donna, 113, 214
Harvey, David, 12
Henrard, Kristin, 142–143n4
Herzfeld, Michael, 109
Hinton, Alex, 215n2
Hinton, Mercedes, 80, 89–90
Hirschl, Ran, 213
historical reconstruction and legal truths, 32
Hoag, Colin, 101, 113
Holston, James, 79–80, 90, 149, 154, 157, 158, 164
Homo Juridicus (Supiot), 190
human person (pessoa humana), 154–157, 162, 166n7
human rights, 4, 205
Huneeus, Alexandra, 5, 113
hyper-individualization, 184

IACHR (Inter-American Commission on Human Rights), 63–68
ICTJ (International Center for Transitional Justice), 47n28
idealized rules, 110
ideological pluralism lending moral weight, 127
ILO Convention 169 treaty, 178, 184
"impression management," 197n32
impunidad (impunity), challenging, 129–130
indigenous peoples: Barí communities, 134–135; collective ownership of lands, 137; militarization of lands, 135; movements of in Latin America, 6; ONIC's claims to represent, 138–139; UNDRIP, 192–193; vision of political autonomy, 129; Wayúu communities, 131–134, 138–139
"insurgent citizenship," 157–158
internal displacement in Colombia, 27–28

international human rights standards, 127
International War Crimes Tribunal, 126
Israeli Embassy bombing (Argentina), 52, 64

Jackson, Michael, 139
Jimeno, Miriam, 41
"John Doe," 154
Jordan, Brigette, 10–11
Judicialization of Politics in Latin America, The
    (Sieder, Angell, and Schjolden), 5
Judicial School of the Argentine Magistracy
    Council, 104–108
"juridification" of revolutionary social rela-
    tions, 213
justice: from active remembrance of victims, 69;
    in AMIA/DAIA attack, 68–70; in areas of
    high violence, 149; coming from citizens,
    not state, 69; contrasted with human rights,
    205; deficit of, 206; as defined in *Black's
    Law Dictionary,* 216n7; from fair, impartial
    judiciary, 69; GMH versus MOVICE views
    of, 33–34; and human persons, 154–156; in-
    security from lack of, 60; in Islam, 208–209;
    meaning of in Portuguese, 155; paradox of,
    205; police cutting corners to ensure, 94;
    ranking different factors of, 51; required
    for law to take root, 212; requiring public
    security, 161–162, 164; scholarship on, 2–5;
    sense of, 205; spatialization of, 7, 12–13;
    "spectrality" of, 205–206; as synonymous
    with law, 207–208; as "thin" concept, 205;
    through PPT hearings, 130–131; as work
    of the courts, 204; worth creative adapta-
    tion, 165
Justice and Peace Law/Law 975 (Colombia),
    25–26, 36, 44, 45n9
justice discourse, 136
justice pluralism, 4–5

Katari, Túpac, 215n3
Kaúl, Abraham, 66–67
Khadduri, Majid, 216n6
Kirchner, Cristina Fernández de, 112, 116–
    117n15
Kirchner, Néstor, 58, 66–67, 72n13, 72n15
Klein, Naomi, 196n24
Klinghoffer, Arthur J., 125–127, 140
Klinghoffer, Judith A., 125–127, 140
knowledge-based activism, 125; knowledge-
    practice, 142n2; prehearings as sites of
    knowledge-making, 131–132, 136–137, 140,
    141–142

Kristeva, Julia, 27
Kulick, Don, 35

labor unions, 133
Lagos, Ricardo, 195n8
Lambek, Michael, 62, 136
Lasser, Mitchel, 101
Latin America, 6
law: after Bolivian revolution, 211–212; appli-
    cability of theory to everyday practice, 108;
    apprehended through ends not means, 100;
    discourse as, 41; as discourse or as language,
    45n11; disenchantment with, 212–213; as
    fetish, 172, 180, 181–182, 186–189; "forms
    of," 212; as governmentality, 171; Judeo-
    Christian dogma in, 190; legal cultures, 5;
    legal language as a tool, 35, 37, 38; legal phi-
    losophy and sociology, 105, 107; legal plural-
    ism, 4–5; legal subjectivities, 7–9; morality
    versus legality, 128; and narrative of victim-
    hood, 35; as revolution, 210; as synonymous
    with justice, 207–208; urban law, 157
Law 975, 25–26, 36, 44, 45n9
Leary, Virginia, 127
Lee, Charles, 148
Leeds, Elizabeth, 83
Lefebvre, Henri, 12, 157
legitimacy-making, 27, 126–127, 137–140
Lickanantay, 176–179, 190–191
Linke, Uli, 36, 40
Lipsky, Michael, 83–84
lithium mining, 182
Little, Walter, 160
Liu, Sida, 138
lucha por la dignidad (struggle for dignity), 29

Macri, Mauricio, 71n4
"making" justice, 95
Mapuche hunger strike, 184–185
Marcola, 79, 86–89
Martinez, Catalina, 47n25
Marx, Karl, 170
Mayllkus, 176–177, 181, 183, 185
Mbembe, Achille, 186, 192
meaning, production of, 35, 39, 44
media coverage: of Atacama 33, 183–185; on
    Atacameños generally, 191; of Peine, 182
Memoria Activa: and AMIA/DAIA, Famili-
    ares group, 54, 56–58, 65–67; case before
    IACHR, 63–68; Ciudadanos de la Plaza
    splinter group, 60–63, *61*; and direct family
    members of victims, 59–60, 62; focus on

justice, 59, 68–69; formation of, 53; as plaintiff, 55; weekly memorial assemblies, 53, 58–60

memory: dependent on justice, 40; individualization of, 62; and legitimacy, 28, 39; production of, 32–34, 38–41; right to, 40, 46–47n25; and right to truth, 38, 47n25; tension between law and, 39; through public ritual, 62

Menem, Carlos, 54, 64, 99, 108, 111, 116n14

Merleau-Ponty, Maurice, 170

Merry, Sally Engle, 5, 15, 17n3, 46n15

Mertz, Elizabeth, 38, 42

Mesa del Diálogo Argentino, 103

Mignolo, Walter, 6

Miklaszewska, Justyna, 2

military: coordination with police, 92; occupying indigenous territories, 135; paramilitary groups in Colombia, 25–26, 30–32, 36, 44, 132–135; taking part in Cúcuta prehearing, 133–134

Mille plateaux (Deleuze and Guattari), 189

Minera Escondida, 179, 181, 183, 195n8

Mingardi, Guaracy, 83, 94

mining in Chile, 194n4; Atacama 33, 183–185, 186, 187, 196n21; Atacameños seeking jobs in, 178; deaths among workers in, 187; energy and water usage for, 174–175; political ecology of in Chile, 171; private copper companies, 172–173, 195n8; public television involvement in, 196n19

Mirrors of Justice (Clarke and Goodale), 4

Miyazaki, Hirokazu, 110, 116n12

modernity/coloniality inextricably coupled, 6

Moodie, Ellen, 161, 162

Morales, Evo, 210–211, 216n8

Morocco, 208, 216n6

mountains' place in Andean ritual, 176–177, 183, 187

MOVICE (Movimiento Nacional de Víctimas de Crímenes de Estado), 27; accusations against, 33; claiming of victims' rights, 34; compared to GMH, 33–34; focusing on state violence, 33; importance of testimonies, 38; justice necessary for memory, 40; mobilizing victimhood, 28; opposing Victims Law and Land Restitution Act, 45n9; power of memory, testimony, 39; and "psychosocial attention," 39; public events to denounce crimes, 41; responding to Justice and Peace Law, 31; on state as patriarchal, 36; threats against, 31; transitional justice

discourse from, 34; victims becoming political actors, 31, 43. See also Colombia

multi-/transnational corporations: aid to trapped miners, 196n21; in Chilean indigenous territory, 178; and emerging markets, 1; justice in local situations, 46n15; and neoliberalism, 6; PPT testimony and rulings against, 123, 128–134, 137, 140–141. See also mining in Chile

Mundy, Martha, 185

Munro, Rolland, 101

naming as power of state, 29

Narotzky, Susana, 189, 193

Nash, June, 177

Nercellas, Marta, 65, 71n8

Nersessian, David, 188

neutral places, danger of, 91

New Left/neoliberalism: alternatives to, 206; in Bolivia, 207, 210, 213; in Brazil, 90, 94, 163; in Chile, 172, 186, 192; in Colombia, 128; and extractivist economics, 6; and media celebrity culture politics, 183; and modern law, 180; in Salvador, 150; scholarship on, 124, 128–129, 162, 172, 213; and sense of justice, 16; stakeholders into shareholders, 172

NGOs: activism in Argentina, 99; concerned with human rights not justice, 205

Nisman, Alberto, 71n4

Nóbrega, José Maria, 156

nonstate armed groups, 95. See also PCC (Primeiro Comando da Capital)

Norero, Aldo, 192

nostalgia, 108–110

objectification process, 141–142

Ochs, Elinor, 46n23

oil exploitation colonization, 135

One Hundred Years of Solitude (García Márquez), 45n6

Ong, Aihwa, 7

ONIC (national indigenous organization of Colombia), 123–124, 129–130, 134–135, 138–139, 142n1

organizational weaknesses in policing, 91–94

Ortner, Sherry, 17n3, 37

Osterweil, Michal, 142n2

Outlawed (Goldstein), 3

Pachamama, 176–177, 181

Pact for Life Program (Brazil), 147–150, 159, 161–163, 165

Pampa Colorada water supply project, 179–183, 195n15

Panourgiá, Neni, 27

paramilitary groups in Colombia, 25–26, 30–32, 36, 44, 132–135

Pastrana, Andrès, 29

past shaped and mobilized, 39

Payne, Leigh A., 38

PCC (Primeiro Comando da Capital): assassination of judge, 88; attacks on state security, 79; imposing own law and order, 82, 96n2; relationship with police, 86–89

Peace and Justice Law/Law 975 (Colombia), 25–26, 36, 44, 45n9

Peine, Chile, 178, 179–180, 182, 189

Pelourinho heritage site, 157, 159–160, 163. See also Salvador, Brazil

Penglase, Benjamin, 162

Pereira, Anthony, 83

Perez Esquivel, Adolfo, 123

pessoa humana (human person), 154–157, 162, 166n7

Pietz, William, 188, 191

Piñera, José, 173–174, 196n24

Piñera, Sebastian, 183, 184, 187

Pinochet, Augusto, 173, 175, 178, 184, 187

Plan Colombia, 29–30

Plaza, Aliro, 181

Plaza de Rodillas, 210

pluralism, justice versus legal, 4–5

Poblete case (Argentina), 111, 116n14

Polanyi, Karl, 136

police in Brazil: collecting, processing of evidence, 92; reform plans for, 94–95; relationship with PCC, 86–89; scholarship on, 89–90; street-level solutions by, 90–94; understaffing, low pay, 92–93; weakness and discretionary space for, 89–90; working in first world, sleeping in third world, 89

political philosophy, 105

Postero, Nancy, 142

Pottage, Alain, 185

Powell, Dana E., 142n2

Powell, Walter, 84–85

power: of fear, 162; and formation of the subject, 46n24; of justice, 205; language of, 41; and security, 165

PPT (Permanent Peoples' Tribunal): denunciation and visibility, 132; hearings held by, 127–128, 134; hechos probados (proven facts), 137; history of, 125–126; as inher-

ently political, 131; legitimacy/authority of, 126–127, 137–139, 141, 142n3; members of, 127; moral force of, 136; as network, 129; petition to for investigation, 128; prehearing in Cabo de Vela, 131–132, 135–136, 138–139; prehearing in Cúcuta, 129, 134–135, 138; purpose of, 129, 131–132, 135–136; responses to, 127–128; verdicts of, 123, 128, 130. See also Colombia

prisoners of freedom, 206

Programa Pacto pela Vida (Pact for Life Program), 147–150

public conscience as source of law, 126

que nem bicho (like an animal), 155

racialization, 185

Rawls, John, 2, 13

"reciprocal construction" of institutions, 7–8

recording of violations, 127

reducción, 203

"refoundation" in Bolivia, 209

Regional Environmental Commission (COREMA), 179–180

reparation for victims, 26

revolution, disenchantment with, 212–213. See also Bolivia

rights discourses, 41

rights ethic versus care ethic, 57

right to the city, 149; human personhood and, 154, 156; and Pact for Life, 165; in Salvador City Statute, 157

right to truth, 38, 46–47n25

Riles, Annelise, 10

Rio de Janeiro, Brazil, 147, 161

Rodríguez Saá, Adolfo, 58

Romero, Simon, 151

Rondon, José Eduardo, 160

Rosen, Lawrence, 208–209

Ross, Fiona, 130, 136

Rúa, Alejandro, 66

rubber bullets, real bullets, 162, 215

rural social movements, 166n11

Russell, Bertrand, 126

Sacaca, Bolivia, 203

Salehi, Ali Akbar, 71n4

Salomon, Frank, 207

Salvador, Brazil: and Bahia, 148, 159–161, 164–165, 166n3; changing attitudes toward security, 159–161; city as "gravely ill," 153;

City Statute (federal law 10.257), 157, 160; cultural heritage of, 158; drug epidemic in, 156–157; importance of citizenship to poor, 153–154; increased violence in, 147–151; informal settlements within, 158; logics of discipline and security, 165; military police strike, 151; mood of "revolt," "fear," "terror," 151; Pact for Life Program, 161–163; Pelourinho heritage site in, 157, 159–160, 163; relearning city, "being smart," 152, 162; road rage in, 153; tourist industry in, 157, 160

Sanford, Victoria, 26

San José miners, 183–185, *186*, 187

San Pedro de Atacama, 177

Santa Clara police precinct (São Paulo), 91–94

Santos, Juan Manuel, 45n9, 47n29

São Paulo, Brazil, 91–94, 147

Sarrabayrouse Oliveira, María José, 108–109, 113

Satan, 188

Schieffelin, Bambi, 35

Schjolden, Line, 5

Schönsteiner, Judith, 178, 182

Sen, Amartya, 2–3, 193

sensual experience, formative power of, 40

Sepúlveda, Mario, 185

"será justicia" (there will be justice), 204

Shivji, Issa G., 127

Shock Doctrine (Klein), 196n24

Sieder, Rachel, 5, 113

Sincracarbón union, 133

Sisa, Bartolina, 215n3

"social license," 178–179

Society of the Spectacle, The (Debord), 194n3

socio-natural logics, 170–171

Soja, Edward, 12

Sokefeld, Martin, 140

Sonis, Natan, 50, 52

South Africa, 209

sovereign violence, logic of, 155

spatialization of justice, 7, 12–13

"spectrality" of justice, 205–206

Spirit of Philadelphia, The (Supiot), 190

SQM (SOQUIMICH), 172

Sri Lanka, 126

state: as agent, 36; as father, 36; power to take and to restore, 28; "state failure" paradigm, 45n7; violence by proxy (Colombia), 26

Stepputat, Finn, 148

stigmatization, effects of, 29

storytelling, 136

Strathern, Marilyn, 136

Street-Level Bureaucracy (Lipsky), 84

Suma y narración de los Incas (Betanzos), 176

Supiot, Alain, 190

Supreme Court of Justice (Argentina), 99–100; disagreement within, 100–101; gap between reality and perceived justice, 110; how to evaluate, 101; internal changes more "legitimate," 103–104; micro and macro views of, 103; nostalgia within, 108–110; professor's/students' views on, 104–108; public demonstrations against, 99; supporting 1930 coup, 111

Supreme Courts compared, 101

Tamanaha, Brian Z., 5

Taussig, Michael, 45n6, 177, 187, 191

testimony process: as performance, 36, 42; as production of memory, 39; strengths and weaknesses of, 130–131

Theidon, Kimberly, 38

Theory of Justice, A (Rawls), 2

Thompson, E. P., 211–212

Timerman, Héctor, 71n4

TIPNIS, proposed highway through, 213

TOF3 (Tribunal Oral en lo Criminal Federal n°3), 65, 73n41

Torres, Ramón, 182

transitional justice, 44–45n5; in Colombia, 26–27; emphasizing retributive justice, 26; language of, 34, 35; public testimony empowering victims, 36; *reconocimiento* (acknowledgment) as goal, 37; resignification under, 30; and state formation, 36; state violence by proxy, 26; survivors appropriating, 32

translegal relationships, 88

transnational corporations. *See* multi-/transnational corporations

Transnational-Ethnicity Inc., 192

truth: as goal of transitional justice, 26, 28; historical versus judicial, 32; right to, 38, 46–47n25

Tsing, Anna Lowenhaupt, 137

umbrella organizations, 139

UNDRIP (Declaration on the Rights of Indigenous Peoples), 192–193

UNESCO world heritage sites, 157

Universal Declaration on the Rights of Peoples (1976), 127

Uribe, Álvaro, 25
U'wa communities, 134

Vaisman, Noa, 51–52
Victims Law and Land Restitution Act (2011, Colombia), 25, 45n9
victims/victimhood: accusations of benefits from, 33; attaining visibility, 26; becoming political actors, 31, 37–38; learning government, NGO bureaucracy, 35; left- and right-wing conception of, 28; memory as only possession, 39; narrative of, 35; obtaining recognition in Colombia, 27–30, 41; privileging some over others, 33; reconstruction from point of view of, 32; self-awareness of, 36–37; of state crimes, 30; as subjects in transition, 38; victim as someone with rights, 34, 40; at workshops, conferences, rallies, 41
Vigário Geral incident, 80

war on terror, 29
water justice, 170–171; always "in the making," 172; claiming native water, 180–181; privatization of water, 174–175, 191; "water-pinching" companies, 175
Wayúu communities, 131–134, 138–139
Weber, Max, 113–114
Willemsen-Díaz, Augusto, 188
Williams, Raymond, 204

Young, Iris Marion, 164
Yugoslavia, 126

Zaidemberg, Roberto, 65
Zaverucha, Jorge, 80
zombie rights, 190–192
Zuppi, Alberto, 58